THE APPRENTICESHIP OF BEATRICE WEBB

THE APPRENTICESHIP
OF BEATRICE WEBB

Deborah Epstein Nord

The University of Massachusetts Press
Amherst

First published in the USA 1985 by
THE UNIVERSITY OF MASSACHUSETTS PRESS
Amherst, MA 01002

Publication of this book has been aided by a grant
from the Rollins Fund

Printed in Hong Kong

Library of Congress Cataloging in Publication Data

Nord, Deborah Epstein, 1949–
    The apprenticeship of Beatrice Webb.

    Bibliography: p.
    1. Webb, Beatrice Potter, 1858–1943.
    2. Socialists—Great Britain—Biography.
    I. Title.
HX244.7.W42N67   1985   335′.14′0924 [B]   83-18235
ISBN 0–87023–427–7

---

*For my mother
and in loving memory of my father*

Contents

PART IV   AUTHORSHIP

Acknowledgements

This book was written and produced with the financial support of the Woodrow Wilson Foundation, the Lane Cooper Foundation, the Hyder Edward Rollins Fund and the New York Foundation; and with the intellectual and moral support of the Society of Fellows in the Humanities of Columbia University and the English Departments of Harvard University and the University of Connecticut. For this encouragement I thank them all.

I also wish to thank the London School of Economics and Political Science for kindly allowing me to quote from the Passfield Papers and from Beatrice Webb's *My Apprenticeship*. Dr Angela Raspin, Archivist at the British Library of Political and Economic Science, gave me invaluable help with research, and for this I am extremely grateful. I should also like to thank Norman MacKenzie, who discussed my work with me and gave generous assistance with the Webb letters.

Many people have helped and advised me, in ways both intellectual and spiritual, and it gives me great pleasure to be able to express my deep sense of gratitude to all of them: my teachers, the late Ellen Moers, Carl Woodring, Philip Collins and especially Steven Marcus; my current and former colleagues, Jerome Buckley, Andrew Delbanco, Joseph Boone, Roger Wilkenfeld and Joan Hall; my readers and critics, Catharine Stimpson, Judith Walkowitz and Ann Douglas; my editors, Julia Steward and Bruce Wilcox; my friends, Ellen Pollak, Loretta Nassar, David Crew and Susan Pennybacker. I am also grateful for the expert proof-reading of Frederick Wegener. Last, I wish to thank my husband, Philip Nord, who remains my best – and my favourite – critic.

Introduction

MYTH-MAKING

It is the fate of many figures of historical importance to be made the subject of myth, and prominent women in particular seem to have suffered from the distorting powers of time, memory and popular prejudice. The very prominence of these women – their power, fame or achievement, their appearance in places where men 'ought' to be – is itself apparently an anomaly to be explained by some freak of personality or circumstance. Because such women depart from expected behaviour by seeming to act like men, their sexual identity is often called into question, caricatured or twisted in historical legend. There is something wrong, so the common wisdom goes, with their femaleness: they are aberrant either in their sexual relationships or in the characteristics of their personalities habitually associated with gender. They are too much like men, or they have no sexuality at all, or they are excessively libidinous.

There are a number of variations on this theme of the reputed abnormality of famous women, and, depending on the culture, the epoch and the specific circumstances of the individual woman, different kinds of distortions crop up in our collective memories. Elizabeth Barrett Browning remains for us the virgin languishing on her couch, the disembodied poetess writing ethereal sonnets and love-letters, not the prodigious translator of Aeschylus and not the woman who left her father's house and lived as wife and mother. George Sand is mythologized in one of two apparently contradictory ways: she was a 'man' or she was a whore; she was 'masculine', dressed in male attire and smoked cigars, or she was the lover of virtually every great male artist in mid-nineteenth century Europe. Left out of the myth are her astounding energy and productivity as a professional novelist. It is not, as Ellen Moers has remarked, 'the management of Sand's sex life that is baffling but the management of her working life'.[1] Queen

1

Elizabeth I of England and Mary Queen of Scots have shared
between them the imagined extremes of sexual abnormality that
George Sand has been able to embody all by herself – the manly
woman and the promiscuous one. 'It is extraordinarily entertaining,' Dorothy Sayers wrote in an essay entitled 'Are Women
Human?',

> to watch the historians of the past . . . entangling themselves in
> what they call the 'problem' of Queen Elizabeth. They invented
> the most complicated and astonishing reasons both for her
> success as a sovereign and for her tortuous matrimonial policy.
> She was the tool of Burleigh, she was the tool of Leicester, she
> was the fool of Essex; she was diseased, she was deformed, she
> was a man in disguise. She was a mystery.[2]

In order to explain the 'mystery' of a woman who inherited and
effectively performed a 'man's' role, it was somehow thought
necessary to dissect her relationship with men and to look into the
suspected irregularities of her hormonal balance.

The real achievements of women can be denied by making
them into 'men' or by apotheosizing their 'femininity'. In her own
lifetime, Florence Nightingale quickly became the 'Lady with the
Lamp', an embodiment of the 'feminine' virtues of self-sacrifice
and saintliness. The Florence Nightingale of popular imagination
is a ministering angel, a woman so completely representative of
conventional 'womanly' goodness that certain modern women,
accepting the myth, consider her a regressive and, therefore,
destructive model of female achievement. But what of the woman
who was administrator, reformer, researcher and statistician,
rebel and pioneer? Lytton Strachey, recognizing the falseness of
the Victorian Nightingale legend, attempted to re-create her
image in history. His portrait of her in *Eminent Victorians* is a
superb example, however, of the substitution of one myth for
another, for all that Strachey did was to turn the 'Lady with the
Lamp' inside out. He changed her from a *'saintly*, self-sacrificing
woman, . . . consecrating with the radiance of her goodness the
dying soldier's couch' into a woman possessed by *'demons'*, a Miss
Nightingale 'more interesting' but 'less agreeable' than the
legendary one.[3] Strachey converts her first to a demonic creature,
then to an 'eagle', and finally to a 'tigress'; she is not merely strong
and determined but predatory. In his account of her relationship

with Sidney Herbert, the Secretary of State for War, Strachey uses animal metaphors to show how Nightingale 'took hold of him, taught him, shaped him, absorbed him, dominated him through and through'. Herbert is the 'stag', a 'comely, gallant creature springing through the forest', and Nightingale the 'tigress', 'fascinated suddenly by something feline, something strong', ready to sink 'her claws in the quivering haunches'.[4] Herbert died before finishing the work at the War Office that Nightingale spurred him on to accomplish, and it was Nightingale's unrelenting prodding, Strachey wants to suggest, that killed him. It is this image of destructive and distorted sexual energy that Strachey offers in place of the selfless saint; these two versions of Nightingale are, however, but two sides of the same counterfeit coin.

Our images of historical couples suffer a similar taint of misrepresentation, particularly when the female of the pair is as eminent as or more eminent than her mate. When a woman is more famous, more ambitious, more successful or even more notorious than her partner, we speak of roles being 'reversed'. In the relationship of George Eliot and George Henry Lewes, for example, was she not really the 'husband' and he the 'wife'? Lytton Strachey was, for reasons too complex to unravel here, fascinated by pairs of men and women who seemed to him to have traded conventional roles: Elizabeth and Essex, Victoria and Albert, Florence Nightingale and Sidney Herbert. He tended to represent the females of these partnerships as not merely dominant but voracious, engulfing and even fatal. As Michael Holroyd has written, Strachey was obsessed with the idea of the overpowering female whose 'terrific overplus of energy crushes the gilded butterfly male'.[5]

For the women in history who have worked with their husbands and achieved prominence in tandem, this problem is even further complicated. These women can be imagined as 'masculine', as emasculating and yet as inseparable and indistinguishable from their male partners. Such is the case of Beatrice Webb, the subject of this study. The Fabians, and the Webbs in particular, have always been the convenient and fruitful subject of caricature. Virginia Woolf, whose often amusing and occasionally insightful swipes at Beatrice and Sidney Webb are sprinkled throughout her diaries and letters, admitted that she found it difficult to avoid 'the half carping, half humorously cynical view which steals into one's description of the Webbs'.[6] This particular difficulty has affected the vast majority of historians and critics who have tried to write about these two leaders of the Fabian Socialists. One of the reviewers of *My Apprenticeship* summed up the 'Webb legend' that had flourished since the turn of the century (he was writing in 1926): 'it is a grim, inhuman legend – a legend of blue-stocking and blue-book – a legend of statistics, economics, infallibility, research, omniscience, lectures, pamphlets, dossiers, calculations, permeation and pedantry'.[7] That a male social and political critic should be guilty of such Gradgrindism was ridiculous and, to some, reprehensible enough; but that a woman should commit the crime of mechanical-mindedness and the presumed neglect of human feeling was absolutely unnatural.

The greatest caricaturist of the Webbs was, of course, H. G. Wells, who saw himself as critic of the Webbs' view of life and accordingly made them into Altiora and Oscar Bailey, the consummate social manipulators of *The New Machiavelli*.[8] His portrait of Beatrice focuses on her suspect sexual identity: Altiora Bailey's better qualities are described as 'masculine', which of course makes them inappropriate in a woman, and her offensive qualities are attributed to her female gender. Here is Wells' first description of Altiora in the novel; it has had an impact on the standard image of Beatrice Webb that Wells himself could never have predicted:

She had much of the vigour and handsomeness of a slender impudent young man, and an unscrupulousness altogether feminine. She was one of those women who are wanting in – what is the word? – muliebrity [the word that the narrator has difficulty remembering means 'womanliness']. She had courage and initiative and a philosophical way of handling questions, and she could be bored by regular work like a man. She was entirely unfitted for her sex's sphere. She was neither uncertain, nor coy nor hard to please, and altogether too stimulating and aggressive for any gentleman's hour of ease. Her cookery would have been as sketchy as her hand-writing, which was generally quite illegible, and she would have made, I feel sure, a shocking bad nurse. Yet you mustn't imagine she was an inelegant or unbeautiful woman, and she is inconceivable to me in high collars or any sort of masculine garment. But her soul was bony, and at the base of her was a vanity gaunt and

greedy! When she wasn't in a state of personal untidiness, . . .
she had a gypsy splendour of black and red and silver all her
own.[9]

What is particularly fascinating about Wells' description – aside
from his view of women as coy, unscrupulous nurses and cooks
who have good penmanship – is his juxtaposition of the hard-
edged 'boniness' and vigorous mannishness of Altiora with her
'gypsy splendour'. There is a suggestion of fierceness and wildness
in Wells' vision of her, something akin to the dangerous nature of
Strachey's Florence Nightingale. And like Nightingale, Altiora is
pictured as an eagle: 'She was a tall commanding figure . . . with
dark eyes that had no depths, with . . . aquiline features and
straight black hair that was apt to get astray, that was now astray
like the head feathers of an eagle in a gale.'[10]

The victims of Altiora's fierceness in the novel are the narrator,
Remington, whose doomed marriage she arranges (she was
'systematic even in matters that evaded system'), and the
innocent, unsuspecting men of affairs she captures for her London
soirées and for potential political manoeuvring. In Wells' caricature of Beatrice Webb, as in other, non-fictional accounts of the
Webbs, it is as if all the legendary manipulative and Machiavel-
lian powers of the Fabians are somehow centred in their most
eminent female leader. Altiora appears to be the force behind
Fabian plotting and 'permeation', and in her these conspiratorial
qualities are joined with what Wells calls 'feminine unscrupulousness'. The historian Robert Scally, describing the Webbs'
courting of imperialist politicians in the 'Coefficients Club', writes
of the machinations of 'Beatrice Webb, the accomplished hostess',
overseer of 'interesting little dinners', and of 'Beatrice, the
Fabian', whose obsession was the 'permeation of potential
leaders'.[11] She commits a double offence in two different but
complementary personae. As the Gradgrindism of the Fabians is
exaggerated in representations of Beatrice Webb, so is this aspect
of manipulation and, appropriately, seduction. Virginia Woolf
described Beatrice not as an eagle but as a spider: she recorded
going to her first Fabian meeting and seeing 'Mrs Webb, seated
like an industrious spider at the table; spinning her webs (a pun!)
incessantly.'[12]

Virginia Woolf felt that her husband had been caught in the
Fabian web, and Wells counted himself among the casualties of

Webb seductiveness as well, but Altiora Bailey's most thoroughly subdued victim in *The New Machiavelli* is Oscar Bailey, Wells' portrait of Sidney Webb. The undeniable biographical facts of the Webbs' marriage are that Sidney pursued Beatrice and that she finally accepted him after long months of resistance. In Wells' novel, however, consistency of characterization demands that Altiora be the aggressor. She discovers Oscar through his writing, then takes occasion to 'meet and subjugate him, and, so soon as he had sufficiently recovered from his abject humility and a certain panic at her attentions, marry him'.[13] While Altiora is 'aggressive, imaginative, and has a great capacity for ideas', Oscar is 'almost destitute of initiative'. While she can be 'just as nice to people – and . . . just as nasty – as she wanted to be', he can only be 'artlessly rude and egoistic'. In fact, the representation of Sidney is, if anything, more distasteful than that of Beatrice, but the two portraits are both distorted and skewed in the direction of *her* strength, wilfulness and drive and *his* ineffectuality, insignificance and weakness. 'She ran him' is Wells' way of summing up the marriage.

Malcolm Muggeridge's 'Mr and Mrs Daniel Brett', in his autobiographical novel *In a Valley of this Restless Mind*, are but pale reflections of Altiora and Oscar Bailey, but they are part of the well-established tradition of Webb caricature. Eleanor Brett has 'angry eyes and an arrogant mouth'; Daniel Brett is 'rubicund and industrious, with a small round belly pushing out his waistcoat and short plump legs'.[14] The Bretts speak in synchronized fashion, like a chorus with two voices and one mind, and they advise the young protagonist that if he wants to find the 'blue-print of a new civilisation', he must 'investigate, . . . collect facts and arrange them'. The Bretts are automatons; they regard people as mere producers or consumers – nothing more than 'dead wood'. Muggeridge's wife Kitty, the daughter of Beatrice Webb's youngest sister, chose to describe her aunt, not in fictionalized form, but in an introduction to the biography of Webb that she wrote with Ruth Adam. The biography itself, if lacking in emphasis or interpretation, is at least evenhanded and thorough; but Kitty Muggeridge's personal reminiscence at the beginning of the book perpetuates much of the Webb mythology and sets an unfortunate tone for the rest of the text.[15]

Kitty Muggeridge's 'Aunt Bo' is a woman whose 'beauty was marred by a lack of tenderness, a kind of domineering masculin-

ity' and who 'in the end could only be described as handsome'.[16]
Like Wells, Muggeridge finds something fierce and wild about her
aunt: 'She walked with the swinging stride of a gipsy and
something untamed in her gave her an air of breeding and "race"
unwarranted by lineage.'[17] Muggeridge describes the sight of
Sidney and Beatrice on a tandem bicycle, 'a small beetle-like
figure, crouched over the handle-bars . . . and, perched majesti-
cally behind him, what appeared to be a large grey bird'. Once
again, the use of animal metaphors suggests Beatrice's threaten-
ing power and Sidney's vulnerability to potential assault. 'Uncle
Sidney' is, in fact, 'a figure of derisory contrast', 'a very small man
with a very big head, pretty little hands and feet which looked as
though they would screw on and off'.[18] The wife is 'masculine' and
'handsome'; the husband's extremities are 'pretty'. What follows
these loaded descriptions of the Webbs' physical appearances in
Muggeridge's introduction is a litany of anecdotes, each one of
which illustrates Beatrice's lack of feeling, meanness of spirit and
disregard for others. The stage for biography is set.

Because of the legendary emphasis on Beatrice Webb's 'mascu-
linity' of personality and intellect, and because of the exaggerated
identification of Webb with the superrational extremes of Fabianism, it has been difficult for biographers and historians to see any
room for the non-rational, the non-mechanical, the non-
'scientific', in her thought or behaviour. Shirley Letwin, whose
unconcealed animosity towards Webb in her *Pursuit of Certainty* is
probably unequalled by any other critic's, appears to be
confounded by any mention of faith, religion or even human
sympathy in Webb's private writings. Whatever seems to be
inconsistent with Letwin's image of Webb is explained by
overweening ambition, cold calculation or self-delusion. Letwin
cannot figure out, for instance, what could have 'inspired
[Webb's] desire for religious faith' in adolescence: was it feigned
only to attract her mother's attention or 'to make herself
interesting as a doubter'?[19] Webb took solace in Herbert
Spencer's notion of the 'Great Unknowable', according to Letwin,
because it 'set her free to worship the scientific method without
asking herself uncomfortable questions' and 'helped to reassure
her that she had not become an unfeeling reasoning machine'.[20]
Webb's real nature, in other words, *was* mechanical, 'scientific'
and 'unfeeling'; her interest in any kind of spiritual experience
was merely a sop to her *amour-propre*. Letwin concludes that

Webb's solution to her superficial and essentially feigned need for faith was to worship science, to make it her religion. Webb's obvious obsessions with religion and with the inability of science to generate values or sustain spiritual needs are ignored by Letwin or dismissed as inauthentic.

Because Webb was active in spheres traditionally reserved for men, her energy, assertiveness, directness and strong physical presence have been regarded by many as 'masculine' characteristics. Because she has been identified as a 'masculine' woman, the characteristics of temperament conventionally associated with 'femininity' that Webb seemed to possess – her religiousness, spirituality, passion and sympathy – have been regarded as suspect or have simply been ignored. It has been difficult for observers and critics of Webb – as it was, as we shall see, for Webb herself – to avoid using the category of gender to describe unconventional aspects of her personality and behaviour, to respond to her as an individual rather than as a failed woman or a counterfeit man. Just as her quest for faith, her desire for the private happiness of marriage and motherhood, and her interest in the writing of fiction did not disqualify her for prominence in the world of politics or in the discipline of social science, neither did her public achievements prevent her from yearning after spiritual, sexual and creative expression.

REVISIONISTS

The revision of Beatrice Webb's public and historical image began for certain readers and critics with the publication of *My Apprenticeship*. The autobiography seemed to contradict many of the standard features of the already thriving 'Webb legend', and reviewers repeatedly commented on the 'surprises' it contained. One reviewer found the 'most interesting, because the most *unexpected*, part of Beatrice Potter's development . . . in the narration of her spiritual growth'.[21] Another suspected that Mrs Webb had probably not yet found the form for presenting her social investigation that was best suited to her: the 'insight, humour, and a heartfelt and contagious sympathy' that parts of *My Apprenticeship* revealed found 'no scope in works like "The Industrial Democracy" and "The History of Trade Unionism"'.[22]

A third reviewer described *My Apprenticeship* as 'a surprisingly human document' in view of the public reputation of Mrs Webb as an 'intellectual statistician with a cold masculine grasp of the intricate phenomenon' of social problems.[23] In an obituary tribute to Webb, R. H. Tawney wrote (with unfortunately unwarranted confidence) of the myth-destroying power of her autobiography. 'The Beatrice Webb of fiction,' Tawney wrote, 'a combination of economic pedant with hard woman of affairs, did not survive the publication of *My Apprenticeship*.'[24]

The effort to demythologize Beatrice Webb was continued by acquaintances who wrote of her in their memoirs and tried to separate her image from Sidney's. These friends of the Webbs perceived aspects of Beatrice often hidden from casual observers, and took pains to expose the error of seeing a monolithic 'Webb' temperament. Desmond MacCarthy, who worked with the Webbs as drama critic of the *New Statesman*, wrote of his fondness for Beatrice (to him she looked like a *'benevolent* hawk') and of his conviction that she did not lack an artistic sensibility, as most people imagined. If she had wanted, MacCarthy claimed, she could have developed a responsiveness to poetry just as she had developed a love for music in her old age, and just as she had 'fostered in herself states of mind she identified with prayer'. 'I remember telling H. G. [Wells],' MacCarthy continued,

> that she had spoken to me about this [her prayerful states], adding 'she is convinced that she shares the experience of mystics'. He was sceptical: 'There's no more mysticism in Beatrice than in a steam engine.' But I think he was so far wrong.[25]

Bertrand Russell dwelt on the differences between husband and wife in his portrait of the Webbs. Beatrice had a wider range of interests than Sidney, and, contrary to the commonly-held opinion that she was interested only in *groups* of people or in those individuals whom she could 'permeate', she took 'considerable interest in individual human beings, not only when they could be useful'.[26] She was also a 'deeply religious woman' according to Russell; she liked to induce 'exquisite visions' in herself by fasting; and she was never 'deflected by personal ambition'.[27] Sidney did not share the 'religious side' of his wife's nature, and lacked, Russell believed, his wife's intellectual sharpness and inventiveness: before marriage, Sidney Webb was 'much less than half of what the two of them afterward became'.[28]

The most striking description of an intimately-observed Beatrice Webb came from Leonard Woolf, who was better able to see beyond a brittle and intimidating exterior than was his wife. In *Sowing*, the first volume of his memoir, Woolf tells of his friendship with the Webbs and includes an extraordinary account of Beatrice. Sidney, Leonard Woolf asserts, had no 'facade' at all: 'he was all the way through exactly what he appeared to be on the surface'. Sidney did not suffer from 'doubts or hesitations', 'headache or constipation'.[29] Beatrice, on the other hand, was not at all what she appeared to be:

> you could not see much of Beatrice without realizing that, beneath the metallic facade and the surface of polished certainty, there was a neurotic turmoil of doubt and discontent, suppressed or controlled, an ego tortured in the old-fashioned religious way almost universal among the good and the wise in the nineteenth century. I do not think tortured is too strong a word, for, if you watched Beatrice Webb when she was not a hostess, not talking, but attending only to her own thoughts, you would occasionally see a look of intense spiritual worry or acute misery cross her face.[30]

Woolf believed, further, that Webb had the 'temperament, strongly suppressed, the passions and imagination' of an artist; and he believed that his own impressions of her extreme internal conflict and strain were confirmed by the contents of her autobiography.

The enthusiasm of reviewers and friends for Webb's *My Apprenticeship*, and their recognition of its value as a clue to her identity, ultimately prompted critics of literature to consider the text and so to enter into the revision of Webb's image in history. F. R. Leavis suggested in an introduction to John Stuart Mill's essays on Bentham and Coleridge that *My Apprenticeship* ought to be read not merely as 'the life's record of a notability' but as 'one of the classics of English literature'.[31] Webb's autobiography belonged in a discussion of Mill's seminal essays because, in its 'classically representative way', it described, as did Mill's own autobiography, 'a most important part of the intellectual history of the nineteenth century'.[32] Leavis placed *My Apprenticeship* within a tradition of Victorian autobiography and within the context of a Victorian debate between 'Benthamite' and 'Coleridgian' attitudes. *My Apprenticeship* is important as intellectual history and as social history, but it is also 'one of the classics', Leavis asserts, because of the quality of its writing: 'we recognize in the writer a potential novelist'. Webb reminds Leavis of George Eliot, not just because both were 'gifted and highly intellectual women' and both closely connected to Herbert Spencer, but because they were similarly 'earnest, strong in sympathetic imagination, and religiously given beneath all the liberal convictions of . . . intellect'.[33] Webb, like Eliot, had a 'novelist's interest in the concrete . . . [and] in the individual life'.[34]

Samuel Hynes, in his admirable essay 'The Art of Beatrice Webb', follows Leavis' lead in seeing Webb as a novelist manqué, as a sort of 'latter-day George Eliot', although he finds evidence for this judgement, not in *My Apprenticeship*, but in the extraordinary and voluminous diaries on which the autobiography is based.[35] In Hynes' view, Webb avoided the writing of fiction as part of a 'willed suppression of the whole realm of feelings'.[36] She rejected art and 'chose instead the most uncreative, self-abnegating course – to give her life over to social research and to the writing, with her husband Sidney, of those "solid but unreadable books" '.[37] The nearly seventy years' worth of diaries that Webb produced, Hynes argues, were the result of a life of suppression and constraint: 'self-expression, . . . if thrust out by the front door will come in by the scullery window, and the novels that Beatrice Webb could not write found a kind of private existence in her diaries'.[38] The diary allowed 'expression to the suppressed artist' and acted as a mechanism of release so that she could 'hold herself to the course that she had chosen'.[39]

Webb's diaries, previously accessible to scholars as part of the Passfield Papers and more recently on microfilm, now appear in print in four volumes, edited by Norman and Jeanne MacKenzie, those indefatigable chroniclers of the Fabians and, in particular, of the Webbs.[40] Readers will now be able to see more clearly the literary talents that Hynes celebrates, and to judge for themselves if this personal document supports the public image of an anaesthetic, rigidly calculating woman.[41] The diaries differ from the autobiography in a number of ways, not the least of which is Webb's decision to omit from *My Apprenticeship* any overt mention of her now much-noted passion for Joseph Chamberlain. The discovery that Beatrice Webb was capable of this obsessive emotion has startled reviewers of the diary, and the MacKenzies themselves have highlighted the Chamberlain affair as the dramatic and thematic centre of the first volume in their general introduction.[42]

Webb's own account of her first thirty-four years in *My Apprenticeship* adds shape and interpretation to the record of the diaries and establishes a quest for 'creed' and 'craft' – belief and work – as the keynote and dominating obsession of her life. The autobiography gives us Webb's image of herself, her creation of self, and directs our attention to the spiritual and intellectual, rather than the romantic, content of her life. It is crucial to the revision of Webb's place in history and to our understanding of her as a woman that we have her record of her life as she transcribed it in the diary and as she recollected and transformed it in the autobiography.

In this study of Webb's autobiography and early years, I seek to continue the reappraisal of her life and work that began with the publication of *My Apprenticeship* but that has not fully succeeded in revising the Beatrice Webb of caricature and legend. Part of the task of a critic who tries to come to terms with the many misrepresentations of Webb is to account for the numerous real contradictions that characterized her life, and to avoid inflation or distortion of a sympathetic, rather than an antagonistic, kind. The literary critic, in his or her desire to claim Webb for 'art', tends to come close to disdaining the very remarkable non-artistic achievements of her life. Her autobiography is a rich and important literary text, and her diaries reveal the talent and intelligence of a keen observer of individuals and society, but it is doubtful that the novels Webb *might* have written would ever have approached the quality of George Eliot's fiction. Revisionists of the Webb myth also have a tendency to cast Sidney Webb as the enemy of his wife's creative spirit. This is a tempting but inadequate point of view, as is the opposite but equally seductive idea that the Webb marriage represented a perfectly matched, perfectly balanced partnership of equals.

The contradictions and inconsistencies of her nature are hard to encompass in any one image or in any one critical study: Webb was a 'religious' Fabian, an 'emancipated' woman who rejected political feminism, an apparent anti-Semite who strongly identified with Jews, a non-Marxist admirer of Soviet Russia, a class snob who married 'beneath' her and felt most at home among Lancashire textile workers, an ambitious woman who gave up personal, individual notoriety for fame in partnership. There do appear, at times, to be two Beatrice Webbs, and my object here is to understand the relationship between the two. What is the connection between 'Altiora Bailey' and the Beatrice Webb described by Leonard Woolf in his memoirs?

One might begin to answer the question of Webb's doubleness by analysing her problematical position as an intellectual, personally ambitious woman who had to confront certain obstructive social and sexual conventions of her time. The conflicts she experienced as an anomalous Victorian woman preceded and contributed to the other political, intellectual and psychological conflicts of her life and work. But it would be a mistake to see Webb – or any other woman, for that matter – as a representative of eternal womanhood, outside of time and place. In a discussion of *My Apprenticeship* in *The Female Imagination*, Patricia Meyer Spacks recognizes Webb's 'case history' as 'paradigmatic' of a woman suspended between the categories of feeling and reason, love and work, 'feminine' emotion and 'masculine' intellect. Spacks appreciates the examination of these dichotomies in the beginning section of *My Apprenticeship*, but she regrets Webb's early abandonment of the subject of female conflict for the subject of work: 'More and more, her autobiography begins to record her work rather than her life'.[43] Spacks unfortunately regards a one-hundred-page section of *My Apprenticeship* on philanthropy and social investigation in late-Victorian Britain as a 'lengthy digression'. She fails to recognize the full purpose or significance of *My Apprenticeship* as a text, because she values it, at least in this context, only as an expression of the 'female imagination' and does not consider its other literary and historical connections.

If, as Leavis suggested, we examine Webb's memoir in the context of Victorian autobiographical literature, we can recognize it as a breakthrough in the history of women's writing rather than as an example of a woman's retreat from introspection or personal confession. Webb's was the first British woman's autobiography to take the classic Victorian form of spiritual crisis and conversion. Like Mill and Carlyle, she wrote of the search for faith and vocation, of the need for belief and work. Like them she considered her work to be emblematic of her life, and regarded her own spiritual and intellectual development as the essence of her existence. It had not been the habit of either female novelists or female memoirists to make these claims for their lives in the form of self-conscious autobiographical writing. If we see Webb's *My Apprenticeship* in this light, we can understand that the dualities and dilemmas which Spacks regards as characteristic of the ambitious, achieving woman are also part of the shared intellectual tradition of Webb's time.[44] In *My Apprenticeship*, conflicts of female identity intersect with the familiar Victorian debate between 'Bentham' and 'Coleridge', between reason and faith, mind and heart, or, in Webb's own terms, 'the Ego that denies' and 'the Ego that affirms'. Webb wrote in a genre that tended to describe and expose conflict because it suited her own experience of internal contradiction. There were inconsistencies in her position as a publicly-powerful woman and as a religiously-minded Fabian, and she represented these apparent contradictions in *My Apprenticeship* as related and overlapping phenomena.

My intention in this study, as I have suggested by its equivocal title, is to examine both the early years of Beatrice Webb's life and the literary record of those years. If *My Apprenticeship* belongs to a classic tradition of Victorian autobiography, as well as to traditions of nineteenth-century women's writing, it does so largely because of the life Webb was able to live in the last decades of the Victorian age. The shape of Webb's search for what she called 'creed' and 'craft' was determined by the convergence of certain historical phenomena of those decades – by changes in the position of women, by the 'discovery' of poverty in the East End of London, by new kinds of social investigation and by the 'socialist revival' at the end of the century. By looking at the two 'apprenticeships', we begin to understand some of the ways in which history gives form to the individual life and, in turn, influences the use of literary genre. By considering the events surrounding the writing of *My Apprenticeship*, as I do at the conclusion of this study, we are able to see further that the resolutions of autobiography often mask the unresolved contradictions of life, and that Webb's memoir, though a historical record, is also a fiction.

Chronology

Because the following study of Beatrice Webb's life and work is organized in a thematic, rather than in a strictly chronological, way, it might be helpful for the reader to be able to consult a brief biographical chronology of the years covered by *My Apprenticeship*.

1858 Birth.

1873 Visits the United States with father and sister Kate. Begins to keep a diary.

1874 Suffers a 'breakdown in health'.

1875 Sent to boarding-school in Bournemouth for one term. 'Converts' temporarily to orthodox Christianity; receives the Holy Sacrament for first time.

1876 'Comes out' in society.

1880 Travels to Italy with older sisters.

1882 Death of mother, Laurencina Potter.

1883 Spring: works as volunteer for the Charity Organization Society.
Summer: meets Joseph Chamberlain.
Autumn: visits Bacup in Lancashire for first time.

1884 Her relationship with Chamberlain fails to end in marriage.
Travels to Germany with Margaret Harkness.

1885 Spring: manages Katherine Buildings, a slum dwelling in East London, with Ella Pycroft.
Winter: father, Richard Potter, suffers a stroke.
The 'Dead Point': a severe depression that lasts into 1886.

1886 Visits Bacup for second time.
February: 'A Lady's View of the Unemployed at the East' appears in the *Pall Mall Gazette*.

1887 Begins social investigation with Charles Booth: inquiry into dock labour.
October: 'The Dock Life of East London' appears in *Nineteenth Century*.

Herbert Spencer asks her to be his literary executor.

1888   Inquiry into the sweating-system and into the Jewish community of East London.

August: 'East London Labour' appears in *Nineteenth Century*.

Testifies before the Lords' Commission on the Sweating System.

1889   April: Booth's *East London* is published.

Visits Bacup for third time.

Undertakes independent study of the Co-operative Movement.

1890   Meets Sidney Webb.

1891   Becomes secretly engaged to Webb.

Joins Fabian Society.

The Co-operative Movement in Great Britain is published.

1892   January: death of father; engagement publicly announced.

February: Spencer drops her as literary executor.

July: marries Sidney Webb.

Part I
Spiritual Quest

1 A Tradition of Victorian Autobiography

If, as Carlyle wrote, 'History is the essence of innumerable Biographies', then the history of the Victorian age may be regarded as the essence of innumerable autobiographies. Carlyle himself found it appropriate to write an autobiographical fiction to accompany and elucidate his 'clothes philosophy'; John Henry Newman, when accused by Charles Kingsley of lying about his religious faith, responded by writing an autobiography as *Apologia*; Darwin sought to amuse himself and educate his children by leaving behind a record of the 'Development of my mind and character'; Trollope took the opportunity in his memoirs to confess that his 'first object in taking to literature as a profession' was to make money; and John Stuart Mill revealed to his Victorian audience, albeit posthumously, that as a young man of twenty he had suffered a 'crisis' in his mental history.[1]

The autobiographies of a number of eminent Victorians belong to a secular tradition that evolved out of the confessional writings of the saints and was inaugurated in the nineteenth century by Wordsworth's *Prelude*. The process of Christian conversion and redemption was translated in this modern secularized form into what M. H. Abrams has called the 'painful process of *self*-formation, crisis and *self*-recognition'.[2] In the Christian 'theodicy of the private life', it is Providence that gives meaning to pain and defines experience; in the modern form it is the individual himself or herself who must, in the very writing of autobiography, both detect and create life's shape, process and meaning.

Beatrice Webb's *My Apprenticeship* belongs to this Victorian autobiographical tradition: the shape and pattern of the life it describes are derived from Webb's experience and memory, but also from the process of writing itself and from the literary models – most of them created by men – that were available to her. Webb's actual relationship to other autobiographical texts is a complex issue, as is the issue of any writer's conscious and unconscious connections to literary tradition. We do know from *My Apprenticeship* that she read John Stuart Mill's *Autobiography*, and from her diary that she read St Augustine's *Confessions*, Thomas Carlyle's *Sartor Resartus*, Goethe's *Faust* and *Wilhelm Meister*, Harriet Martineau's *Autobiography* and George Sand's *Histoire de ma vie*.[3] She read all of these works in late adolescence and early adulthood, during a prolonged period of spiritual and psychological crisis. These texts and the very vocabulary they established for understanding the growth of an individual influenced both the way Webb lived her life and the ways in which she thought about it.

The '*grammar* of our experience', Frank McConnell writes with reference to the enormous influence of *The Prelude* on subsequent literature and lives, 'goes far toward determining the nature of the experience itself'.[4] Wordsworth's autobiographical epic, together with other autobiographical works read by Webb and by other Victorians, created an archetypal way of perceiving the shape of a life, a way that was at once the product and the initiator of cultural terms and conventions. These conventions could determine what an autobiographer might include, how he would begin and end, what themes he would use to give shape to an objectively formless chronology.[5] In this process of selecting, ordering and interpreting the events of a life, the autobiographer would transform his past into a kind of fictional narrative. Webb incorporated the terms of other nineteenth-century autobiographies into the way she conceived of her life as she lived it and as she remembered it.

LOSS OF FAITH AND THE CRISIS OF UNBELIEF

A general pattern of de-conversion and subsequent rebirth characterizes the genre of autobiography to which *My Apprenticeship* belongs. The autobiographer describes a loss of orthodox faith; a period of crisis, of acute despair and dejection, when the old faith is found to be inadequate; a search for new faith to fill the void of unbelief; and a rebirth in newfound faith and vocation.[6] Wordsworth's crisis in *The Prelude* resulted, at least in part, from a loss of faith – a loss of faith in the efficacy of the French Revolution and of the power of human reason to bring about a new moral and social order. The Victorians who followed Wordsworth in writing autobiographies of crisis and conversion suffered from a similar loss of faith in some orthodoxy, often religious but occasionally, as in the case of John Stuart Mill, political or philosophical.

One recent critic has described this fall from orthodoxy as an 'experience of exile from an initial state of security', an Edenic state of psychological safety that is intimately related to the child's belief in parental dogmas.[7] Edmund Gosse, in *Father and Son*, and William Hale White, in the *Autobiography and Deliverance of Mark Rutherford*, both describe long and painful processes of de-conversion from orthodox Christianity; and for Gosse especially, the progress of spiritual disillusionment recapitulates the progress of relations between parent and child. The gradual widening of a temperamental distance between Gosse and his father culminates in a revelatory moment of de-conversion, almost a travesty of the traditional epiphanic moment:

> Over my soul there swept an immense wave of emotion. Now, surely, now the great final change must be approaching. I gazed up into the tenderly-coloured sky, and I broke irresistibly into speech. 'Come now, Lord Jesus,' I cried, 'come now and take me to be for ever with Thee in Thy Paradise.' . . . And I raised myself on the sofa, . . . and waited for the glorious apparition. . . .
>
> Presently the colour deepened, the evening came on. . . . The tea-bell rang – last word of prose to shatter my mystical poetry. 'The Lord has not come, the Lord will never come,' I muttered, and in my heart the artificial edifice of extravagant faith began to totter and crumble. From that moment forth my Father and I . . . walked in opposite hemispheres of the soul, with 'the thick o' the world between us'.[8]

Gosse ends the account of his spiritual journey with this liberating moment of anti-conversion; but 'Mark Rutherford', in a reaction far more characteristic of the hero of Victorian autobiography, trembles at the emptiness of unbelief and passes through a painful crisis, a depression and agony of spirit. Carlyle's evocation of Diogenes Teufelsdröckh's crisis of faith in *Sartor Resartus* – the 'Everlasting No' and the 'Centre of Indifference' – and John Stuart Mill's description in his *Autobiography* of the mental crisis of 1826 are paradigmatic expressions of the Victorian prelude to secular conversion. Carlyle employs the industrial metaphor of the 'dead immeasurable steam-engine' and Mill calls on Coleridge's 'Dejection' ode to convey the sense of numbness, purposelessness and loss of desire that characterize a period of transition between the loss of old faith and the recovery of an altered one.[9]

After faltering in his Calvinist faith, 'Rutherford' exhibits the classic symptoms of spiritual paralysis and suicidal despair that mark a Carlylean sojourn in the 'Mill of Death':

> Towards morning I got into bed, but not to sleep; and when the dull daylight of Monday came, all support had vanished, and I seemed to be sinking into a bottomless abyss. I became gradually worse week by week, and my melancholy took a fixed form. I got a notion into my head that my brain was failing. . . . For months – many months, this dreadful conviction of coming idiocy or insanity lay upon me like some poisonous reptile with its fangs driven into my very marrow. . . . I prayed incessantly for death.[10]

He has been 'plunged in the Valley of the Shadow' and cannot rise out of it: he is fixed in spiritual limbo.

VOCATION

'Rutherford's' crisis of faith is equally a crisis of vocation. It is after he delivers one of his first sermons as minister of an Independent chapel that he collapses and takes to bed; and it is not until after he finds a new kind of work among the poor of London that he regains belief. His agnostic friend Edward Mardon warns him that he cannot solve his spiritual 'perplexities' until he knows what he wants to *do*: work and faith, action and belief, are inextricably linked in this quintessentially Victorian view of vocation. Salvation comes to 'Rutherford', as to other autobiographers of the age, through the Gospel of Work, through learning what to preach and then dedicating one's labour to the enlightenment and regeneration of society. Teufelsdröckh, rising 'newborn of Heaven', senses himself to have been elected, 'as it were *preappointed* for Clothes-Philosophy'. He will reveal to a moribund society the knowledge of rebirth and will preach revolution, a 'Phoenix Death–Birth', a death-into-life, for the human community.

Although the spirit of Romanticism – particularly as it is embodied in a Wordsworthian communion with nature – has regenerative powers for a number of Victorian autobiographers, it is through a *rejection* of Romantic self-consciousness that they are able to define a reborn self and carve out new forms of belief and work.[11] Byronic world-weariness and egotism must be exchanged for a spirit of renunciation, sacrifice and dedication to humanity. Finding Byron's despairing state too disturbingly similar to his own, Mill turns to the 'anti-self-consciousness theory of Carlyle'; Carlyle, having closed his Byron a number of decades before, had derived his theory from Goethe, in whom he found an antidote to the melancholy of the faithless Romantic hero. Goethe, too, had experienced the living-death of the 'Everlasting No', but he had transcended 'inward imprisonment, doubt and discontent' to rise to 'freedom, belief and *clear activity*'.[12] It was Goethe's profound knowledge of despair and Mephistophelian nihilism, and his will to overcome them through 'Annihilation of *Self*', that made the poet such a compelling example for Carlyle, as for other Victorians.[13] According to Teufelsdröckh, the 'first preliminary moral Act' must be '*Selbst-todtung*': ' "It is only with Renunciation (*Entsagen*)," ' he quotes the master, ' "that Life, properly speaking, can be said to begin." '[14]

When Teufelsdröckh exhorts his reader – and himself – to 'Produce! Produce!', he is signalling a good deal more than the belief in what M. H. Abrams has called a 'strenuous economic activism'.[15] Only action and creation can obliterate doubt and conquer self; only work directed outwards, away from self, can fulfil the requirements of an exemplary form of vocation. Work and, indeed, production become sacred means to transcendence of self. Abrams contrasts the 'visionary quietism' of the Romantic poet-seer with the 'economic activism' of the Victorian prophet. The Carlylean Gospel of Work removes salvation from the Romantic realm of individual experience and places it within a decidedly social sphere.

Production might take any number of forms, and the common good might be advanced in many ways: through the invention of theories of social regeneration, through dedication to the service of humanity and, indeed, by a commitment to certain kinds of literary expression. The writing of autobiography could itself be understood as part of the fulfilment of vocation. The Victorian imperative of social usefulness and the habit of renunciation precluded the possibility of autobiography as overt celebration of self, and autobiographers conceived of their personal histories as moral exempla and as inspiriting instruction. Herbert Spencer considered it a 'provoking necessity' that 'an autobiography should be egoistic'; John Stuart Mill rather coyly denied that any part of his autobiographical narrative could possibly be of interest 'as being connected with myself'.[16] Spencer knew that the writing of autobiography was, of necessity, an act of 'egoism', but he and other autobiographers of his age found ways of translating solipsism into selflessness in the explanations they offered for writing about their own lives.

Edmund Gosse describes his *Father and Son* as an 'educational and religious' record, a 'diagnosis of Puritanism'.[17] 'Rutherford' offers his readers comfort and hopes to free them from the solitude that he himself had suffered. And Carlyle, certainly the most highly self-conscious of Victorian autobiographers about the relationship between literary form and idea, uses individual experience as a way of preaching self-reformation and of demonstrating the 'Clothes Philosophy': as symbols embody and reveal the abstract, so do individual experience, individual being, flesh and bone embody and reveal the 'divine ME', the abstract and infinite MEness of the self. In the hands of the Victorian autobiographer, the Romantic 'doctrine of experience' becomes a philosophy of instruction and social amelioration.

BENTHAM V. COLERIDGE: THE DIALECTIC OF VICTORIAN AUTOBIOGRAPHY

The discovery of faith and vocation in the autobiographical works with which I am concerned takes place within a context of dialectical struggle – generational, philosophical or psychological. The autobiographer portrays himself as a man caught, like Faust, between two opposing forces that do battle for his soul; and he recounts a movement toward some form of synthesis rather than an unequivocal victory of one antagonistic force over another. Many were torn, in a post-Darwinian age, between the spirit of science and the spirit of religion. For others the conflict manifested itself as one of Doubt against Faith, or as Materialism against Idealism. In many cases, the autobiographer perceives his parents – or, more commonly, his father – as the embodiment of one particular mode of thought and feeling that he must reject, modify or oppose.

Edmund Gosse introduces his autobiography with the very fact of struggle: 'This book,' he writes, recalling Matthew Arnold's 'Stanzas from the Grand Chartreuse', 'is the record of a struggle between two temperaments, two consciences and almost two epochs. . . . Of the two human beings here described, one was born to fly backward, the other could not help being carried forward.'[18] In his *Apologia*, Cardinal Newman describes an ongoing conflict between the pernicious Rationalism of the eighteenth century and the deeper philosophy and faith shared by both the Romantic poets and the Oxford Movement. And John Stuart Mill identified the particular dialectic that determined his identity as the struggle between Bentham and Coleridge.

Mill's essays, 'Bentham' (1838) and 'Coleridge' (1840), might profitably be read as companion pieces to his *Autobiography*, for in them he attempted to examine in less personal terms the two forces – the 'two great seminal minds of England in their age' – that most influenced his own mind and that bore upon the mental crisis and personal evolution that are described in the *Autobiography*. Bentham and Coleridge represented the two poles between which Mill's ideas, personality and ambitions were shaped, and they stood for a duality that pervaded much of nineteenth-century thought. These two essays are of central importance, then, to the reading of Victorian autobiography: they constitute a debate, a background, a dialogue, against which various individual struggles are played out.

The autobiographer seeks to find his place within the debate between Rationalism and Romanticism. Carlyle arms himself against the rationalist philosophy of his youthful education with the idealism of German Romanticism. He rails against political liberalism, *laissez-faire* economics, ethical hedonism and associationist psychology, against a mechanical and soulless England where

Man's whole life and environment have been laid open and elucidated; scarcely a fragment or fibre of his Soul, Body, and

Possessions, but has been probed, dissected, distilled, desiccated, and scientifically decomposed.[19]

Idealist Germany opposes mechanical and empiricist England as
Coleridge opposes Bentham and as, in Dickens' *Hard Times*,
Sleary's Circus opposes the Gradgrind and Bounderby schools of
thought and practice.

Even those autobiographies that appear to be specifically
religious, that seem to have at their centres the split between belief
and unbelief, revolve around some version of a Bentham/
Coleridge opposition. Gosse and 'Rutherford' find Romanticism,
and Wordsworth in particular, as an antidote to the desiccated
and repressive Calvinism of their upbringings; they react, not
merely against orthodox faith but against an arid religiosity that
does not admit feeling, love of beauty or, indeed, true spirituality.
'Rutherford' describes the stifling and oppressive Sunday atmosphere created by his 'rigid Calvinist Independent' parents, and
this Sunday spirit becomes an emblem for the familial faith he
wants to abandon, much as the London Sabbath gloom of *Little
Dorrit* stands as a symbol of the repressive and guilt-creating
Calvinist childhood that Arthur Clennam suffered in his mother's
home.

Gosse writes even more harshly than 'Rutherford' of the
Calvinist home in which, he says, his soul was 'planted, not as in
an ordinary open flower-border or carefully tended parterre, but
as on a ledge, split in the granite of some mountain'.[20] His parents
had joined a tiny group of Plymouth Brethren 'on terms of what
may almost he called negation – no priest, no ritual, no festivals,
no ornament of any kind'.[21] Directed by their religion, they
renounce story-telling ('not a single fiction was read or told to me
during my infancy'), forbid the singing of secular song, and toss
the servants' Christmas pudding into the ash heap. Gosse rejects
their religion not so much for its dogma as for its lack of humanity.
The aridity of his father's Calvinism and that of James Mill's
Benthamism had the same result: the stifling of creativity and
emotion in the oppressed spirits of their sons.

Even Cardinal Newman explains his attraction first to the
Oxford Movement and then to Catholicism in terms of a reaction
against rationalism, the 'great evil of the day'. Liberalism, the
destroyer of faith and dogma, is as much Newman's enemy as it is
Carlyle's. Newman runs towards dogma, as Gosse and 'Ruther-

ford' run away from it, because he too distrusts reason and wants to embrace a truly felt faith. Catholicism, with its doctrine of infallibility, enables the believer to resist the rational extravagances of human thought and saves him from speculation and scepticism. Newman, embracing religious orthodoxy, and Gosse and 'Rutherford', rejecting it, find in their own interpretations of Romanticism a renovating spirit.

In Mill's essays he envisions, not the defeat of Benthamism in his own life or in history, but a dialectical relationship between Benthamite and Coleridgian ideas that would ultimately result in a synthesis of the best elements of each school. One of his aims in writing the essays was to suggest that each of these 'seminal minds' had its own essential contribution to make to an adequate understanding of humanity and of human institutions. 'In every respect,' Mill wrote, 'the two men are each other's "completing counterpart": the strong points of each correspond to the weak points of the other.'[22] Mill sees the history of opinion as an oscillation between two conflicting streams of thought, between the beliefs of two sorts of men who appear to be enemies but are in fact allies: 'The powers they wield are opposite poles of one great force of progression.'[23] Mill understood this movement of thought in history partly through his own experience of intellectual crisis. He needed to reconcile Bentham and Coleridge for the sake of his own mental equilibrium; he needed to enlarge and modify Utilitarianism by bringing the spirit of culture to bear on the spirit of political economy. His *Autobiography* traces the 'progression' of these opposing modes of thought in his own life.

When Mill came to write his essay on Bentham, more than ten years after the crisis of 1826, he identified the inadequacies of Utilitarian thought as the very inadequacies of his upbringing: Benthamite philosophy lacked any power to aid in the ethical or spiritual life of the individual or of the group. Bentham might assist the body politic in achieving its ends but could do very little in helping to determine *what* those ends should be. His synthesis was incomplete, according to Mill, because his analysis failed; and his analysis failed because in his survey of human nature he overlooked too many crucial elements. Mill understood, because of the interplay between his own intellect and psyche, that the psychological and temperamental limitations of the philosopher resulted in the limitations of his philosophy.

Bentham seemed to value neither the motive of conscience nor the motive of altruism in the 'regeneration of mankind'. And perhaps most important of all to Mill, most closely connected with the crisis that Benthamite philosophy ultimately helped to produce in his own life, was Bentham's ignorance of dejection, that state which Mill looked to Coleridge to define:

> He knew no dejection, no heaviness of heart. He never felt life a sore and weary burden. He was a boy to the last. Self-consciousness, that demon of the men of genius of our time, from Wordsworth to Byron, from Goethe to Chateaubriand, and to which this age owes so much both of its cheerful and of its mournful wisdom, never was awakened in him.[24]

Mill guessed that Bentham was a 'boy to the last': he never passed through the fiery baptism of the 'Everlasting No' or the sad emptiness of the 'Centre of Indifference'. He never adopted the philosophy of maturity, the 'anti-self-consciousness theory of Carlyle'; and he never underwent the kind of crisis that was central to the experience of so many of the great Romantics and of the Victorian writers of spiritual autobiography.

After the mental crisis of 1826, Mill gave greater attention to the 'internal culture of the individual', and found encouragement for this not only in Coleridge and Wordsworth but in certain Continental thinkers. Mill discovered that the Saint-Simonians and Comte and what he called the 'Germano-Coleridge' school understood the role of altruism in human society and the importance of a spirit of community. The Saint-Simonian scheme of socialism, of 'labour and capital . . . managed for the general account of the community', seemed to Mill to lack practicability; but he believed that the expression of such an ideal was in itself of benefit to society.[25] If Mill later became a socialist of sorts, it was from a sense of the central importance of selflessness and of collective effort in the achievement of social, political and individual happiness.[26]

Mill found that it was essential to put faith in social sympathies and to include genuine religious belief as an important element in man's social and intellectual progress, as Bentham had not. Here again, Coleridge could provide an antidote, for he strove 'to bring into harmony religion and philosophy', to make clear that the Christian faith consists not only of 'divine truth' but of the ' "perfection of the human intelligence" '.[27] 'Of unbelievers (so-called) ... there are many species,' Mill wrote in the *Autobiography*, 'including almost every variety of moral type. But the best among them ... are more genuinely religious, in the best sense of the word, than those who exclusively arrogate to themselves the title.'[28] After the crises of his youth, Mill could more easily count himself among the 'religious unbelievers'.

John Stuart Mill never arrived at a radical rejection of Benthamism, and he adopted only those particular aspects of a Coleridgian vision that would broaden and make more humane the Utilitarianism of his father. The political and social ideology – liberalism – to which he devoted himself throughout his career did not represent an actual rupture with his own past. This return to a 'higher', a more elevated and even more authentic, version of the parental dogma is not uncommon in the recorded life-histories of Victorian autobiographers. After 'Mark Rutherford' finds his new mission among the poor of Drury Lane, he marvels at his reformed faith: 'I felt as if somehow, after many errors, I had once more gained a road, a religion in fact, and one which was essentially *not new but old*, the religion of the Reconciliation.'[29]

It is, for both Mill and 'Rutherford', the process of questioning and re-fashioning belief that is crucial; and it is a real breakdown in the ability to sustain faith and work that is at the centre of this experience. For although the autobiographer may not ultimately reject completely the ideologies and values of his origins, he invariably conceives of this psychological and often physical breakdown as a moment in the process of *conversion*. The secularized autobiography of the Victorian age inevitably depends for its language and structure on the narrative of religious conversion. We shall see how, in the case of Beatrice Webb's *My Apprenticeship*, conversion to secular faith gives shape to her life's story and how, ultimately, like Mill and 'Mark Rutherford', she re-encounters essential elements of the faith she inherits in the faith she adopts.

2 *My Apprenticeship*: the Shape of a Life

How can a man learn to know himself? by reflection never – only by action. In the measure that thou seekest to do thy duty shalt thou know what is in thee. But what is thy duty? The demand of the hour.

Goethe

In the Introduction to *My Apprenticeship*, Beatrice Webb writes that beneath the surface of daily existence, her life had been determined by an opposition, a 'continuous controversy between an Ego that affirms and an Ego that denies'. With this phrase she signals an entry into the familiar world of Victorian dichotomies, into a private world of her own that normally remained hidden from public scrutiny, and into a world that bore the mark of Goethe's influence. Her words echo *Faust* – '*der Geist der stets verneint*' – and reflect the Goethe of Carlyle, the Goethe that was perceived as part Saint and part Sceptic.

Webb first read Goethe when she was sixteen, and she continued for many years to consider him a 'master, from whom I should learn the "art of life" '. 'Goethe was read with care and love,' she recalled in 1885, 'my relationship with him was intensely *personal* – his influence over me was for the time supreme.'[1] As a girl, she notes in *My Apprenticeship*, she was an omnivorous reader, but with 'an unusually restricted literary taste':

Of all the great authors whose works I tried to read, only Goethe dominated my mind. For many years I felt towards him as if he were an intimate friend, sharing out his wealth, and revealing to me an entirely new ideal of personal morality, of the relation of art to science, and of art and science to the conduct of life.[2]

Goethe could instruct her how to live because, as Carlyle suggested, he had faced the same questions, the same doubt and despair, the same controversy between affirmation and denial, and had emerged with 'the attainment of inner harmony' that depended, Webb believed, on the solution of this controversy. He also pondered questions which came to be of central importance in the scheme of Webb's inner debates: the question of the role of science in determining a pattern of life and of the need for other influences to guide the hand of science.

Webb's explanation of the exact nature of these two 'Egos' appears stilted and confused, for she tries desperately to offer the explanation on as abstract and impersonal a level as possible in order to suggest the universality of such an internal struggle. But her brief discussion of the two questions generated by the continuous controversy between Egos defines the obsessions of mind and spirit that dominate her autobiography and dominated her life. The first question raises the possibility of a science of society that might enable man to forecast the future and thereby shape it. The second, and more intensely personal, of the two involves the need for religion to determine the ideals on which society will be based:

> assuming that there be, or will be, such a science of society, is man's capacity for scientific discovery the only faculty required for the reorganisation of society according to an ideal? Or do we need religion as well as science, emotional faith as well as intellectual curiosity?   (p. viii)

The affirming Ego believes in both the efficacy of social science and the additional need for a religious ideal to give ethical direction to science. The denying Ego is the doubter, the sceptic, who questions the value of both religious faith and social science. In her autobiography, Webb will offer her tentative answers to these questions as a 'philosopohy of work or life'. As she is no philosopher, she will present her beliefs in 'the simpler form of personal experience'.

She was, however, a social scientist, and *My Apprenticeship* is the autobiography not only of a Victorian and of a woman, but of a sociologist as well. Webb arrives at a rather extreme version of the Victorian autobiographer's standard denial of egoism – 'I have neither the desire nor the intention of writing an autobiography' –

but she defends her record of the events and private struggles of her life in a new way. She justifies her autobiography as a sociologist's means of revealing her philosophy and her identity:

> the very subject-matter of my science is society; its main instrument is social intercourse; thus I can hardly leave out of the picture the experience I have gathered, not deliberately as a scientific worker, but casually as a child, unmarried woman, wife and citizen. For the sociologist . . . is in a quite unique manner the creature of his environment. Birth and parentage, the mental atmosphere of class and creed in which he is bred, the characteristics and attainments of the men and women who have been his guides and associates, come first and foremost of all the raw material upon which he works. . . . It is his own social and economic circumstances that determine the special opportunities, the peculiar disabilities, the particular stand-points for observation and reasoning – in short, the inevitable bias with which he is started on his way to dis-covery. (pp. 1–2)

The vocation of social science combined with the creed, socialism, that constitutes her 'inevitable bias', can best be made intelligible through an explanation of the social milieu from which she came and against which she reacted. Here, the justification of the autobiographer and the logic of the sociologist merge.

THE POTTER FAMILY: DOMINANT ORTHODOXIES AND ALTERNATIVES

Beatrice Webb's 'inevitable bias' – her eventual political and social attitudes and prejudices – evolved, at least in part, through a rejection of certain elements of what she saw as the Potter family orthodoxy. Like the autobiographers described in the preceding chapter, she regarded the evolution of her beliefs as inseparable from her familial experience and, like them, she attributed her own childhood unhappiness and feelings of loneliness and neglect to the inadequacies of her parents' *ways of thinking*, to their ideas as well as to their personalities. She writes in *My Apprenticeship* that the Potter household was dominated by the spirit of capitalist enterprise, and that the family's participation in the habitual comings and goings of upper middle-class life created what Webb called a 'nomadic' existence, characterized by perpetual movement and change:

> The world of human intercourse in which I was brought up was in fact an endless series of human beings, unrelated one to the other, and only casually connected with the family group – a miscellaneous crowd who came and went out of our lives, rapidly and unexpectedly. Servants came and went; governesses and tutors came and went; business men of all sorts ... came and went; perpetually changing circles of 'London Society' acquaintances came and went. . . . Our social relations had no roots in neighborhood, in vocation, in creed, or for that matter in race; they likened a series of moving pictures – surface impressions without depth – restlessly stimulating in their glittering variety. (pp. 40–1)

Richard Potter, Beatrice's father, also came and went, making frequent business trips to Canada, the United States and Holland in his capacity as director of the Great Western Railway, president of the Grand Trunk Railway of Canada, and investor in the Hudson Bay Company and the Dutch Rhenish railways. In her autobiography, Webb attributes to her father the ethic of amorality that she finds to be characteristic of a mid-Victorian 'capitalist at large'. He was fickle in politics and in religion: he abandoned the Radicalism of his father and casually attended Anglican services without ever having been confirmed into the Church of England. She argues that he was a highly successful capitalist, both as director of railways and owner of Gloucestershire timber yards, precisely because his 'conception of right conduct was a spacious one, of loose texture, easily penetrated by the surrounding moral atmosphere'. Potter dismissed as 'moral pedantry' conduct that was dictated by anything other than pragmatism or personal allegiance. His daughter takes him to task for having no fixed principles, no fixed faith and, above all, 'no clear vision of the public good'.

There is a symbolic appropriateness to Richard Potter's involvement with the railway, that emblem of the equivocal nature of Victorian progress. Dickens put the railway at the centre of *Dombey and Son*, a novel that exposes the confusion of business morality with human morality, the way in which family life is corroded by the ethic of the 'cash nexus'. The railway runs through Staggs Garden with a kind of amoral oblivion, blithely destroying old ways of life and communities and playing havoc with notions of time and distance. The constant change and movement of the Potter household, and the ambition, unencumbered by ethics, of Richard Potter, are understood in Dickens' vision of the effects of industrial capitalism on family life.[3]

If Richard Potter appeared chameleon-like to his daughter, Laurencina Potter, Beatrice's mother, appeared unbending in her dedication to strict Utilitarian politics and *laissez-faire* economics. Mrs Potter was raised on Adam Smith, Malthus and Nassau Senior, and her closest intellectual confidant was Herbert Spencer. Her belief in the law of self-interest was absolute: it seemed to her the 'bounden duty of every citizen to better his social status, to ignore those beneath him, and to aim steadily at the top rung of the social ladder' (p. 16). She considered it self-indulgent 'to pay more than the market rate, to exact fewer than the customary hours or insist on less than the usual strain'. Webb sums up her mother's philosophy of life and work in a mid-Victorian maxim worthy of Thomas Gradgrind or Josiah Bounderby: ' "The man who sells his cow too cheap goes to hell." ' Webb's father minimized the importance of a consistent faith, and her mother's social philosophy was at odds with what she understood to be a truly Christian spirit.

When F. R. Leavis suggested that Webb's autobiography 'carries on from much the point at which Mill's stops', he had in mind the apparent continuity between the ethos of James Mill's tutelage and the atmosphere of the Potter home.[4] In their autobiographies, Webb and John Stuart Mill write of a quiet rebellion against the same orthodoxies, against a rigid Utilitarianism and the ethos of political economy. In similar but far more self-destructive rebellion is Dickens' Louisa Gradgrind, a fictional representation of the casualties suffered by the child raised on Utilitarian principles. When Webb writes of her childhood conception of 'labour' as an abstraction, as an 'arithmetically calculable mass of human beings', 'never visualized as separate men and women', she recalls Louisa coming face to face with the individuality of a 'Coketown Hand' for the first time. Heretofore 'Hands' had been to her a mass of creatures, like ants or beetles, or like a body of water that sometimes rose and then fell but was never separated 'into its component drops'.[5] Water was also the metaphor associated with the working class in Webb's childish mind: the headlines she saw on her father's library table – ' "Water plentiful and labour docile", "The wages of labour are falling to their natural level" ' – gave a 'queer physico-mechanical twist' to her conception of labouring men (p.41).

Webb[6] saw the spirit of *laissez-faire* embodied not only in her mother but in Laurencina Potter's intellectual soulmate, the 'philosopher on the hearth' of the Potter household, Herbert Spencer. The Potter home was visited by many men of science, philosophy and politics – by James Martineau, Frederic Harrison, J. A. Froude, Sir Joseph Hooker, Tyndall and Huxley – but the family's most intimate friend among Victorian intellectuals was Spencer. The Potter parents' differences of temperament were reflected in their divergent attitudes toward the 'incessantly ratiocinating philosopher'. Richard Potter felt great affection for him, but displayed complete indifference to his ideas: 'he would walk with him, he would fish with him, he would travel with him . . . but argue with him or read his books he would not'. Laurencina Potter, on the other hand, found in Spencer an ally with whom she could talk and argue in evening debates that lasted long after her husband had grown bored and gone to bed.

Webb's relationship to Spencer was an important and an ambivalent one. Spencer acted as 'liberator' to all of the Potter daughters, taking them on nature hikes in the Gloucestershire woods and freeing them from the boredom and constraint of the classroom; but in Beatrice Potter's life he played the unique role of first intellectual mentor:

> It was the philosopher on the hearth who, alone among my elders . . . encouraged me in my lonely studies; who heard patiently and criticized kindly my untutored scribblings about Greek and German philosophers; who delighted and stimulated me with the remark that I was a 'born metaphysician', and that I 'reminded him of George Eliot'; who was always pressing me to become a scientific worker.   (p. 28)

Spencer's role in Webb's development was complex. She reacted vehemently against the Individualist ethic he shared with her mother; she came to condemn his 'failure to attain to the higher levels of conduct and feeling'; and she eventually saw his warped personality as the sad result of the 'bankruptcy of science when it attempts to realize the cause or the aim of human existence'. But from him she first learned to regard social institutions as 'organisms' to be observed and explained, to understand the usefulness of *facts* – 'a gift said to be rare in a woman and of untold importance to the social investigator' – and she inherited from him an interest in the evolution of institutions which was later expressed in her historical approach to social investigation (pp. 27, 38). To use Webb's own terms, she fiercely rejected the articles of his Creed while using the tools of his Craft as a basis for her own innovations. 'There is indeed no limit to what I owe to my thirty or forty years intimacy with this unique life,' she writes, 'no less as a warning than as a model' (p. 29).

If Richard Potter's capitalist ethic and Laurencina Potter's Spencerian dogmas of Individualism and *laissez-faire* formed the dominant orthodoxies of the household and, at the same time, left their daughter with a sense of disturbing rootlessness and spiritual emptiness, it was the example of Beatrice Webb's grandparents and of Martha Jackson, the 'household saint', that offered a set of alternative principles by which to live. Richard Potter Sr and Lawrence Heyworth were both Northern industrialists, self-made men, 'non-conformists in religion and Radicals in politics', both elected to Parliament after the Reform Act of 1832. Potter, called 'Radical Dick', the son of a Yorkshire tenant farmer, had a cotton warehouse in Manchester and supported Free Trade, the Anti-Corn Law League, the abolition of slavery, Catholic Emancipation and the protesters at Peterloo.[7] Heyworth, from a family of Lancashire domestic weavers and cotton hands, prospered as a Liverpool merchant, trading primarily with South America, and shared the Radical political sentiments of Richard Potter Sr.[8] Webb describes these two typical representatives of the political and economic developments of nineteenth-century industrial England at the beginning of *My Apprenticeship*, not only to suggest something of her parents' origins, but to offer her grandparents' spirit, their association with community life, their principled and active dedication to the egalitarian thrust of Radicalism as a contrast to the rootless and seemingly unprincipled atmosphere of the life of her immediate family. The Potter and Heyworth ancestry and their Northern origins, from which Webb's parents had all but cut themselves off, came to represent for her a way of life that held meaning, religious purpose and a true collective and communal spirit. 'I was reared in Toryism,' she once told an interviewer, 'but as I grew up, the Radicalism of my ancestors revived in me.'[9]

Martha Jackson, called 'Dada', had acted as companion to Mrs Potter, and subsequently became nursemaid to her daughters. She was actually a distant Heyworth relation – a poor relation – whose familial connection to the Potter family was not, oddly enough, revealed to Beatrice Potter until she was in her twenties. Webb notes, in comparing the influences on her of Herbert Spencer and Martha Jackson, that he was 'in intellect towering above her, but in emotional insight depths below her'. She herein identifies one of the dichotomies that dominated her own life: the debate, familiar to so many Victorian autobiographers, between intellect and emotion, between reason and feeling. Webb came to associate Martha Jackson with the earnest world of her grandparents, with the spirit of community she discovered in the Northern industrial towns of their birth and, most importantly, with religion: 'The most far-reaching and influential of Martha's gifts was her revelation of the meaning of the religious spirit' (p. 20). This spirit, absent in the conduct and temperament of the Potter parents, made 'Dada' seem to Webb the embodiment of an 'overpowering consciousness of love' and the dispenser of justice, of an 'equalitarian beneficence'.

The complex of associations and principles that Martha Jackson embodied for Webb – the Northern roots of her grandparents' Radicalism, a sense of community and cooperation, a spirit of religion and love, an attitude of unsentimental and evenhanded benevolence – later emerged as themes in the process of Webb's conversion to socialism. Those characteristics of personality and temperament that she associated with Herbert Spencer became identified with the Individualist ethic she rejected. The first reflections of Webb's debating Egos are visible in her connections to these two early mentors, one spiritual and the other intellectual. Spencer convinced her that a science of society was indeed possible and, at the same time, caused her to question the adequacy of science in solving social problems. Martha Jackson alerted her to the need for 'religion as well as science, emotional faith as well as intellectual curiosity'. Richard Potter was a conventionally religious man but, unlike 'Dada', his behaviour betrayed a lack of spiritual and moral purpose that caused Webb to question not only the ethic of capitalism but that of organized Christianity. And Laurencina Potter's political and economic orthodoxies, combined with a personal coldness and aloofness, served ultimately to alienate her daughter from a rigid Utilitarian point of view and from a way of dealing with people according to the rules of political economy.

YEARS OF CRISIS AND THE SEARCH FOR FAITH

Webb writes of the years between early adolescence and marriage as a prolonged period of intermittent anxiety, depression and confusion. There were two moments of acute crisis during these years, one in the mid-1870s and the other in the mid-1880s: the first of these inaugurated a search for faith and the second a search for vocation. In the 1870s, Webb experienced an adolescent depression and consequent conversion to orthodox Christianity. Although this conversion was promptly followed by a loss of faith, she continued to feel the need to find 'a creed by which I could live' and, in the years spanning her two breakdowns in health and spirit, she explored various solutions to the problem of belief. Her second crisis, one of sexual and social identity, was precipitated by a forced withdrawal from the work that she had newly embraced as her life's purpose. This crisis ended in a renewed commitment to vocation; it marked the beginning of her apprenticeship as a social investigator; and it set in motion her gradual conversion to the creed of Socialism. The faith she had so determinedly sought in the years between the crises of adolescence and young womanhood grew ultimately out of the vocation she adopted as she approached her thirtieth year.

Beatrice Webb's childhood was marked by depression and ill-health, and by a painful sense of aloofness from other members of her family. She often took refuge in the laundry-room of the house, where she felt comforted by the warmth of the newly-dried sheets and table-cloths and by the attention of the servants, or in 'secret places, under the shade of grub and tree, in the leaf-filled hollows of the wood and in the crevices of the quarries' where she would daydream about love scenes and death-bed scenes and 'conjure up the intimacy and tenderness' lacking in her life. Her sense of isolation was related to the continual illness that led to fleeting plans of suicide:

Indeed, almost continuous illness, bouts of neuralgia, of indigestion, of inflammation of all sorts and kinds, from inflamed eyes to congested lungs, marred my happiness; and worse than physical pain was boredom, due to the incapacity of ill-health. . . . I have a vivid memory of stealing and secreting a small bottle of chloroform from the family medicine-chest as a vaguely imagined alternative to the pains of life and the ennui of living; and of my consternation when one day I found the stopper loose and the contents evaporated.   (p. 58)

Although her ill-health and accompanying depression seem to have been chronic, there were certain distinct periods in her life in which she became immobilized by emotional crisis. These 'breakdowns', as she herself called them, recurred until very late in life; and two such instances occurred during her first thirty-three years and are recorded in *My Apprenticeship*.

The nine Potter daughters were educated by German, French and English governesses at Standish, their Gloucestershire home. Beatrice, however, could never sustain a season of regular schoolroom hours: 'after a few weeks or months . . . I always took to my bed, the family doctor prescribing "no lessons, more open-air exercise, if possible a complete change of scene" ' (p. 59). So she invented her own method of 'self-culture'; she would read whatever books interested her, and write reviews or summaries of them in her diary. At the beginning of 1874, at age sixteen, she was reading, translating and commenting upon *Faust*. What most impressed her about *Faust* was Goethe's demonstration of the failure of knowledge to make men contented. Faust, after all, reaches the 'zenith of human knowledge' and neverthe-less contemplates suicide. Webb remarked in her notes on *Faust* that his resolve to commit suicide is broken 'by the feeling which the church bells and the songs of the choir on Easter morning awaken in him' (8 January 1874). In the following months, her own life would seem to mimic, in adolescent fashion, the pattern she perceived in *Faust*: a painful period of unhappiness and illness would end in a phase of extreme Christian devotion.

A few months after she had begun to translate *Faust*, she resolved to 'make a faith' for herself:

I am really trying to gain a firm belief for myself. I think it is no good going to others to have your belief cut out for you; you must examine, study, both the Bible and the lives of those who follow the Bible and those who don't. It is no sin to doubt, but it is a sin, after you have doubted, not to find out to the best of your capability why you doubt, and whether you have reason to doubt. . . . I must make a faith for myself, and I must work, work, until I have.   (p. 72)

By the following autumn, after a tiring London Season, she was 'in bad health and desperately unhappy', suspected that the only cure for it might be 'to go heart and soul into religion', and lamented that she had not been brought up to believe 'that to doubt was a crime'. Through the autumn months, her health deteriorated and she was bedridden:

I am suffering from an indisposition which is decidedly trying to one's health of mind as it . . . makes one discontented and low-spirited. I have never felt so low-spirited as I have this autumn. I have felt for the first time in my life how much unhappiness there is in life. *But one has not been given the choice of existing or not existing.*   (p. 74)

Webb notes that after this the 'breakdown in health became serious' and that, as a consequence, she was sent to board at a fashionable girls' school in Bournemouth; it was at Bournemouth that she sought 'mental security in traditional Christianity'.

Following, in her own manner, the pattern of *Faust*, she received the Holy Sacrament for the first time at Easter, 1875. She reached a height of religious devotion and solemnity that transformed even the language and tone of her diary:

Easter Eve. The day before I receive for the first time the Holy Sacrament. The last month or two has been a very solemn epoch in my life, and may God grant that I may never cease remembering the vows which I have made before God and man, that I intend to become a true Christian, that is, a true disciple and follower of Jesus Christ, making Him my sole aim in life. And now I am going to receive the great sacrament, which He Himself instituted as a perpetual means of remembering His visit on earth.   (p. 75)

Her devotion continued through the months of 1875: she lived an ascetic life of religious study, tried to purge herself of the sins of vanity and lying, continued to take the sacrament, resolved never to 'come out' and to make her 'aim in life the understanding and acting up to religion'.

By the winter of 1875–6, she had begun to struggle with growing doubts about certain aspects of Christian dogma, and her orthodoxy had begun to wane. She left Bournemouth at the beginning of 1876, torn between the opposing demands of her faith and her powers of reason, and continued to debate theology with her cousin Margaret Harkness, whose close friend she had become at boarding school and whose adolescent seriousness matched her own. 'I agree with you,' Margaret responded to her cousin's queries about the nature of God, 'in feeling the greatest reverence for the Good, the Beautiful and the True, but I cannot see how we can argue from there, that they are God or of God. All I really believe is that the universe is the production of one universal mind which I call God. . . . I doubt if you have ever been such a sceptic as I.'[10]

Spring of 1876 took the entire Potter family to London for the Season, and here Beatrice's encounters with 'currents of thought at that time stirring in the minds of those who frequented the outer, more unconventional and . . . more cultivated circles of London society' caused a 'sudden revolt of intellect' and further undermined her traditional Christian beliefs. She wondered, however, if a new and higher faith would replace the one rejected:

> I have indeed altered my religious belief in this last six months to an extent I should never have thought possible a year ago. I see now that the year I spent at Bournemouth I was vainly trying to smother my instinct of truth in clinging to the old faith. And now that I have shaken off the chains of the beautiful old faith, shall I rise to something higher, or shall I stare about me like a newly liberated slave, unable to decide which way to go, and perhaps the worse for being freed from the service of a kind master.   (p. 81)

Christianity had provided comfort in a period of adolescent depression; conversion had grown out of a temporary psychic need, and could not be sustained beyond the point at which her intellectual curiosity took precedence over those slowly subsiding needs.[11] Even after her de-conversion from Christian orthodoxy occurred, however, her search for Creed continued.

The years following this adolescent episode were marked by
continual musings on the need for faith, by an interest in Herbert
Spencer's 'Religion of Science' and by a final refuge-taking in an
idiosyncratic habit of prayer. In the autumn and winter months of
1876, she not only read the works of Spencer but developed an
interest in Eastern religions. Buddhism seemed a likely alternative to the Christian Church and Bible; Buddha and his
philosophy appeared to her to be 'logically and ethically superior
to Christ and the teachings of the New Testament'. What
appealed to her in Buddhism, as she understood it, were its
renunciation of the world and the flesh, its offer of Nirvana and its
'superficial likeness to the philosophy of modern science', or 'an
agnosticism even more complete than that of Herbert Spencer'
(p. 85). Living in what she called a 'stronghold of capitalism,
surrounded by the pleasure-grounds of London', she distrusted
the adulation of personality and the influence of worldly experience. Yet Buddhism found in her no convert: its poetry and
mystery fascinated her, but its most significant impact on her was
the further loosening of her bond to traditional Christianity.[12]
Neither Christianity nor Eastern religion would suit her, and it
was not long before she came to believe that she had found a
spiritual resting-place in the 'Religion of Science'.

'The God was the Unknowable,' she writes in *My Apprenticeship*,
'the prophet was Herbert Spencer. Prayer might have to go, but
worship would remain.' Webb first read *Social Statics* and *First
Principles* in the winter of 1876–7, when she was eighteen, copied
long passages from these works into her diary, and exclaimed, at
the end of a long quotation from *Social Statics*, 'Who could wish for
a grander faith than this!' She read Spencer for the first time, not
as a social scientist, not as a scientific guide to the evolution and
organization of society, but as the proponent of a substitute
religion. She looked for a God in Spencerian theory and, though
she eventually came to reject the 'Unknowable' as a force to
worship, at this earlier date she felt 'happy and contented' at the
mystery she perceived in the 'Great Unknown':

> The consciousness of the Unknowable, the 'Great Mystery
> underlying all things' is the fundamental idea which has
> prompted all religions and which is the ground of reconciliation
> between Science and Religion – Both alike declare it in their
> truest moments – Indeed these first chapters of Mr Spencer's

First Principles appear to me to be most truly religious as well as scientific – and written in a tolerant tone, quite untainted by any antagonism to Religion. (13 December 1877)

She perceived in Spencer's philosophy not only a divinity to worship, but a true marriage of Religion and Science.

Spencer's theories, because of what she sought in them, could not long sustain her, and in the final years of the 1870s and first years of the 1880s she was bothered by an awareness that she lacked the kind of real faith that would support her in times of unhappiness. 'The religion of science,' she wrote, 'has its dark side':

It is bleak and dreary in sorrow and ill-health. And to those whose lives are one continual suffering it has but one word to say – suicide. If you cannot bear it any longer, and if no ties of duty turn you from extinguishing that little flame of your existence – depart in peace: cease to exist. It is a dreadful thought. It can never be the religion of a 'suffering humanity'. The time may come, and I believe it will come, when human life will be sufficiently happy and full to be unselfish. But there are long ages yet to be passed, and generations of men will still cry in their misery for another life to compensate for their life-long sorrow and suffering. (p. 94)

Spencer's 'Unknowable' provided insufficient comfort. Ultimately she came to reject his *laissez-faire* bias as the most glaring fault of his social analysis, but among her first reasons for questioning Spencer's wisdom was what she later called his 'materialism'; she found that *she* had 'an inclination to doubt materialism more than . . . spiritualism'.

She needed the solace of Christianity, but she found it still an immoral religion: the idea of working diligently and believing blindly for the sake of one's own salvation seemed to her a doctrine of selfishness. In the religion of the future there might be true unselfishness, true spirit of community and altruism. But was her own happiness, she wondered, the result of faithlessness: 'does my want of happiness come from my want of belief in the old faith which has helped so many thousands along this weary way?' (p. 95).

In 1878, she visited Prague with her family, and was particu-

larly struck by the Jewish Quarter, by the 'unity' of the Jews that
seemed to survive 'misery, squalor and death' and by the beauty
and music of a Jewish service (12 and 13 October 1878). Her
response to a silent mass at St Peter's, during a trip to Italy in
1880–1, was even more enthusiastic, and she became convinced
during this visit that although her 'logical or intellectual faculty'
made her a sceptic, her 'emotional faculty' demanded fulfilment:
'I possess another faculty – the emotional – which is the dominant
spirit in all my better and nobler moments. This spirit unceas-
ingly insists that there is something above and around us which is
worthy of absolute devotion and devout worship.' 'Could not the
agnostic,' she asked herself, 'if he felt that his nature was not
sufficiently developed to live without an emotional religion, could
not he renounce his freedom to reason on that one subject, and
submit to the authority of the great religious body on that subject
of religion?' (pp. 96–8). She was reading *Daniel Deronda* with great
interest during her Italian journey, and found that she admired in
George Eliot's novel 'the preference she gives to emotive over
purely rational thought' (2 February 1881). The controversy
between the two Egos was moving toward a temporary resolution; Webb was still looking for a church. The death of her mother
in 1882 found her ready for a renewal of religious faith, and
pushed her towards the refuge of prayer and work.

The death of Laurencina Potter in the spring of 1882 did not
lead to a period of crisis in her daughter's life, but rather acted as
an impetus to believe and to work. The sense of purpose and new
energy released by her mother's death culminated in dedication to
daily study and prayer. '[A] new and wondrous faith has arisen
within me,' she wrote in her diary, 'a faith in goodness – in God. I
must pray, I do pray and I feel better for it' (p. 100). For the first
time since she had left Bournemouth she took communion, and
she lamented the intervening six years of 'more or less dreary
materialism'. She retained the habit of prayer, a habit she could
never successfully explain to either her friends' or her own
satisfaction, throughout her life. In the ten years between her
mother's death and her own marriage, prayer enabled her, she
writes, 'to survive, and to emerge relatively sound in body and
sane in mind'. She associated it with the determination to work
diligently, not for the ends of personal vanity, but towards a
common good. In the months following the death of her mother
she wrote:

Now I have within me a definite ambition . . . it has taken possession of me and filled a vacancy. . . . I know more decidedly than ever what materials and what tools I want – the mastery of some synthetical philosophy, to bind together isolated groups of ideas and experiences, experience of human nature by careful observation and experiment! and certain necessary tools, such as a fair knowledge of numbers and their relation, and some power of correct expression.   (13 August 1882)

She began at this time a regimen of early-morning study to prepare herself for some as-yet-unknown vocation. For eighteen months, she noted in 1884, 'duty and faith still burnt clearly', but those months of peaceful work and prayer ended in the second crisis of Webb's early life.

In November 1884, she recorded that her eighteen months of faith had come to an end and that a period of depression had begun:

Have seldom felt more strangely ominous than I do now; as if death were approaching – Personally it would be welcome. . . . It is curious this feeling of life being *ended*. . . . How is it that anyone cares for life? I have always hoped for better and better has never come.   (26 November 1884)

This feeling of utter bleakness and sense of life's being over was caused in part by what appeared to be the end of a problematic relationship with the Birmingham Radical, Joseph Chamberlain, but in *My Apprenticeship* Webb never refers directly to the passionate nature of this relationship or to her sometimes fervent desire to marry Chamberlain. She alludes only to a 'black thread of personal unhappiness woven into the texture' of her account of the events of her life in the mid-1880s. She does record in the autobiography, however, in words recalling both Mill's and Carlyle's rejection of the goal of happiness, a new-found determination to begin to 'live for others, and take what happiness comes to us by the way' (p. 272). The path of personal happiness and gratification having been blocked, she decided to make service and work her goals.

But this decision too was thwarted. Her father suffered a stroke in November 1885, and Webb was tied to home as his nurse and constant companion. The experience of work ceased to be available to her – 'I was deprived of the narcotic of work, and . . . this abstinence was tormenting'. She found herself with neither the fulfilment of personal relationship nor the satisfaction of useful activity; her despair and dejection reached Coleridgian proportions:

> Life seems to my consciousness a horrible fact. Sometimes I wonder how long I shall support it. . . .
> I look out tonight on that hateful grey sea, the breaking and the vanishing of the surf on the shore; the waves break and vanish like my spasms of feeling; but they return again and again, and behind them is the bottomless ocean of despair. . . .
> Now and again deceived by a movement of physical energy, and then falling back on the monotony of despair. No future but a vain repetition of the breaking waves of feeling.   (p. 273)

She had reached the 'dead point'. Months of anxiety, gloom and 'suicidal thoughts' followed. In January 1886, she composed a will in which she left her books to Margaret Harkness, ordered her diaries destroyed, and claimed that: 'If Death comes it will be welcome – for life has always been distasteful to me.'[13]

This depression ended under the dual influences of work rewarded and a revival of religious fervour. 'Two days after that wail of egotistical misery,' writes Webb, referring to the diary entry just quoted, 'there came a letter! Not a love letter, dear reader, but a prosaic communication from the editor of the *Pall Mall Gazette*.' She had written a letter to the editor offering her views on the state of unemployment in East London, of which she had had some experience while rent-collecting in an East End dwelling. On 13 February 1886, she pasted in her diary the very brief note that she had received from the *Pall Mall Gazette* that requested her permission to publish her name at the heading of her 'article', and wrote above it: 'A turning point in my life.'[14] What had been offered as a letter-to-the-editor appeared as a column entitled 'A Lady's View of the Unemployed at the East'. This 'slight recognition of my capacity as a writer on social questions' indicated to Webb that her ambition might be satisfied, that her intelligence and opinions might be respected, that she could, in fact, work.

A month later, she was experiencing the 'holy influence' of

religion once again, and taking the sacrament. Webb returned to this ritual of the church she could not join as she had done after her mother's death. She was again at Bournemouth, the scene of her first rush of Christian devotion, and she speculated on the effect of her old associations with this place on her renewed religious feeling. The sacrament seemed to her 'the great symbol of sacrifice – of the sacrifice of individual life and happiness' (15 March 1886). 'The bleak suicidal despair has vanished,' she wrote in her diary, 'given way to a steady, religious melancholy. . . . It will be a sad life; God grant that it may be a useful one – that I may dedicate myself earnestly and without trembling to a search after the truths which will help my people' (4 April 1886). Frederic Harrison, a Gloucestershire neighbour and friend, heard in the spring of 1886 that Beatrice Potter had become a Catholic (28 May 1886). She had not taken this radical step, but in the withdrawal to Bournemouth that had been necessitated by her father's condition, she had settled into a monastic and apparently satisfying existence of faith and work. She read St Augustine, continued the self-training of a student of society by reading history and philosophy, and fortified herself to renounce not only the worldly life of London Society but the possibility of private happiness as wife and mother.

In the years following the crisis of 1885–6, Webb continued to profess a Carlylean faith in work as saviour and a Wordsworthian sense that she was fulfilling the mission chosen for her by a power greater than herself. She also continued her self-styled practice of praying, and frequented St Paul's for communion services. 'Faith' and 'work' were the constantly recurring keynotes of her diary entries: 'My life must be summed up in the two words: Work and Pray'; 'My work, now, absolutely absorbs me – when I am too tired to work, I pray'; 'The Faith in my own capacity to do this work burns in communion with my faith in the great Spirit before whom all things are equally small – it brightens or darkens with this higher faith' (p. 274; 25 October & 28 March 1888). When she began a new diary book in March 1887, she copied out the following quotation from Zola on the flyleaf: '*L'Avenir est aux laborieux qui se mettent chaque matin devant leur table, avec l'unique foi dans l'étude et dans leur volonté.*' The Victorian notion of vocation – of faith coupled with work for the good of humanity – evolved in her consciousness as she emerged from her 'silent agony' of 1885–6. She was now aware of having a 'special mission to society at large' and of being 'but an instrument to be handled or thrown on one side, by a Greater Power' (21 July 1888). Like Wordsworth, she felt herself to be among the elect and, like Carlyle and Mill, she found work for the common good to be the cure for 'despairing self-consciousness'.

VOCATION AND CONVERSION

During these 'years of apprenticeship', when faith and work set the tone of her daily life, Webb discovered her vocation and, in so doing, began the gradual conversion to Socialism that is the central theme of *My Apprenticeship*. This conversion, from Individualism to Collectivism, had its roots in her rejection of the ethos of her home, and was set in motion when she took up the craft of social investigation. The faith toward which she gravitated was generated out of the work she did in the 1880s, and out of the political temper of the decade. Her first crisis resulted in a temporary devotion to orthodox Christianity; her crisis of the 1880s ended in a commitment to the work of social investigation and a translation of the remnants of Christian faith into the 'faith' of Socialism.

Webb adopted her vocation in the atmosphere of what she calls the 'mid-Victorian Time-Spirit', a spirit that combined belief in the powers of science with the 'impulse of self-subordinating service . . . transferred, consciously and overtly, from God to man'. '[I]t is hard to understand,' she wrote in the 1920s, 'the naive belief of the most original and vigorous minds of the 'seventies and 'eighties that it was by science, and by science alone, that all human misery would be ultimately swept away' (p. 126). Science could demonstrate how the purpose of life might be fulfilled, and the purpose itself would be determined by this transfer of the impulse of service from God to society. If science was to be the method and service the purpose, Webb 'drew the inference that the most hopeful form of social service was the craft of a social investigator'. Herbert Spencer had encouraged her work in the natural sciences, and advised her, in 1883, to take up the 'absorbent organs in the leaves, roots and seeds of plants' as a line of inquiry, but she was not 'interested in rocks and plants, grubs and animals, not even in man considered as a biped'. 'What roused and absorbed my curiosity,' she writes, 'were men and women, regarded – if I may use an old-fashioned word – as "souls", their past and present conditions of life, their thoughts and feelings and their constantly changing behavior' (p. 133). Auguste Comte represented to Webb and to many of her contemporaries a culmination of the 'mid-Victorian Time-Spirit'. The union of a glorification of science with a 'religion of humanity' suited Victorian intellectual needs and made the 'science of society' appear a logical and morally justified vocation. The craft of social investigation, sanctioned by the ethos of the 1880s and by the philosophies of men like Comte, was not yet recognized 'in the laboratories of the universities', and Webb's apprenticeship took place in the field and at her own desk, at first under her own supervision and ultimately under the direction of one of the first of English scientific social investigators, Charles Booth.

The state of poverty of masses of English people was of concern not only to those burdened by what Webb calls a 'consciousness of sin' – the 'collective or class consciousness . . . that the industrial organization which had yielded rent, interest and profits on a stupendous scale, had failed to provide a decent livelihood and tolerable conditions for a majority of the inhabitants of Great Britain' – but also to those who feared the power of the working classes and to those for whom poverty was a challenging and even fashionable intellectual issue (p. 174). Even the Potter family opened its eyes to the causes of the lockouts and strikes of the early 1880s: Richard Potter, 'with a puzzled expression, sought enlightenment from Carlyle's *Past and Present*'; Kate Potter (later Courtney) volunteered as a rent-collector in the East End of London; and during the London Season of 1883, Beatrice Potter joined the Charity Organisation Society.

The stages of Webb's professional and political transformations will be discussed at length in the third part of this study, but in the remaining pages of this chapter, I shall sketch briefly the course that her work took in the 1880s in order to complete the story of conversion that forms the central theme of her autobiography. As Webb went from one project to another, rejecting certain established kinds of work and inventing new ones, she moved closer and closer to a rejection of Individualism and to an acceptance of Collectivism. Like 'Mark Rutherford', who discovered a new form of faith only after he had found vocation, Webb was brought to the 'Creed' of Fabianism only after she had made social investigation her 'Craft'.

The 'mid-Victorian Time-Spirit' and the 'consciousness of sin' that pervaded certain sections of Webb's own class made 'slumming' and charity-work likely activities for a young woman looking for some way of translating what she had learned at her own desk into useful action. During the London Season of 1883, Webb became a philanthropic 'case-worker', visiting the homes of the poor in order to determine which families were 'deserving' and which 'undeserving' of charitable assistance from private organizations. She was attracted to this work with the Charity Organisation Society because of its ostensibly 'scientific' approach to the problem of poverty but, after a few months of acting as what she called 'an intruder in the poor man's hovel', she became disillusioned with the entire project of philanthropy. She came to feel that charity would never solve the enormous problems of chronic poverty, and that she was neither investigating nor comforting nor even dealing justly with the poor. Webb was also convinced that the destitute poor of London were not representative of the stable working class, and she wanted to observe working people, not in a state of crisis, but under conditions of relative normality. For this, she turned her interests northward and took her first step as a social investigator in Bacup, the Lancashire home of her Heyworth ancestors.

In the autumn of 1883, she adopted the first of the disguises she would resort to as a 'participatory observer' of working-class life. It was Martha Jackson who took her to Bacup and introduced her as 'Miss Jones', Welsh farmer's daughter. In a series of letters to her father, woven into the text of *My Apprenticeship*, Webb describes the working, religious and social life of the Bacup factory-workers and artisans. Her visits to the factory, the chapel, the Co-operative store and to individual homes convinced her of the importance of the role of dissenting Christianity and of Co-operation in the life of the community. She felt personally comforted and warmed by the spirit of religion and community she observed, and she gained infinite respect for the way these men and women attempted to govern their own lives with collectivist energy. 'Mere philanthropists are apt to overlook the existence of an independent working class,' she wrote to her father, 'and when they talk sentimentally of the "people" they

really mean the "ne-er-do-weels" ' (p. 152). She returned home
with a vision of working-class life based on community, cooperation, and religious spirit that she could compare not only to the
lives of impoverished Londoners but to the life, governed by the
Individualist and capitalist spirit, of her own family.

Just over a year later, in January 1885, she continued her
investigation of the lives of the poor as a resident rent-collector for
the owners of an East End working-class dwelling, Katherine
Buildings. Here she could observe the people, not as 'failures'
applying for charity, but as functioning members of an East End
world. As a rent-collector, she hoped to be regarded as 'part of the
normal machinery' of the inhabitants' lives, rather than as a
detective or an upper-class lady doing a bit of 'slumming'. She
and Ella Pycroft, her co-worker, chose the tenants for the
buildings, collected the rents and looked after the maintenance of
the dwelling. But she carried on with the apprenticeship for her
real vocation – that of social investigator – as she performed these
other duties, for here was an opportunity to acquire skills of
observation and inquiry. Webb kept a complete account of the
tenants of Katherine Buildings: she interviewed them about their
money, their employment, their health, their families, their
personal histories. In this way, she began to learn about the
structure of employment in the East End, and about its effects on
the lives of the workers. She gradually came to understand that
the 'lady collectors' could have little impact on the tenants they
supervised if conditions of labour remained unchanged.

Webb's residence in the East End was cut short by her father's
stroke and by the consequent necessity to return home.
Psychological crisis followed this forced withdrawal from work,
and she returned to Bacup in the autumn of 1886 as if for
sustenance. She again had praise for the Bacup community, and
was particularly impressed with the effects on working conditions
of factory legislation, having witnessed the disastrous consequences of unregulated labour at the East End. '[O]vertime is
forbidden for women and children,' she wrote to her father, 'and it
is here that one sees the benefit of the factory acts, and consequent
inspection' (p. 159). Her belief in *laissez-faire* policies had been
gradually worn away by her contact with its bitter and squalid
results in London, and with the benefits of regulation in the
North. She wrote home of the pleasures of the 'higher working-
class life' of Bacup, of its 'charm of direct thinking, honest work

and warm feeling', and of her discovery of the 'real part played by
religion in making the English people, and of dissent teaching
them the art of self-government' (p. 164). She also wrote about her
fears for the future of the community if religious faith should lose
its hold. What would serve to unite the people, to sustain them
individually and enable them to act collectively: 'I . . . wondered
what would fill the void it would leave, what inspiring motive
would take its place?' (p. 165). An animating force was needed in
the life of the community as well as in her own.

Her father's partial recovery allowed Webb to begin her
apprenticeship as social scientist in earnest. In February 1877,
she began to assist her cousin Charles Booth in his mammoth
study of the life and labour of the people of London, a project
which combined, for the first time, qualitative and quantitative
methods of sociological study. Webb learned her vocation as an
observer of dock-workers, the sweating-system and the Jewish
community of East London, and, as she mastered her vocation,
she moved farther and farther away from the politics and
economics of Individualism. Booth and his assistants, having
originally undertaken to prove that poverty was not as rampant in
London as Socialists and 'sensationalists' had been arguing,
succeeded instead in exposing a degree of poverty that no one else
had yet imagined. The question had to be asked, then: 'How had
this morass of destitution and chronic poverty arisen during a
period of unprecedented national prosperity?' (p. 240). The
answer was to be found in the conditions of employment of the
people and not in the devil drink, the influx of 'aliens' (Jews) into
the East End, the insidious effects of indiscriminate charity or in
the innate degeneracy of the lower classes. Webb herself concluded that 'uncontrolled competition' and 'individualism run
wild' had to be checked by legislation, by the organization of
labourers and by certain limited kinds of municipal socialism.

Webb was anxious to explore solutions to the problems of
poverty, unemployment, social and economic inequities and the
oppressive conditions of work, so she left the study of London
poverty and set out, in 1889, to begin a study of the history of the
Co-operative Movement in Britain. Webb sought an explanation
for the differences between the 'sweated workers of East London
and the Lancashire textile operatives', and found it in the
'collective regulation of the conditions of employment, whether by
legislative enactment or by collective bargaining'. She had

recognized the importance of Co-operation in the lives of the Bacup workers, and she now realized that it exemplified the will to self-government that she had found lacking among the workers of the East End. Was there any 'practicable alternative', she wondered, 'to the dictatorship of the capitalist in industry?' Did Co-operative societies fulfil the ideal of self-employment and successfully eliminate the role of the capitalist entrepreneur? She discovered that the outstanding achievement of the Co-operative Movement was the organization of industry 'from the consumption end', under the collective control of workers as producers *and* consumers.

As she wrote her work on Co-operation, she grew closer to an understanding of the need for Collectivism, but she had no direct contact with organized socialists, with either the Social Democratic Federation or the newly-established Fabian Society. She began to feel the need for a framework of socialist theory to bolster the 'objective' results of her investigations, and she eagerly read a slim volume of essays published by the Fabians in 1889 that had been given to her by a friend. The essay that most attracted her attention was that written by Sidney Webb because, as she wrote to J. C. Gray of the Co-operative Union in passing the book on to him, '*he has the historic sense*'. The concept of 'the inevitability of gradualness' struck a responsive chord in Beatrice Potter, for she and Sidney Webb shared the same intellectual fathers: 'Owing mainly to the efforts of Comte, Darwin, and Herbert Spencer,' wrote Sidney Webb in his Fabian essay, 'we can no longer think of the ideal society as an unchanging State. The social ideal from being static has become dynamic' (p. 391). Here was a socialism that, unlike the English Marxism of the Social Democratic Federation, looked to the Victorian political and social theorists on whom Beatrice Potter had been raised. Within a very short time of reading these essays, she declared herself, in the pages of her diary, a socialist 'at last'.

Less than a month after she had proclaimed the completion of her conversion to Socialism, Beatrice Potter met Sidney Webb. She was still working on her study of the Co-operative Movement, and felt the need to consult someone who knew a great deal about the history of labour in Britain. Her cousin Margaret Harkness, now a journalist, novelist and intimate of London labour union leaders, suggested a meeting with Sidney Webb, and brought them together in her rooms across from the British Museum. 'A list of sources,' Beatrice wrote, 'accessible at the British Museum, including the then little known Place manuscripts, various State trials, old Chartist periodicals, and autobiographies of working-class agitators, was swiftly drafted, then and there, in a faultless handwriting, and handed to me' (pp. 292–3). Beatrice and Sidney Webb did not begin the partnership of marriage until July 1892, but their partnership of work had begun by the early months of 1891. The 'fellowship' on which their marriage would be based was here established in 'a common faith and a common work'. The apprenticeship had been completed: she had found faith, vocation, a spiritual and political home, and a working partnership. The crises of spirit and identity, as they are described in *My Apprenticeship*, seemed to be behind her, and the struggle of the two Egos – one sceptical and the other believing – appeared to be resolved in the coupling of the science of society with the 'faith' of Socialism.

My Apprenticeship, with its themes of crisis, search for faith and conversion, belongs then to an English literary tradition shared by Mill, Carlyle, W. H. White, Edmund Gosse and Cardinal Newman. Webb rejected the orthodoxies of political economy, Individualism and traditional Christianity; she sought a creed to replace those outworn; she underwent crises of faith and identity; and she found new faith through work and the practice of vocation. As Mill struggled between Bentham and Coleridge, Webb struggled between a spirit of affirmation and a spirit of denial, of faith and scepticism. As Carlyle eschewed the celebration of selfhood and embraced the celebration of work and duty, so did Webb. And like Gosse, White and Mill, she rebelled against an inherited set of principles associated with a parental lack of feeling, of tenderness, of true spirituality. *My Apprenticeship*, however, reflects a major difference of authorship: because it is the work of a woman, its familiar themes take on new dimensions of meaning, and it introduces conflicts and obsessions endemic to the sex of its author which intersect with those associated with Victorian male writers of autobiography. The following chapters will suggest ways in which *My Apprenticeship* is peculiarly a woman's work, the ways in which it departs from a tradition created by men and resembles both the fiction and memoirs of the nineteenth-century women who preceded Beatrice Webb.

Part II
The Divided Self

3 Female Traditions of Autobiography: Memoir and Fiction

The Woman in me kneels and weeps in tender rapture; the Man in me rushes forth, only to be baffled. Yet the time will come when, from the union of the tragic king and queen, shall be born a radiant self.

Memoirs of Margaret Fuller Ossoli

If the primary theme of *My Apprenticeship* is Beatrice Webb's quest for 'Creed' and 'Craft' through a working out of the conflict between the 'Ego that affirms' and the 'Ego that denies', its secondary theme – its subtext – is the resolution of that other division of self she experienced as an intellectually ambitious Victorian woman. Growing up in an age that clearly separated the spheres of men and women, she found it all but impossible to reconcile her longings for public achievement with her desire for the private happiness of marriage and domesticity. Like Margaret Fuller, she aspired to some integration, some 'union', of the two beings who seemed to co-exist uncomfortably within her. Like Fuller and like so many other accomplished Victorian women, she could not understand two seemingly irreconcilable impulses – one appropriately womanly because sanctioned by society, and the other abnormally manly because it was not – without using the language of gender and without claiming possession of a double or divided nature.

My Apprenticeship shares this theme of division with memoirs of other nineteenth-century women and with some of the major works of fiction by Victorian women novelists, and, in its way, it represents an amalgam of these two genres of women's writing. Like memoir, it is the factual record of a life, but like fiction, it achieves what other memoirs by nineteenth-century women did not: a structural and thematic coherence through the explicit exposition and resolution of female conflict. According to recent examinations of women's memoirs, there appear to be two dominant strains in non-fictional writings by women about their own lives. First, there is the memoir of the public woman who is loath to emphasize her public life or to make claims for its importance. These personal histories are tinged with embarrassment, self-denial and ambivalence about professional success.[1] There is also, however, the memoir of the woman writer who, as Nancy Miller has suggested, avoids discussion of her intimate life, of the emotional and physical experiences that are peculiarly female, and who shapes her life's story according to the *'transcendence* of the feminine condition *through writing'*.[2] Both versions of the female self lack what another critic has called 'the crucial motive of autobiography – a desire to synthesize, to see one's life as an organic whole'.[3] The first kind of female memoirist retreats from self-analysis and interpretation of intellectual experience or ambition; the second takes refuge from self in tracing only the literary or professional trajectory of her life.

The memoirs of women like Charlotte Tonna, Harriet Martineau and Annie Besant in England, Margaret Fuller and Jane Addams in America and George Sand in France are to be distinguished from the autobiographies of those Victorian men whom I have discussed, because of their largely unstructured, episodic and discursive natures. These women did not write the kinds of autobiographies that Northrop Frye has identified as prose fictions, autobiographies 'inspired by a . . . fictional impulse to select only those events and experiences in the writer's life that go to build an integrated pattern'.[4] Only the women novelists of the nineteenth century, notably Charlotte Brontë and George Eliot, could identify, interpret and resolve, however tragically or infelicitously, the conflicts that determined and shaped their own – and other women's – lives.

The autobiographies of Mill, Gosse, Carlyle, White and, indeed, Beatrice Webb assume the intrinsic interest and importance of the mental and spiritual lives of the autobiographer; they depend upon the translation of private experience into public document, and upon the assumed propriety of that translation. They also rely, as Frye suggests, on the perception of an 'integrated pattern' of life and on the resolution of internal struggle. The female memoirist, although she may have experienced spiritual crisis, did not presume to make it the focus of public interest or the thematic centre of her recorded life's history. She did not claim the right to 'fictionalize' her life – to assert its integrated pattern – or to make the content of private, psychological experience into public narrative. And for most nineteenth-century women of ambition and achievement, the resolution of struggle and the satisfactory discovery of sexual and spiritual identity remained painfully elusive and, therefore, virtually impossible to describe.

The novelists, however, could achieve resolution in fantasy – in fiction – and they could avoid intellectual presumption and the stigma of egotistical display through a form of anonymity. The recorded lives of Jane Eyre, Maggie Tulliver and Lucy Snowe did not expose Currer Bell or George Eliot to public scrutiny and certainly did not implicate directly the private lives of Charlotte Brontë or Marian Evans. It was as necessary to the Victorian woman's survival to keep an inner life of conflict masked as it was to keep illegitimate aspirations hidden. The writing of autobiography was, like the expression of ambition or private struggle, prohibited: both demanded an impermissible form of attention for the female self.

If one contemplates the tone of self-effacement and embarrassment that characterizes the earliest memoirs of English women, it hardly seems surprising that nineteenth-century women had not yet developed the habit, already common among their male contemporaries, of self-consciously 'fictionalizing' their lives in autobiography. When the very first women's memoirs appeared in the seventeenth century, most were disguised as biographies of husbands, and many female memoirists shared the self-abnegating posture of Lady Fanshawe, who wrote of her offspring: 'My dear husband had six sons and eight daughters, born and christened, and I miscarried six more.'[5] 'Scribbling' women, like the Duchess of Newcastle in the seventeenth century and Laetitia Pilkington in the eighteenth, wrote memoirs defending themselves against the condemnation of those who mocked them for their writing and begrudged them their means of gaining a livelihood. They used memoir as apology, defence and ingratiation: 'I am determined to . . . please even my greatest Enemies,' Mrs Pilkington began. 'I hope this [memoir] will convince the world that [I] was never yet reduced to the Meanness of Falsehood or Tricking.'[6] The Duchess of Newcastle took great pains to assure her readers of her chastity, her gentility and her feminine refinement. She abhorred, she wrote, an unchaste thought; found that it troubled her conscience to kill a fly; preferred to dine on boiled chicken and water; and was addicted only to those things in fashion, thought or life that were 'lawful, honest, honourable, and modest'.[7]

Quaker contemporaries of Pilkington and the Duchess of Newcastle who joined them in the enterprise of memoir avoided the disapproval of readers and had no need for apology because they wrote, not to call attention to themselves, but to bear witness to God's influence upon their lives.[8] By the middle of the nineteenth century, the propriety of a woman's writing the story of her own life for the purposes of publication was still in doubt. When an American edition of the *Personal Recollections* of Charlotte Tonna, the Evangelical writer of moral tales, appeared in 1849, Harriet Beecher Stowe wrote an introduction to it that began with a defence: 'However the fastidious may be shocked by the autobiography of a lady, published during her lifetime, we think the world is much indebted to her for it, and that the reasons for such a work, as stated by herself in its commencement, are given with dignity and good sense.'[9] Tonna's reasons were simple: she wished to avoid becoming 'the heroine of some strange romance' in a posthumous biography, to record the facts of her life so as to prevent their distortion after her death. But Harriet Beecher Stowe felt compelled to assure her audience that the 'good sense' and 'dignity' of Tonna's intentions guaranteed the propriety of her literary venture.

In the second half of the nineteenth century, women felt somewhat freer to write about their own lives, but those who did usually confined themselves to accounts of the travels, adventures and public causes with which they had been associated. Women who had lived in exotic places with their diplomat or missionary husbands, nurses who had served in the Crimea with Florence Nightingale, actresses like Fanny Kemble and Lily Langtry, literary ladies like Eliza Linton and Margaret Oliphant, and pioneer reformers like Josephine Butler and Dr Elizabeth Blackwell, wrote 'Reminiscences', 'Recollections', 'Diaries', 'Journals', 'Memorials' and 'Revelations'.[10] These women felt free to write of the public events and achievements of their lives, but did not often assume that their personal struggles or spiritual crises would be of equal interest to their readers. Nor did those female memoirists who did choose to reveal certain aspects of their private selves often detect some ultimate purpose or teleological design in the pattern of their lives.

THE VANITY OF DAYDREAMS

The taboos against self-advertisement that shaped the autobiographical writings of nineteenth-century women are reflected in the recurring subjects of their memoirs. The accounts of adolescence and young womanhood in the memoirs of numerous Victorian women seem to hinge upon a complex of connecting prohibitions against vanity, daydreaming, fantasy and ambition. The fear of making a fiction of one's life and the embarrassment of possessing unallowable ambition are expressed in the female memoirist's early guilt about indulging in fantasies of professional or romantic success. Daydreaming was regarded as 'vanity', a sinfully egotistical and foolishly futile exercise in wishing for gratification of illegitimate desires.

When Robert Southey told Charlotte Brontë in his now-classic letter that 'Literature cannot be the business of a woman's life', he also warned her that the 'daydreams' in which she habitually indulged were likely to produce in her a 'distempered state of mind' and make her 'unfitted' for a woman's 'proper duties'.[11] Here Southey cautioned against both the desire for fame and the activity of fiction-making, for both corrupted a woman's determination to do what the poet laureate assumed it was her duty to do: care for home and hearth, husband and children. The memoirs written by Brontë's contemporaries attest to the power of Southey's admonition about the perceived dangers of ambition, and share a preoccupation with the pernicious role of daydreaming in their own lives.

If the *Confessions* of Augustine served as a model for the autobiographical efforts of certain modern men, the sixteenth-century life of St Theresa of Avila provided a similar inspiration for Victorian women. Theresa occupied a place of particular importance in the lives and writings of nineteenth-century women, for she represented to them a woman who had struggled against the demons of an inner life – vanity and a taste for romantic literature among them – and achieved greatness through service, sacrifice and vocation.[12] In their memoirs, Harriet Martineau and George Sand both recalled adolescent longings for a martyrdom like Theresa's; Malcolm Muggeridge called Beatrice Webb 'another St Theresa, . . . fierce but sublime'; and George Eliot used Theresa's epic life as an ideal against which to measure the accomplishments of Dorothea Brooke.[13] Modern women like Dorothea, Eliot suggested in her 'Prelude' to *Middlemarch*, aspired to a 'life beyond self' and suffered the conflicting demands of ambition and convention.

Theresa's path to saintliness began in vanity, as Augustine's ultimate goodness had its roots in sin. In her *Life*, she describes an early obsession with books of chivalry: 'I thought there was no harm in it when I wasted many hours night and day in so vain an occupation. . . . So completely was I mastered by this passion that I thought I would never be happy without a new book.'[14] She began to take pains with her appearance, to use perfumes, to engage in unnamed 'other practices' that she had believed were innocent. Alarmed at this behaviour, her father took Theresa to a convent where a patient sister explained to her the sinfulness of her fantasy world of romantic adventure. Soon after this, Theresa records, she took the veil, the first step towards heroism and the founding of her own order.

Some three centuries later, Charlotte Tonna gave an apologetic account of her own childhood fantasies in her *Personal Recollections*: 'I acquired that habit of dreamy excursiveness into imaginary scenes and among unreal personages, which is alike inimical to rational pursuits, and opposed to spiritual-mindedness.'[15] This regrettable habit made her 'qualified, both by nature and by habits of thinking', to become a writer of novels, a course she felt compelled to take in order to support herself after the death of her father. Marriage to a young officer 'saved' her, she tells us, from this occupation; and in her later years, after conversion to strict Evangelicalism, she came to view all non-didactic fiction as 'an abomination to God'.

Another nineteenth-century woman who lamented her own talent and 'busy imagination' was the mother of Edmund Gosse, from whose journals he quotes in his own autobiography. As a devout member of the Plymouth Brethren sect, she considered the writing of fiction sinful, and fought against her own inclinations to story-telling. 'The longing to invent stories grew with violence,' she wrote of her childhood, 'everything I heard or read became food for my distemper. The simplicity of truth was not sufficient for me; I must needs embroider imagination upon it, and the folly, vanity and wickedness which disgraced my heart are more than I am able to express.'[16] Like Theresa, Gosse's mother fought an obsession, a bad habit that had been a source of pleasure and had become a mania.

Harriet Martineau believed herself to have received a permanent stigma as a result of inhabiting realms of fantasy as a young girl. Martineau, who suffered from deafness, suggests in her *Autobiography* that this infirmity had been greatly exacerbated by daydreaming, 'seriously aggravated by nervous excitement at the age when [she] lived in reverie and vanities of the imagination'.[17] These 'reveries', like Tonna's 'dreamy excursiveness' and Mrs Gosse's inventions, were cause for shame and deserving of punishment.

The guilt associated with these accounts of daydreaming and their connection, particularly in the case of Theresa, with personal vanity and 'chivalric' themes, might lead one to conclude that the fantasies which so chagrined these women were sexual in nature. In *A General Introduction to Psycho-Analysis*, Freud claims that of the two kinds of daydreams – those that spring from 'the egoistic cravings of ambition' and those that originate in 'erotic desires' – *ambitious* fantasies predominate in young men and *erotic* fantasies in young women, '*whose ambition centres on success in love*'.[18] This final qualification points to a certain haziness in the distinction between the motives of ambition and those of erotic desire, and Freud goes on to add, in fact, that in the daydreams of men, 'the erotic requirement can often enough . . . be detected in the background, all their heroic deeds and successes . . . really only to win the admiration and favour of women'.[19] I would suggest that both erotic fulfilment and satisfied ambition were features of Victorian women's daydreams, and that both, because reflections of the desire for illicit recognition and gratification, were sources of female guilt.

The central Victorian statement on the meaning of female daydreaming is 'Cassandra', a fragment on the position of women and a form of memoir by Florence Nightingale.[20] This partly fictional, partly autobiographical work of impassioned prose is from Nightingale's unpublished 'Suggestions for Thought to Searchers after Religious Truth', which Elaine Showalter has described as a major work of English feminism, a bridge between the writings of Mary Wollstonecraft and Virginia Woolf.[21] In 'Cassandra', Nightingale warns the parents of young women like herself that their daughters' mental lives are dominated by dreams of 'passion, intellect, [and] moral activity', that some aspire to work in 'the light of intellect' while others live out in fantasy the sexual passions of which they are presumed innocent. But almost all young women, Nightingale asserts, mingle ambition and romantic desire in their daydreams:

> What are the thoughts of these young girls while one is playing Schubert, another reading the *Review*, and a third is busy embroidering? Is not one fancying herself the nurse of some new friend in sickness; another engaging in romantic dangers with him, such as call out the character and afford more food for sympathy than the monotonous events of domestic society; another undergoing unheard-of trials under the observation of someone whom she has chosen as the companion of her dream; another having a loving and loved companion in the life she is living, which many do not want to change?[22]

This passage from 'Cassandra' indicates that Freud's description of male daydreams – heroic deeds against an erotic background – might serve as well for the daydreams of at least certain Victorian women.

What does appear to be different about the daydreams of Victorian females is not their content but their relative importance in the lives of ambitious middle-class women and the degree of guilt they seemed to stimulate. In his *Autobiography*, Herbert Spencer writes about his boyhood 'castle-building' as a habit beneficial to his character. (His protegée Beatrice Webb later used the same term to refer to her daydreams, but, as we shall see, she regarded the habit of 'castle-building' as shameful and frivolous.) Such fancies, Spencer observed, constituted 'a play of the constructive imagination, and without constructive imagination there is no high achievement'.[23] H. G. Wells, Webb's contemporary and fellow Fabian, records with a good deal of amusement and no hint of embarrassment his boyish fantasies of military dictatorship and conquest.[24] And Bertrand Russell remarks in *Portraits from Memory* on the good fortune that enabled him to realize his childhood dreams of fame – 'of receiving flattering letters from learned foreigners who knew me only through my work'.[25] These three men avoid any discussion, either direct or oblique, of erotic fantasies, but they recall without compunction the ambitious daydreams that prepared them for success. Their fantasies were not dangerous, as Southey believed Charlotte Brontë's to have been, because far from deflecting these men from their 'duties', daydreams represented an acceptable sign of healthy aspiration.

Victorian women regarded such fantasy not as a symptom of health but as an illness to be purged or an incubus to be shed. In 'Cassandra', Nightingale explains that daydreaming is at once the plague and the very sustenance of young women's lives. She describes the struggle to break the shameful habit: 'We fast mentally, scourge ourselves morally, use the intellectual hairshirt, in order to subdue that perpetual daydreaming, which is so dangerous.'[26] The fight to subdue fantasy, however, must always end in vain, for the dreams 'against which [women] so struggle, so honestly, vigorously, and conscientiously . . . *are their life*, without which they could not have lived'.[27] The habit is both life-giving and soul-destroying, and it becomes, therefore, an addiction. Nightingale's point is that women have no other lives to live, no aspirations they might realize, no activities that might engage their minds and spirits. They are confined and constricted, and they can only turn in on themselves for the ephemeral but addicting satisfactions of fantasy. 'I mourned that I never should have a thorough experience of life,' Margaret Fuller wrote. 'I was always to return to myself, to be my own priest, pupil, parent, child, husband, and wife.'[28]

RELIGION AND WORK: AMBITION IN THE PRIVATE AND PUBLIC REALMS

How to have a 'thorough experience of life' without violating the rules that circumscribed a Victorian woman's sphere of activity was a question often solved temporarily by the embracing of religious devotion. St Theresa's entry into convent life served as a model for the renunciation of worldliness and vanity that was, at the same time, an expression of ambition and a bid for heroism. The religious fervour of Victorian girls – their passion for martyrdom and the monastic life – cannot be understood simply as a rejection of the world or as evidence of redirected adolescent sexuality: it must also be perceived as one of the few acceptable means of claiming recognition for the self and of channeling or sublimating (rather than repressing) energy and aspiration. Theresa, as George Eliot emphasized, led a *heroic* life. Self-sacrifice, renunciation and saintliness – behaviour that to the twentieth-century eye appears self-punishing and neurotic – seemed to the Victorian girl available routes to importance and achievement.

Religious devotion called for an essentially invisible, silent and private involvement with God, sanctity and self. The energies of ambition and sexuality were directed inward, as in the chronic habit of daydreaming, rather than outward into the realm of visible, public action. Harriet Martineau, who recalled in her autobiography that she craved a martyrdom like Theresa's, also revealed that her childhood devotion to religion answered intellectual, as well as spiritual, needs. At the centre of her religious life was the constant reading of *Paradise Lost*, what she called her 'first experience of moral relief through intellectual resource'.[29] Born nearly four decades after Martineau, Annie Besant felt a similar devotion to Milton's epic, and took to reciting whole sections of it in dreamy tones.[30] Her daydreams, she records, were filled with 'brooding over the days when girl martyrs were blessed with visions of the King of Martyrs', and she experimented with fasting and occasional self-flagellation.[31] Besant's later fanaticisms, whether Atheistic, Fabian or Theosophical, all had this element of passion and near-hysterical enthusiasm, but all expressed as well her never-easily-fulfilled desire for 'sacrifice to something felt as greater than the self'.

George Sand described an episode of adolescent conversion in her *Histoire de ma vie*. When Beatrice Webb read Sand's memoir and wrote of it in her diary notebook in March 1878, she was particularly struck by the notorious Frenchwomen's religious fervour and youthful desire for a convent life. Here was a woman, more infamous for her romantic liaisons than famous for her prolific novel-writing, who had shared Webb's own attraction to monasticism. At the Couvent des Anglaises, at age fifteen, Sand was seized by an ardent religious passion that echoed both Augustine's and Theresa's: she had heard a voice declaring '*Tolle, lege*' in the chapel of the convent, and of her subsequent ecstasy she recorded: '*Je brûlais littéralment comme Sainte Thérèse.*'[32] After conversion, she fixed on a vocation in the convent, and was prevented from taking vows immediately only by a sister who counselled delay.[33] The monastic life meant glory and prominence in a world removed from public scrutiny and disapprobation, a separate, insulated world in which the aspiring nature could risk ambition. Renunciation of the public sphere was heroic and, for the moment, satisfying. 'I have been a chosen one,' Margaret Fuller wrote of herself, '[for] the lesson of renunciation was early, fully taught.'[34] To renounce was to be chosen.

None of these nineteenth-century women stopped, however, where Theresa did: they all went on, beyond the realm of daydreams and of religious enthusiasm, to a life of secular work and activity. In each case, the struggle to cross over into the public sphere was long and taxing, for as disturbing as their religious excesses may have been to family and friends, their determination to work outside the home appeared far more deviant and, therefore, much more alarming. Religion was a private matter for home or convent; work, particularly the kind of activism embraced by Martineau, Besant and Nightingale, was a public matter that took women beyond the drawing-room.

The prelude to work outside the domestic sphere was very often a course of self-directed study and, though the drawing-room could accommodate this, the unmarried daughter's familial duties could not. 'The family uses people,' Nightingale declared in 'Cassandra', 'not for what they are, nor for what they are intended to be, but for what it wants them for – for its own uses.'[35] The Nightingales, a fine example of the Victorian middle-class family intent upon blocking the ambitions of a daughter, wanted Florence for reading aloud, playing the piano, taking carriage rides and paying visits.[36] She accepted these demands, and satisfied her own desires to prepare for a career in nursing only through secret, early-morning reading by candlelight: she studied hospital reports and Blue Books, and filled notebooks with a 'mass of facts, compared, indexed, and tabulated'.[37] But, Nightingale wondered in 'Cassandra', '[i]f a man were to follow up his profession or occupation at odd times, how would he do it? Would he become skillful in that profession?'[38]

Harriet Martineau grew up in a similarly demanding middle-class family, and learned early that her relations would fiercely resist the intellectual efforts that were for her a 'refuge from moral suffering'. She too was expected to sit and sew, read aloud, practise her music and be ready to receive callers, and she too had to hide her work 'either early in the morning, or late at night'.[39] When the hidden writing was finally made public in the form of tales of political economy in the *Monthly Repository*, Martineau could hardly believe her good fortune at having taken that leap beyond domestic life. The discipline of continuous writing, the satisfactions of publication, the excitement of touching the world of business and of men seemed unparallelled joys to her: 'It was truly *Life* I lived,' she remembered in her *Autobiography*, 'during those days of strong intellectual and moral efforts.'[40]

Florence Nightingale wrote of the restorative powers of a woman's encounter with even the cruellest realities of life. When women can shake off the exhaustion bred of passivity, they are reborn into the world. Jane Addams, ill and depressed after the death of her father, first observed the squalour of an urban slum from the top of a double-decker bus in London's East End while on a European trip recommended by her physician. At this sight, she wrote in *Twenty Years at Hull House*, she was seized with 'despair and resentment' and was further dismayed to realize that the only context out of which she could respond to this disquieting reality was a literary one. We women, Addams thought, waste our time 'lumbering our minds with literature' instead of seeking contact with the real. When, after a second visit to London a few years later, she resolved to begin a settlement house in Chicago, it was as much for the sake of young, middle-class women as it was for that of the poor: she wanted a place 'in which young women who had been given over to study might restore a balance of activity . . . and learn of life from life itself'.[41]

THE TOLL OF ANOMALOUS CHOICES

Once the right to activity was won, it became nearly impossible to reconcile that activity with the more traditional destinies of women. The limitations of time and energy and the pressures of social convention made work and marriage – or work and love – appear to be mutually excluding alternatives. Achieving women who married and suffered for it, and women who avoided marriage altogether, concluded that matrimony and the exercise of an independent mind were incompatible experiences. Annie

Besant, who fits the former description, concluded after her divorce that women who 'get themselves concerned about the universe at large' would do well to hesitate before marrying.[42]

After a long life of celibacy, Harriet Martineau felt convinced that her 'strong will' and 'anxiety of conscience' made her fit only to live alone: 'The older I have grown,' she wrote in the *Autobiography*, 'the more serious and irremediable have seemed to me the evils and disadvantages of married life, as it exists among us at this time. . . . My business in life has been to think and learn, and to speak out with absolute freedom.'[43] And Florence Nightingale, who rejected a number of persistent suitors, declared that for some women marriage means the 'sacrifice [of] all other life' and an annihilation of self behind the destinies of men.[44]

The rigidity of separation between private and public spheres and the seeming futility of trying to reconcile them forced some women to cling fiercely to the choices they had made, to dismiss the attractions of a married life, and to become confirmed renouncers of the possibility of 'personal' happiness. To take the risk of rejecting a traditional life was to create an all-consuming need to succeed at an uncommon one. But, though they rebelled against convention, they could not escape the debilitating effects of those conventional standards and expectations that had early on become embedded in their own minds and spirits. Their memoirs recall moments of crisis, when ineradicable conflicts erupted and internal divisions brought on psychic paralysis, breakdown, periods of prolonged invalidism and suicidal impulses.

Such episodes of crisis, though they appear as features of numerous female memoirs, are seldom given full interpretation by those women who experienced them, and are rarely, if ever, made to seem pivotal in some coherent pattern of life. Women might recount their breakdowns and depressions with great vividness, with even greater authenticity of description perhaps than did someone like Mill, but they do not imagine their lives moving ineluctably toward crisis and then moving, in a transformed and transcendent state, away from it. The meaning of conflict and crisis seems never to be fully conscious in these women's memoirs, perhaps because conflict went unresolved, untranscended, or perhaps because crisis – illness and even invalidism – was itself often an involuntary solution to inner struggle. The attentive reader discerns, however, that such episodes all reflect the impossibility of achieving an integration of self – a reconciling of love and work, of the needs of others and the needs of self, of the impulses that seemed normal and 'womanly' and those that seemed deviant and 'manly'.

'A man's ambition with a woman's heart,' Margaret Fuller wrote of herself, 'is an evil lot.' The price she paid for this division, she believed, was chronic invalidism. Emerson wrote in Fuller's *Memoirs* that she was a lifetime victim of pain and disease, but that she 'read and wrote in bed, and believed that she could understand anything better when ill. Pain acted like a girdle, to give tension to her powers.'[45] Her illness seemed to her intimately connected with work, and appeared, paradoxically, to be both the facilitator of mental activity and the miserable result of it. Her father, she wrote, 'overeducated' her too early and too fast:

> The consequence was a premature development of the brain
> that made me a 'youthful prodigy' by day, and by night a victim
> of spectral illusions, nightmares and somnambulism, which at
> the same time prevented the harmonious development of my
> bodily powers and checked my growth, while, later, they
> induced continual headache, weakness and nervous affections
> of all kinds.[46]

She was convinced that her intellect made her ill, and yet, according to Emerson, it thrived on illness.

Her brain was at odds with her body and stunted its growth, as her 'man's ambition' was at odds with her 'woman's heart'. She described herself as a 'wandering Intelligence' with 'no real hold on her life'. Her heart, her feelings, her body too, were a woman's, she felt, but her mind was a man's: 'Soon I must return into the Intellect, for there, in sight, at least, I am a man.' This dissociation became complete when she lay in bed working: she suspended the activities of her body and gave her mind free rein. To live in the realm of intellect seemed both a curse and a freedom, and the illness that accompanied it contained within it that same contradiction.

For certain women, illness was both the result of unresolved psychological tensions and a liberator from the duties imposed upon them by virtue of their sex. Florence Nightingale and Harriet Martineau both suffered extended periods of invalidism and, in doing so, freed themselves from the demands made of them, not as wives, but as daughters. The unmarried woman who did not break altogether with her family made herself subject to its demands indefinitely by her very singleness. As a young woman, Nightingale pleaded with her intransigent family to be allowed to train as a nurse and, repeatedly unsuccessful, she suffered chronic depression and illness. After eight years of argument and struggle, when she was finally able to leave the parental roof to begin work in London, she wrote to her mother: 'You must now consider me married or a son.'[47]

Her family's demands on her time, however, and their insistence that she stop behaving like a poor woman or a slut (who else would need or want to care for the sick?), continued well after she had been to the Crimea and returned a national heroine. The Nightingales ceased to try to control their daughter's life when she, at age thirty-seven, began a gradual retirement into invalidism. In 1857 she collapsed, would not eat, and took to her bed; all those around her assumed she was about to die. She died in 1910, after some *fifty-three* years of continued writing and work carried out, for the most part, from her bed. The only way to stop those near her from imposing on her was to remove herself from their view. She told Benjamin Jowett, master of Balliol, that he was her closest and dearest friend because she could correspond with him rather than see him: he was not in London to distract or interrupt her. All relations were to be sacrificed to her work, and yet her fear of loneliness only increased as she grew older.[48]

The comments in Beatrice Webb's diary on Harriet Martineau's *Autobiography* include a sympathetic mention of Martineau's 'five years' peaceful illness with immense opportunities for quiet and serious thought' (31 March 1877).[49] In 1839, when she was thirty-seven (also the age at which Nightingale took to her bed), Martineau retired to a six, not five, year confinement after collapsing while on the continent. This retirement closed the 'anxious period . . . so charged with troubles that when I lay down on my couch of pain in my Tynemouth lodging . . . I felt myself comparatively happy in my release from responsibility, anxiety, and suspense'. This period was marked by 'extreme tension of nerves under which I had been living . . . while the three anxious members of my family . . . were on my hands'.

Her mother, who accompanied her everywhere and was going blind, would not allow her to employ a maid or nurse, so that Martineau took care of all domestic chores, acted as companion to her mother, and stayed up late at night to mend and sew. The reader of Martineau's *Autobiography* is not, therefore, surprised to find that for many months after her retreat to Tynemouth, Martineau would wake from a dream in which her mother had fallen from a precipice, bannister or cathedral spire (how appropriate for a reader of Milton), '*and that it was my fault*'.[50] Like Nightingale, she prevented intrusion only by retreating and then suffered the guilt produced by retreat. The pattern was circular and vicious: to withdraw was to be free to work, and to work was to feel a kind of guilt that could make one ill.

When the roles of worker and nurturer collided, or when a choice was forced upon these striving women between the conventional womanly role and a life of public activity, they often collapsed under the burden of what seemed like a life of contradiction. The act of caring for a sick or dying parent, usually a father, often brought on depression and suicidal feeling.[51] In many cases, a father might act as tutor or sole mentor in matters of the intellect, or as a buffer between daughter and a mother who thwarted ambition. The loss of that link with a world of thought and of the potential defender against motherly obstruction, coupled with an immersion in the 'womanly' task of nursing, acted to intensify confusion of identity and the difficulty of choice between roles.

Jane Addams' 'black days', the 'nervous depression' against which she fought for years, initially followed the death of her father, the focus of her young life. Her mother had died when she was an infant and, as a child, she wrote, she 'centered upon [her father] all that careful *imitation* which a girl ordinarily gives to her mother's ways and habits'.[52] Mr Addams died during the summer of his daughter's graduation from the Rockford Seminary and just before she was to enter the Women's Medical College of Philadelphia. The 'dark days' – hospitalization and a six-months' stay in bed with 'spinal difficulty' – necessitated her withdrawal from medical school.

'I was very glad,' she wrote with hindsight, 'to have a physician's sanction for giving up clinics and dissecting rooms and to follow his prescription of spending the next two years in Europe.'[53] There she discovered that 'there were other genuine reasons for living among the poor than that of practicing medicine upon them' and had a glimpse of another sort of vocation. She had venerated science and chosen to study medicine because she believed that only through such study could a woman grow 'accurate and intelligible' and 'detect all self-deceit and fancy in herself'. After seeing the settlement houses of the East End, she realized that a woman might work intelligently and usefully without attempting to reshape her mind through the study of science.

When George Sand returned to her home at Nohant from the Couvent des Anglaises, she found that at her stage of life decisions had to be made and proper roles assumed. Her grandmother, who had raised her and presided over Nohant, expected her to marry, but Sand felt herself afraid of *'ce mari, ce maître, cet ennemi de mes voeux et de mes espérances'*, and wished to postpone the inevitable moment of marriage. Her grandmother became ill, and Sand found herself in a maternal role for the first time: *'Un jour vint où nous changeâmes de rôle et où je sentis pour elle une tendresse des entrailles qui ressemblait aux sollicitudes de la maternité.'*[54] Now independent of all parental influences, she began a course of study, with emphasis on philosophy and religion, and simultaneously developed a suicidal *'manie'*. She suffered from a continual conflict within, from the oppression of her situation at Nohant and from a brain exhausted with serious thought. What was she, and what would she do?

Her grandmother died, and within a short time Sand married Casimir Dudevant, an error that she sensed almost immediately. The moment of decision, in which she felt forced to choose between marriage and a life of work and mental exertion, was a moment of crisis. The experience of *'les sollicitudes de la maternité'* made the role of wife and mother seem her natural course, and a life of study that excluded the possibility of love and family seemed to her a kind of desolation. But could the pursuit of art and learning be reconciled with marriage to a man of her class? Her sense that they could not, that a husband would of necessity be *'l'ennemi de mes espérances'*, was confirmed by marriage to Dudevant. Depression, loneliness and boredom followed upon the birth of her much-loved son; within eight years, she left Dudevant for a writer's life in Paris.

For most of these Victorian women, crisis did not bring in its wake the discovery of reconciliation: continued conflict or a life of rigidity and exclusion were more often the outcome. Florence Nightingale, in perhaps the most extreme example of an unyielding response to conflict, simply remained in bed. But most chose to retreat in some way from a puzzle of inner discord that appeared insoluble: how to be both worker and wife; how to speak out for what they believed and still exist comfortably and decorously in what Annie Besant called 'the double-harness' of marriage; how to be both independent and loved; how to be active and yet possess the passive virtues of conventional womanhood; how to be visible and yet invisible? These conundrums were best solved for the mid-Victorian woman, not in the texts of memoirs that remained faithful to the inconclusiveness of actual life, but in the realm of the imagination, in the fictions they wrote and read.

FICTIONAL RESOLUTIONS

In 1928, Virginia Woolf looked back on the 'epic age of women's writing' and saw the fiction of the major Victorian women novelists as an essentially autobiographical mode. Woolf was accurate in this description of the novels of Charlotte Brontë and George Eliot, but she was wrong, I suspect, when she opposed that autobiographical mode to what she called 'art': someday, Woolf hoped, women could begin to 'use writing as art, not as a method of self-expression'.[55] It was surely 'art' when Brontë took that 'buried suffering smouldering beneath her passion', which Woolf so aptly identified, and translated it into fiction, making the frustrations of her sex the focus and structure-giving themes of literature.

In *Jane Eyre*, *Villette* and *The Mill on the Floss*, Brontë and Eliot bring spiritual crisis and the difficulty of transcending inner division into conscious thematic focus, and portray the course and imagined resolution of 'buried suffering' in dramatic terms. All three novels are concerned with a woman's difficulty in achieving balance and integration of self. Jane Eyre, Maggie Tulliver and Lucy Snowe all have a great need to be loved, and an equally pressing need to assert the singular nature of their identities. They are each to some degree split between a hidden, inner life and an incomplete outer life, and their nearly insurmountable task is to bring the inner life into public being while, at the same time and without detriment to that task, learning to love and be loved. To accomplish this is to grow into female adulthood, not an easily performed feat but always an implicit ideal in the works of Brontë and Eliot. Each heroine follows a path of vacillation between renunciation and fulfilment, a path that ends ultimately in some form of resolution: for one, a mate who makes possible both self-abnegation and gratification; for a second, premature death that represents regression and a return to wholeness; and for a third, a *vision* of true synthesis.

In her childhood, Jane Eyre is neither loved nor is she in any sense free to do or be what she likes. The problem for her, as for Maggie Tulliver and Lucy Snowe, is to find an antidote to these two inextricably linked deprivations. Jane first mistakenly seeks fulfilment of both her need to love and her need to act and assert her will in the same place: at the side of an unregenerate Edward Rochester.

Jane falls in love with Rochester, at least in part, because she can help him, protect him, even save his life at one point, and because she enjoys in his presence a 'full and delightful life'. But the balance of power and dependence between them shifts as the outward fact of Jane's social inferiority, Rochester's need to engulf her, and Jane's too great vulnerability to her own need for love come into play. Even before Jane learns of the circumstances that would permanently establish Rochester's power over her (his inability to make her his legal wife), she signals the danger inherent in her worship of the 'creature of whom I had made an idol'.[56] In her subsequent rejection of Rochester, she regains an 'inward power', and in renouncing 'love and idol' she recaptures respect for herself. As the deprivation of her youth made her susceptible to the seductions of an overwhelming love, so the succumbing to that love and her need to escape 'stagnation' make her anxious for independence, for fierce self-reliance and for the renunciation of gratification.

Renunciation of the world represents a form of strength for Jane, as it did for many of the Victorian women whose memoirs I have touched upon. Brontë and Eliot are able to isolate and examine this phenomenon of renunciation and, to some degree, to expose its underlying motive and meaning. Brontë begins with such an analysis in *Jane Eyre*, in which she embodies her heroine's vacillation between self-denial and fulfilment in an alternation of male lovers. Rochester offers Jane the satisfaction of passionate love: he is the Byronic lover who dominates and attracts. St John Rivers offers a heroic asceticism, an absence of passion, the opportunity for self-sacrifice: he is the lover of renunciation who repels. But St John also offers Jane the chance to work and to save

again, first as a schoolteacher and then as a missionary. Brontë
solves this unsatisfactory split between subservience and sexual
love on the one hand and accomplishment and physical repulsion
on the other by exposing St John's passionlessness as tyranny and
death, and by transforming Rochester into a chastised and needy
man.

Jane loses the freedom she had initially enjoyed under St John's
influence, just as she proceeded to lose the early freedoms of
Thornfield. As she had once redressed this shifting balance by
leaving Rochester, so she regains power by running from St John
back to Rochester: 'It was *my* time,' she declares about her break
from St John, 'to assume ascendancy. *My* powers were in play and
in force.'[57] The momentum of this ascendancy can be maintained
because Rochester has reverted to the helpless creature who had
long before needed the support of Jane's shoulder to reach the
horse that had thrown him on the road. Her newly-inherited
wealth has made her independent, and his new poverty has
compounded his physical dependence. No longer can he be her
employer or her benefactor-husband. She will be able to love *and*
to save, to be loved *and* to assert her will. The problematic of the
novel is solved: passion and liberty are discovered in the same
place, thanks to a transformed hero and the caprice of fortunes.

The 'heroine of fulfilment', as Elaine Showalter has called Jane
Eyre, is, however, a renouncer still. She can have both Rochester
and power but only at the expense of Rochester's own self-
sufficiency and wholeness; she can have only a diminished
Rochester. Within the terms established by Brontë's novel, Jane
can achieve equality and love only if the man she had so
passionately desired is impoverished and wounded, his own
potency in some way modified. The social limitations of Brontë's
world and the consequent imaginative and literary limitations
within which she composed her plot are ultimately responsible for
the crippling – some would say castrating – of Rochester. Jane had
to find a way of 'exercising her faculties', not in the wide world she
saw from the roof of Thornfield, but within the domestic sphere of
conventional marriage. Rochester is a casualty of the need to
derive from a single, limited source what might better be achieved
in a realm beyond the hearth.

The drowning of Maggie Tulliver at the conclusion of *The Mill
on the Floss*, like the crippling of Rochester, is at once a tragic result
and a resolution of the otherwise insurmountable conflicts that

governed the Victorian heroine's life. Maggie's death returns her to the childhood state of spiritual and physical harmony with her brother that had signalled unity and integrity of self. Between the years of earliest childhood and the moment of death brother and sister separate, Maggie ceases to be her brother's equal and intimate companion, and she experiences a growing contradiction between her outward activity and her inward desires.

Adolescence forces Tom and Maggie to adopt the roles deemed appropriate to their respective sexes, and we know that for Maggie the lessons of sexual differentiation are learned with pain and difficulty. She finds that the world will not tolerate her tomboy ways, her unruly dark hair, her penchant for book-reading or her desire to master the Latin that Tom is taught at school. By the age of thirteen, Maggie has been tempered by the experience of frustration and of 'conflict between the inward impulse and the outward fact'. She learns to behave with passive decorousness, accommodating herself to the tedium and limited scope of her life. She lives authentically in the world of 'Waking dreams' as a daydreamer thrown back on herself.

Maggie's solution to the painful distance between her 'passionate longings' and the 'still, sad monotony' of her actual life is renunciation in the form of religious piety. Eliot comes closer than any other woman novelist or memoirist of her time to a full understanding of the place of renunciation of the lives of Victorian girls. By enthusiastically following the path of self-denial, Maggie turns the reality of deprivation – of not being able to have or do what she wants and needs – into a consciously chosen virtue. By outdoing her own enemies at inflicting suffering upon herself, she might achieve an alternative form of heroic fulfilment:

> [S]he sat in the twilight forming plans of self-humiliation and entire devotedness, and in the ardour of first discovery, renunciation seemed to her the entrance into that satisfaction which she had so long been craving in vain.[58]

It is just such a desire for martyrdom and ennobling self-abnegation that draws Maggie into a friendship with Philip Wakem.

Philip is Maggie's lover of self-denial, as St John had been Jane Eyre's, and, like St John, he offers the possibility of self-sacrifice as well as an entry into the world of intellect and spirit. But, like

Edward Rochester at the close of *Jane Eyre*, Philip is needy and deformed, and Maggie's caring for him represents a suppression or chastening of her own sexual nature. Philip himself understands that Maggie is engaged in a 'narrow, self-delusive fanaticism', an attempt to 'stupefy' herself into resignation. When she runs off with Stephen Guest, Philip is able to see that Maggie's feelings for her cousin's fiancé had 'proceeded from one side of [her] character, and belonged to that partial, divided action of [her] nature'. When Leslie Stephen complained that Maggie's passion for Stephen was 'not congenial to her better impulses' and therefore a lapse in Eliot's novel, he had not fully grasped what Philip Wakem had understood: that Maggie had become a divided creature, a young woman whose integrity of self had been fragmented by years of struggle against convention and of self-styled martyrdom. The unsuitability of Stephen Guest, Maggie's lover of a limited but urgent form of gratification, reveals the distortion of taste and temperament that she had suffered.

As Maggie Tulliver had become estranged from Tom, so had she grown estranged from that part of her nature which had long been contained and only obliquely and distortedly expressed. It is in death that she transcends both the immutable circumstance of inner division and her break with Tom, by reverting to a time when physical being had not yet been splintered off from spiritual life. Maggie drowns in the state of unselfconscious and innocent intimacy with another being that she had never again managed to achieve after earliest girlhood: 'brother and sister had gone down in an embrace never to be parted: living again in one supreme moment, the days when they had clasped their little hands in love, and roamed the daisied fields together'.[59] Maggie Tulliver could not achieve adulthood; she could not attain the unity of internal impulse and external reality or of physical and spiritual needs that would enable her to live happily as a woman. So she returns to the phase of her life before division had become an irrevocable fact.

When Charlotte Brontë came to write *Villette*, she chose the condition of radical self-abnegation as a subject for dramatization and analysis. Lucy Snowe, in large part because of her experience of loss and lonely survival, exists in a state of virtual negativity. She lives as an observer and voyeur, witnessing the human drama but renouncing participation in it. All life, passion and imagination are kept locked within her; not allowed any outward expression, they turn back on themselves and become morbidly distorted. 'I seemed to hold two lives,' Lucy writes of her earliest self, 'the life of thought, and that of reality; and, provided the former was nourished with a sufficiency of strange necromantic joys of fancy, the privileges of the latter might remain limited to daily bread, hourly work and a roof of shelter.'[60]

Lucy Snowe's customary aloneness and alienation from those around her is accelerated and magnified in her isolation during the Long Vacation at Madame Beck's. Even the 'prop of employment' is withdrawn from her; and she is forced to care for a 'deformed and imbecile pupil' – forced, that is, into total selflessness and sacrifice. Her despair is complete: illness, sleeplessness, delirium follow. In the Confession, collapse and symbolic rebirth that follow Lucy's nightmare state, she makes an implicit, if hesitant, commitment to the world of the living and to the life that had been confined within her. As a result of this restoration to life, Lucy is able to recognize the failings and insensitivities of a man she had admired – Graham Bretton – and to appreciate the pedagogical attentions of another – M. Paul.

With Paul Emanuel and Graham Bretton, Charlotte Brontë establishes a new pair of male lovers that subverts and, in part, corrects the dichotomy between love and work that she represented in the lovers of *Jane Eyre*. In Dr John, Brontë reproduces the beauty and coldness of his namesake, St John Rivers, but she transfers St John's offer of independence from the unloving hero to the loving hero, M. Paul. The gift of a school – what St John had given Jane and what the Brontë sisters themselves envisioned as the means to escape perpetual economic dependence – comes to Lucy Snowe from Paul Emanuel, a refashioned Edward Rochester, a Napoleon turned schoolteacher and mentor. The cigar smoke that had wafted into the garden of Thornfield on the night of Rochester's proposal now lingers on the books and pamphlets Lucy Snowe discovers in her desk: the sensual and the intellectual have been merged in M. Paul.

The importance of love between teacher and pupil in *Villette* does not, however, derive solely from the erotic power of superior knowledge and intellectual mastery; it rests too in the male teacher's ability to impart to his younger female student those skills that will enable her to do without him. M. Paul helps to end Lucy's homelessness, her divided existence, her habitual renunciation, and then he leaves her alone for what she paradoxically calls the happiest years of her life. Lucy has been left with home, vocation, the knowledge of Paul's love for her and with but a vision of the co-existence of love and work. Brontë refuses to commit her novel to a definite ending, to tell her readers if Lucy Snowe will live out her days in the company of Paul Emanuel or only in the presence of his memory. The crippling of Rochester and the drowning of Maggie Tulliver reflect the same problem that underlies the inconclusive ending of *Villette*: the demand that the Victorian woman novelist reconcile in fiction what she knew could never be easily reconciled in life.

When Brontë invites her readers to complete the novel for themselves, it is as if she wishes to suggest that only in the imagination can such a thoroughly satisfactory reconciliation take place. She clearly indicates, however, what 'union and a happy succeeding life' would be like for Lucy Snowe, what 'sunny imaginations' might hope for: a woman established in her vocation, independent, possessed of both power and sufficient wealth, who welcomes home in her self-sufficiency a lover who values her for her very strength and intelligence, for what he regards as her 'passionate ardour for triumph'. Charlotte Brontë can evoke in her readers' imaginations the felicitous resolution of inner division and chronic conflict that female memoirists of her time could not; but she underscores in her inconclusive ending of *Villette* that such resolutions are fictional and that reality – her own autobiographical reality included – eludes transcendence, consummation and wholeness.

4 *My Apprenticeship*: Autobiographical Resolution

> To be on the right side of ordinary is the perfection of
> prudence in a young woman, and will save her from much
> heartburning and mortification of spirit.
>
> Beatrice Webb, Diary, November 1882

My Apprenticeship is the autobiography of a woman who lived on
the 'wrong side of ordinary' and suffered the consequent 'heart-
burning' and 'mortification of spirit'. Beatrice Webb experienced
her failure to be an ordinary woman as a conflict between
'masculine' and 'feminine' selves: one self desired unrestrained
mental and professional activity, while the other was anxious for
the private, domestic contentments of marriage and family. In
Webb's autobiography, this conflict of sexual identity intersects
with a specific spiritual conflict – between the believing 'Ego' and
the sceptical 'Ego' – that characterizes the autobiographies of
numerous male Victorians. 'It is impossible,' Webb wrote, 'for a
woman to live in agnosticism. That is a creed which is only the
product of one side of our nature' (p. 98). The 'womanly' aspect of
her nature, the faculty of faith and 'emotive thought' – a term she
owed to George Eliot – had to be incorporated into whatever
philosophy she adopted and whatever action she undertook.
Webb sought to resolve the convergent crises of faith and sexual
identity in a mode of existence that would combine 'manly'
scepticism and 'womanly' belief, public striving and private
contentment.

The problems of the anomalous female that regularly appear in
the memoirs of nineteenth-century women are also found in
Webb's autobiography: the sense of inner division, the elusiveness
of integration of self, the struggle against fantasy, the self-

admonishment for vanity and egoism, the difficulties of study and work, the question of marriage and its tyrannies. In *My Apprenticeship*, however, these separate problems are raised to the level of structure-giving themes, as they are in the autobiographical novels of Brontë and Eliot. Webb took excerpts from her diary, the private notebooks in which she wrote for seventy years and the equivalent of many of the unstructured memoirs written by nineteenth-century women, and wove them into a thematically coherent whole, interpreting them by creating from them a pattern and teleological form.

The conflicts expressed in these diary passages are resolved in *My Apprenticeship*, as they are not in the memoirs of Martineau, Nightingale, Besant, Addams and Sand. As male Victorians resolved spiritual and intellectual crises in their autobiographies, as Brontë and Eliot resolved – however problematically – the conflicts of their heroines, so does Webb depict the integration of her divided self, the resolution of her sexual and spiritual struggles, in the denouement of *My Apprenticeship*. As conversion to Fabianism, a political philosophy that ostensibly accommodated both science and faith, transcends the struggle between the two 'Egos', so marriage to Sidney Webb, a husband who was also a partner in work and faith, transcends the conflict between the 'masculine' and 'feminine' selves. And, as these conflicts intersect in the autobiography, so do their resolutions merge, for conversion to Socialism and marriage to Sidney were convergent means by which Webb sought to make her life whole.

THE POTTER FAMILY: CONTRADICTORY ATTITUDES TOWARD THE ROLE OF WOMEN

The attitude, either articulated or unexpressed, of Webb's family toward the role and essential nature of women was neither monolithic nor consistent: it engendered conflict in Webb, rather than confidence and clarity about her sexual identity. Beatrice Webb was second to the youngest of nine sisters, many of whom were intelligent, talented and enterprising, most of whom married men of substantial social position and wealth, and none of whom, save Beatrice, established herself in a career or had a public life in her own right.[1] Beatrice was the last to marry, and the only one to experience life as an idiosyncratic female and rebel within her class. Her difference from her sisters was due, at least in part, to her position as the eighth daughter, born just before the only and long-awaited Potter son, who lived but four years and who, during that time, was the emotional centre of his mother's life. Webb describes her earliest years 'creeping up' – rather than growing up – 'in the shadow of my baby brother's birth and death'. Her earliest memory is one of displacement by her brother: 'The first scene I remember was finding myself naked and astonished outside the nursery door, with my clothes flung after me by the highly trained and prim woman who had been engaged as my brother's nurse' (p. 57).

Her place in the constellation of her mother's affections was unavoidably determined, according to Webb, by the temporal relationship of her life to her brother's death:

> The birth of an only brother when I was four, and his death when I was seven years of age, the crowning joy and devastating sorrow of my mother's life, had separated me from her care and attention; and the coming of my youngest sister, a few months after my brother's death, a partial outlet for my mother's feelings, completed our separation. 'Beatrice,' she wrote in a diary when I was yet a child, 'is the only one of my children who is below the average in intelligence.' (pp. 11–12)

Linked for Webb are her failure to be as well-loved as her brother while he lived or to fill the gap in her mother's affections after he died, her early alienation from her mother, and her mother's assessment of her intelligence.

The irony of that assessment is apparent, as is the irony of Laurencina Potter's remoteness from the daughter with whom she ultimately had most in common: 'we had the same tastes,' Webb wrote of her mother and herself, 'we were puzzling over the same problems, and she harbored, deep down in her heart, right up to middle life, the very ambition that I was secretly developing, the ambition to become a publicist' (p. 12).[2] Webb felt rejected by her mother, yet strongly identified with her intellectual aspirations and ambition to have a life outside of the domestic sphere. The very activities that seemed to keep Laurencina Potter from her daughters, to make her a 'remote personage . . . poring over her books in her boudoir' and a subject of some ridicule in the family, were those that later gave Beatrice the fortitude to pursue her own interests and ambitions. 'When I work with many odds against me,' she wrote just after the death of her mother, 'for a distant and perhaps unattainable end, I think of her and her intellectual strivings which we were too ready to call useless, and which yet will be the originating impulse of all my ambition, urging me onward towards something better in action and thought' (p. 17).[3] At the height of her confusion about the course her life would take, when she was thirty, unmarried and determined to carve out some useful place for herself in society, Webb sensed that her mother finally belonged more to her than to any of her sisters:

> I feel that she at last knows me and tries to cheer my loneliness and to encourage my effort – now that her outward form lies decaying in the earth. She seems now to belong more to me, than to the others – the others have their husbands and children – I have nothing but my work with the fitful warmth of friendship. (p. 18; 18 June 1888)

But if Webb wanted to gain her mother's love, to accomplish in fact what her mother had only dreamed about, to win her mother's posthumous respect, she also wanted to avoid the disappointments her mother had suffered, the disappointments which fed Laurencina Potter's emotional estrangement from Beatrice and from her other daughters. Webb's ultimate ambivalence about her own role as a woman had its origins, commonly enough, in the complexity of her feelings about her mother: she wanted to emulate Laurencina, to affirm her link with her mother's ambitions; but she feared the coldness of her mother's demeanour, hated the rejection she had suffered, wished to avoid the frustrations which, she suspected, grew out of the very ambitions she shared and caused the very remoteness she detested. Webb craved and recognized the importance of that which her mother's complement, Martha Jackson – 'Dada' – supplied to everyone in the Potter household: 'she nursed them when they were ill, comforted them when they were in trouble, and spoke for them when they were in disgrace'. It was Dada's benevolence, her nurturing kindness and religious spirit that Webb would identify as truly 'feminine' principles of behaviour.

Webb's ambivalent feelings about her mother are expressed in her description of Laurencina Potter's 'divided personality', and in her remarks on the doubleness of her mother's appearance:

> The discords in her nature were reflected in her physiognomy. In profile, she was, if not ugly, lacking in grace: a prominent nose with an aggressive bridge, a long straight upper lip, a thin-lipped and compressed mouth, a powerful chin and jaw, altogether a hard outline, not redeemed by a well-shaped but large head. Looked at thus, she was obviously a managing woman, unrelenting, probably domineering, possibly fanatical. But her full face showed any such interpretation of her character to be a ludicrous libel. Here the central feature, the soul of the personality, were the eyes, soft hazel brown, large but deeply set, . . . eyes uniting in their light and shade the caress of sympathy with the quest of knowledge.   (pp. 13–14)

The mother in profile was harsh and rejecting, the mother in full face sympathetic and striving. This surface doubleness, Webb goes on to say, had its internal counterpart in the 'controversies' of her mother's consciousness. Webb inherited these very 'controversies': they included the conflict between what Webb called, in her own case, the 'Ego that affirms' and the 'Ego that denies'. 'Her soul,' Webb says of her mother, 'longed for the mystical consolations and moral discipline of religious orthodoxy. . . . But she had inherited from her father an iconoclastic intellect' (p. 14). Her mother studied the Greek Testament and the Church fathers with devotion, but she had been raised as a student of political economy, of Adam Smith and Nassau Senior. What begins in *My Apprenticeship* as a description of the 'divided personality' which characterized her mother's problematic nature, ends as an identification of her own inner conflicts with those of her mother. This textual shift suggests the complexity of Webb's relationship to her mother, and signals the consequent complexities of her relationship to her own sexual role.

Webb's mother may have found daughters a disappointment and mourned the absence of a son, but Webb's father was the only man she ever knew 'who genuinely believed that women were superior to men'. This peculiarity of Richard Potter's struck the women of his family as an unwarranted 'over-appreciation' of those females among whom he lived: 'We girls thought him far too long-suffering of Mother's arbitrary moods; she thought him far too acquiescent in his daughters' unconventional habits' (p. 11). The paradoxical accompaniment to Potter's belief in the superiority of women was his undisputed control of all important familial events and decisions. This apparent contradiction was not lost on his daughter:

> Yet in spite of this habitual self-subordination to those he loved, notwithstanding his 'noble amiability', to use an epithet of Herbert Spencer's, he controlled the family destinies. My mother lived where it suited him to live, and he came and went as he chose; his daughers married the sort of men he approved, notwithstanding many temptations to the contrary. (p. 11)

He might have revered women and their intelligence, but he accorded them no power or any real freedom of choice in matters of the most crucial importance.

Richard Potter also seemed to contradict himself in the matter of Beatrice's position as unmarried daughter. He went about marrying off his daughters as successfully and as expeditiously as he possibly could: he invited prospective suitors to Standish as soon as his daughters were of 'coming out' age, and arranged professional advancements for the men he wished his daughters to marry.[4] It was clear in the Potter family that, although learning might be an avocation, marriage was the business of a woman's life. After Laurencina Potter died, however, and Beatrice, as the oldest unmarried daughter, became the female head of the household, Richard Potter preferred that his eighth daughter remain single. Her assistance as manager of household economy, director of the servants, hostess, surrogate mother to Rosy Potter, confidante in business matters and private secretary, was so essential and so valuable to her father that, Webb writes, 'he more than once suggested that if I "did not want to marry" I might become his recognized business associate'.

This common, contradictory notion about the need for the unmarried daughter to remain unattached in the face of the accepted urgency about marriage for women, was both a burden and a blessing for Webb. It freed her from the pressure to marry a man she disliked at a time she disliked, and it allowed her to develop certain economic and managerial skills; but it also replaced marriage with other unlooked-for and inescapable responsibilities. Her father's seemingly contradictory attitude contributed to her confusion about what sort of woman she was expected to be or wanted to be. If marriage was of central importance in the lives of her sisters, why not in hers? And, if marriage had not been considered a pressing issue while her father was alive, how was she to feel when it became one just as his death seemed imminent? When, in 1889, Richard Potter suffered a stroke and thought he was dying, he then expressed to Beatrice his desire that she marry:

> In the long hours of restlessness [Webb wrote in her diary] he broods over the successes of his children, and finds reason for peace and satisfaction. 'I want one more son-in-law' (a proof that he feels near his end, as he has discouraged the idea of matrimony for me . . .), 'a woman is happier married: I should like to see my little Bee married to a good strong fellow.' (p. 387)

What her father did not realize, Webb went on to say, was that the ' "little Bee" of long ago' had disappeared, 'leaving the strong form and determined features of the "glorified spinster" ' in her place. Richard Potter had unwittingly contributed to this metamorphosis.

While Potter cultivated Beatrice as his confidante and housekeeper, her married sisters worried about her single state and shook their heads over her insistence upon studying algebra, history and philosophy. The Potter 'sisterhood' 'became anxious', Webb notes,

> lest my mania for study should interfere with the prospect of a happy and successful marriage. 'Beatrice's intellect, or rather what she attempts to develop into an intellect,' sister Georgie was reported to have said to sister Mary, 'what's the good of it? It's no use to her or anyone else – it's all done to make a show before old and young philosophers.'

Acting upon such logic, her sisters tried to coax her away from her studies:

> Spurred by some such vision of matrimonial futility (for what sensible woman would want a philosopher for a husband?), my

sister Mary broke into my room early one morning to find me
. . . straining hand and brain to copy out and solve some
elementary algebraical problems. 'What nonsense this is,' she
began, half chaff, half-compliment, 'trying to be a bluestocking
when you are meant to be a pretty woman.' (pp. 104–5)

Webb deviated from a code which demanded that she 'graduate
into the goodly company of prosperous matrons, thus adding to
the corporate influence of the family', and, as she remarks,
continuing the metaphor, 'a code needs a court to interpret it'.
The jury of 'enquiry and presentment' in her case was the 'solid
phalanx of seven married sisters, with the seven brothers-in-law
in reserve as assessors' (p. 113). Knowing that she would be found
guilty of breaking the laws of convention, she chose to evade
judgment, to 'withdraw all [her] own aspirations from family
discussion'. Isolation and loneliness within the large family circle
was the result.

DIARY, VANITY, FAITH AND PRAYER: ADOLESCENT 'SIN' AND REDEMPTION

One of the consequences of this isolation was the diary Webb
started to keep in early adolescence. Her very first, intermittent
entries began in 1869, when she was eleven, and she began to
write regularly on a trip to the United States with her father in
1873. The diary notebooks contained 'confessions of spiritual
shortcomings', descriptions of travels and events, and reviews of
books she read in her efforts at self-education. Its reason for being,
however, was the pressing need for emotional release and the
'unwonted pleasure of self-expression'. Webb regarded the diary
as 'an old friend, one who has been with me since I first had
experiences and wished to tell them to some one'; but she also
thought of it as her 'phantom self'. 'It would be curious to
discover,' Webb mused,

> *who it is*, to whom one writes in a diary? Possibly to some
> mysterious personification of one's own identity, to the
> Unknown, which lies below the constant change in matter and
> ideas, constituting the individual at any given moment. This

unknown one was once my only friend; the being to whom I went for advice and consolation in all the small troubles of a child's life.   (p. 271)

The diary was a consolation in times of loneliness and trouble; it also represented to Webb the kernel of her identity, the undefinable constant of her personality that would not change and might some day publicly emerge. It gave her strength, she notes, to go back over the pages of this 'history of a woman's life', and to watch 'the inevitable work its way in spite of my desperate clutches at happiness, which were seemingly fore-doomed to failure' (p. 271). This detection of the working-out of the 'inevitable' in her diary, of the inexorable unfolding of the purpose of her life, despite apparent failure, became the impetus for *My Apprenticeship*, for the writing of an autobiography with teleological structure.

The very first diary entries that Webb includes in *My Apprenticeship* record her earliest struggles with daydreaming and vanity. Here she introduces the theme of her battle against what she considered to be 'egoism', a battle she waged privately throughout most of her life in the pages of her diary. She admonished herself for the egoism of romantic fantasy and the egoism of ambition: both involved a spirit of competition which she felt to be one of her greatest failings. Reading novels, she wrote at the age of eleven, stimulated her propensity for 'building castles in the air', the expression for daydreaming that Herbert Spencer also used, but, as we have seen, with different intent. It was the inadequate education of girls, Webb concluded at this early age, that led them to a total immersion in the reading of fiction, with the following results:

The whole of their thought . . . is wasted on making up love scenes, or building castles in the air, where she is always the charming heroine without a fault. I have found it a serious stumbling-block to myself; whenever I get alone I always find myself building castles in the air of some kind; it is a habit that is so thoroughly innured in me that I cannot make a good resolution without making a castle in the air about it.   (p. 61)

In a few years' time, the private vanity of daydream had escalated to the more public vanity of flirtation. In the autumn of 1872, when Webb was fourteen, she expressed to her diary her disappointment with herself and her idleness. 'But one thing I have learnt', she wrote with resolution,

> is that I am exceedingly vain, to say the truth I am very disgusted with myself; whenever I am in the company of any gentleman, I cannot help wishing and doing all I possibly can to attract his attention and admiration; the whole time I am thinking how I look, which attitude becomes me, and contriving everything to make myself more liked and admired than my sisters. (p. 61)

The element of competition with her sisters caused her to feel shame, as did the element of sexual fantasy in her thoughts about men. She addressed herself – and her diary – on this subject, with bluntness and self-mockery:

> And now my dear friend I want to tell you something seriously, because nobody else will have a chance of telling you – You are really getting into a nasty and what I should call an indecent way of thinking of men, and love, and unless you take care you will lose all your purity of thought, and become a silly vain self-conscious little goose. Do try and build no more castles in the air; do try to think purely and seriously about Love. I often think you are something like Rosamund Vincy in Middlemarch. (6 March 1874)

The absurdity of contemplating Beatrice Webb as Rosamund Vincy should suggest the extreme nature of the reaction that Webb – and other young women like her – had to their own experiences of fantasy and desire for male attention. It seemed to Webb that the only cure for this plague was 'to avoid gentlemen's society altogether.' The norms and customs of her class, however, made this kind of avoidance an impossibility.

The daughters of the upper and upper-middle classes were required to busy themselves with the activities of the London 'Season', that important part of the year during which Victorian families like the Potters left their country homes for London, to mix with others of their class for social and business reasons, and to marry off their children. A period of months in the spring devoted to 'riding, dancing, flirting and dressing up, in short, entertaining and being entertained' allowed no possibility of avoiding the company of men and the agonies of conscience that it produced. 'I discovered that personal vanity,' she writes,

> was an 'occupational disease' of London Society; and that any one who suffered as I did from constitutional excitability in this direction, the symptoms being not only painful ups and downs of inflation and depression but also little lies and careless cruelties, should avoid it as the very devil. By the end of the season, indigestion and insomnia had undermined physical health; a distressing mental nausea about one's own and other people's character, had destroyed all faith in and capacity for work. (p. 48)

Vanity, 'castle-building', the desire to outdo one's female companions, were inescapable hazards of the London Season, for the 'Season' was a duty, the object of which was clearly and explicitly marriage.

Competition among women was the dominating spirit of the 'Season', as competition among men was that of business and 'big enterprise'. What university and professional training were for the sons of wealthy parents, the 'Season' was for their daughters, the 'reason being that marriage to a man of their own or a higher social grade was the only recognized vocation for women not compelled to earn their own livelihood' (p. 44). In her experience as a young woman in London Society, Webb finds the origins of her ultimate political bias and her tendency to discount her father's 'faith in the social value of a leisured class'. Either 'by attraction or repulsion', this experience determined the social ideals of every daughter of the upper and upper-middle class. For someone like Margot Asquith, whose memoir Webb recommends for its portrait of a woman intensely attracted to Society, the activities of the 'Season' continued to be the focus of her life, even after marriage. In Webb's case, the revulsion she felt at her own 'mania' for the 'experimental display' of personality contributed to her rejection of many of the social patterns and customs of her class.

Long before she developed the political and social critique of her society which redeemed her from the 'occupational disease' of the London 'Season', Webb found the antidote to vanity in religion. The adolescent religious conversion described in the first part of this study followed upon Webb's discovery of her curse of vanity and 'castle-building'. Conversion was her solution to what she regarded as egoism, to daydreaming and to her desire to be admired. As in the case of Maggie Tulliver, piety and renunciation of gratification offered themselves as answers to the crises of sexual identity. The reason, Webb felt at the age of fourteen, that she could not fight off temptation, was the absence in her life of adequate faith: 'I feel my faith slipping from me, Christ seems to have been separated from me by [a] huge mass of worldliness and vanity' (p. 61). Just before she left for Bournemouth, the place of her conversion, she wrote in her diary that she was in the 'most unhealthy state of mind' of 'thinking of nothing but myself', and had concluded, also like Maggie, that the 'only real happiness is devoting oneself to making other people happy' (p. 74). As a result of her Bournemouth conversion, she resolved to make the aim of her life the 'understanding and acting up to religion' and swore never to 'come out' in Society. She had decided to renounce worldliness and thereby avoid its dangers.

But Webb's attraction to religion did not derive simply from the desire to evade and renounce worldly temptation; its impetus was not a wholly negative one. She sought not just renunciation, but vocation as well. As in the instances of Maggie Tulliver and such contemporary women as Martineau, Besant and Tonna, who were drawn to piety and a vision of martyrdom, Webb's religious strivings expressed a positive search for faith, the need for a place of usefulness in the world and a desire for an active show of aspiration. When Webb returned from Bournemouth a year later, she experienced a de-conversion from Christian orthodoxy and succumbed to her parents' wishes that she 'come out' during the following London 'Season', but her need to 'make a faith' for herself had remained intact.

Webb concluded that it was 'impossible for a woman to live in agnosticism'. 'That is a creed', she argues,

which is only the product of one side of our nature, the purely rational, and ought we persistently to refuse authority to that other faculty which George Eliot calls the emotive thought? And this, when we allow this faculty to govern us in action; when we secretly recognize it as our guide in our highest moments. Again, what is the meaning of our longing for prayer, of our feeling happier and nobler for it? Why should we determine in our minds that the rational faculty should be regarded as the infallible head in our mental constitution? The history of the human mind, shown in the works of the greatest of the race, proves that what has been logically true to one age has been logically untrue to another; whereas we are able to sympathize and enter into the almost inspired utterances of the emotive thought of philosophers and poets of old. . . . But perhaps the real difficulty is that the emotional faculty, though it gives us a yearning, a longing for, perhaps even a distant consciousness of, something above us, refuses to formulate and to systematize; and even forces us to see moral flaws in all the present religious systems.   (pp. 98–9)

The moral flaws she detected in those 'present religious systems' prevented her from adopting any one of them as her own, but did not stop her from expressing the impulses of her 'emotive thought' in prayer.

In prayer, she could express all of the emotions that found no outlet either in Spencer's evolutionary philosophy or in the rites of the London 'Season'. She could never adequately explain the meaning of prayer because, she said, like poetry prayer eluded definition by words with 'predominantly intellectual meanings'.[5] She could, however, say with certainty that prayer had always been associated with music and forms of architecture, with poetry, painting and nature, and with the 'great emotional mysteries of *maternity, mating* and *death*'. These 'mysteries' are clearly linked to her consciousness of being female, to the destinies of women, to her sexuality, to the death of her female parent. Prayer, religious inspiration, 'emotive thought' – these were Webb's means of expressing what she regarded as the 'feminine' aspects of her nature, aspects which she feared were inhibited by her pursuit of a systematic and logical explanation of the workings of the universe.

WORK: THE BARRIERS OF EGOISM AND SOCIAL CONSTRAINT

The means to discovery of a creed which would satisfy both faculties – the intellectual and the emotional, the 'masculine' and the 'feminine' – were found to be study, work and the discovery of craft. But work brought her face to face with the spectre of egoism, and challenged the constraints of social position. To make the claim that she was worthy of devoting herself to study and of distinguishing herself from her sisters and from other young women of her class by engaging in 'brain work', raised the question of vanity and egoism once again for Webb. How could she comfortably, without guilt, demand the right to be different from others, to spend her time in study, to have a career? She berated herself for her 'jealous ambition', her 'natural love of impressing others' and the 'vanity motive' which entered into her desire to work. She struggled to subordinate her 'interest in self and its workings to a greater desire to understand others', to add Goethe's 'sympathy for all around him' and Ruskin's 'love and reverence, and religious yearning' to what she considered her egoistic compulsion to be admired (pp. 116, 256; 14 December 1879). Study provided her with the happiest hours of her day, but it stimulated her ambition in a way that troubled her. Could she, with any justification, dignify her 'amateurish' efforts with the name of 'work'? 'Why should I,' she challenged herself in her diary, 'wretched little frog, try and puff myself up into a professional?' (24 March 1883).

A week after asking herself this question, however, she was railing in her diary against the constraints of her position and class that prevented her from becoming a professional: 'At present I feel like a caged animal, bound up by the luxury, comfort and respectability of my position. I can't get a training that I want without neglecting my duty' (31 March 1883). A woman in Webb's position who wished to make a career for herself had to contend with the twin inhibitions of her own fear of presumption and the limitations placed upon her by her social world. When she did not feel powerless and insignificant – like a 'wretched little frog' – she felt that the power and strength she did possess were confined and contained by the circumstances of her social position. She alternated between exaggerated humility about her abilities and rage against the external barriers to personal achievement. Like Jane Eyre, she felt caged and angry.

Webb's time of self-education coincided with a period in which she was called upon to carry out the duties of the unmarried daughter. She acted as her father's companion in business and as her youngest sister's guardian; she also had to spend her time 'entertaining and being entertained by the social circle to which she belonged'. The only legitimate counter-claim on her time that was recognized by the society in which Webb lived was the making of a 'good marriage', the 'masterpiece' to which this apprenticeship of social exercise was to lead. How could she reconcile the 'rival pulls on time and energy, on the one hand, of family affection, backed up by the Victorian code of domesticity; and, on the other, of a domineering curiosity into the nature of things, reinforced by an awakening desire for creative thought and literary expression?' (pp. 112–13).

Reconciliation at this point in Webb's life was impossible. Only the ability and stamina to lead a number of different lives at once could solve the problem of 'rival pulls on time and energy'. 'I became,' Webb writes of this period of her life, 'an exceptionally energetic woman, carrying on, persistently and methodically, several separate, and in some ways conflicting, phases of life – undergoing, in fact, much of the strain and stress of a multiple personality' (p. 111). Her 'frantic attempt' to 'combine three or four lives in one' gave her a feeling of schizophrenia, altered – she thought – her looks, and caused that sense of division so common among the heroines of fiction and the writers of memoirs whom I have discussed. Webb's 'real life' was all internal, her external life all empty movement:

> Now my life is divided sharply into the thought part and the active part, completely unconnected one with the other. . . . My only hope is that the ideal one is hidden from the world, the truth being that in my heart of hearts I'm ashamed of it and yet it *is* actually the dominant internal power . . . It is a curious experience, moving about among men and women, talking much, as you are obliged to do, and never mentioning those thoughts and problems which are your *real life*, and which absorb, in their pursuit and solution, all the earnestness of your nature. This doubleness of motive . . . must bring with it a feeling of unreality. (p. 118)

The life of thought was her 'real life', the power that dominated her existence, but it found no means of expression, and she was ashamed of it, as she had been of the similarly guilt-provoking castles-in-the-air of her childhood. As romantic fantasy had caused her shame in early adolescence, so personal ambition was a source of shame for her as a young woman.

JOSEPH CHAMBERLAIN AND THE CRISIS OF SEXUAL IDENTITY

Webb could sustain this divided existence, with admitted difficulty and tentativeness, until she was confronted with the possibility of marriage to a man to whom she was powerfully drawn. Before meeting Joseph Chamberlain, her active relationships with men had never truly interested her. 'The commonplaces of love,' she confessed, 'have always bored me' (16 March 1884). But Chamberlain, with his 'gloom and seriousness, with absence of any gallantry or faculty for saying pretty nothings', fascinated her and, what is more, was able to force her into choosing between a life of study and work and a life in which personal ambition would be sacrificed for the sake of marriage. As a dutiful daughter she might still live a secret, internal life of thought and aspiration, with the hope of someday realizing her private, hidden goals; as wife to a man of power, position and of her own class, she could no longer sustain that hope of realization. The possibility of marriage brought division of self to the point of crisis.

Webb's relationship with Chamberlain is not recorded in any detail in *My Apprenticeship*. When she referred to her autobiography as a memoir 'with the love affairs left out', she was thinking specifically of the affair with Chamberlain. And yet, her descriptions of him in the autobiography reveal both her powerful attraction to him and her profound resentment of the intellectual tyranny which ultimately prevented their union. She also makes clear in *My Apprenticeship* that the result of their failed relationship was a devastating crisis of identity for her.

When she first came to know Chamberlain in the early 1880s, he was a Radical leader and dedicated proponent of social reform, and she was still under the influence of Individualist and *laissez-faire* philosophies. Although, ironically, Webb later became a Fabian Socialist and Chamberlain turned Tory Imperialist, the source of their differences of opinion lay in her 'stubborn' adherence to the tenets of Spencerian Individualism and in her resistance to Chamberlain's radicalism. It is the fact of their ideological differences and of his dictatorial temper that Webb emphasizes in her descriptions of Chamberlain in the autobiography. Dinner-table conversation at one of their first meetings revealed to her the 'fundamental antipathy' between

Chamberlain's mind and Spencer's, and, by association, between Chamberlain's and her own. 'By temperament he is an enthusiast and a despot,' she proclaimed of him after one encounter, '[and] running alongside this genuine enthusiasm is a passionate desire to crush opposition to his will, a longing to feel his foot on the necks of others' (p. 121). She continues her analysis of his manipulative powers as she describes him speaking at a rally in Birmingham:

> You could watch in his expression some form of feeling working itself into the mastery of his mind. Was that feeling spontaneous or intentional? Was it created by an intense desire to dominate, to impress his own personality and his own aim on that pliable material beneath him?
>
> . . . every thought, every feeling, the slightest intonation of irony or contempt was reflected on the faces of the crowd. It might have been a woman listening to the words of her lover! (pp. 122–3)

In *My Apprenticeship*, Webb reverses the connection between the private and public tyrannizing of the man: in the autobiography she uses the analogy of woman and lover to illuminate Chamberlain's public, political behaviour; in life – as recorded in her diary – his private behaviour had the quality of political domination.

At the time of their meeting, Joseph Chamberlain was forty-seven, twice-widowed, dapper, charming and a man approaching the peak of his political power – Webb used to refer to him as 'the great man' in her diary. 'He had energy and personal magnetism,' she wrote nearly twenty years later, 'in a word, masculine force to an almost superlative degree' (1 January 1901). As a husband, he would have fulfilled her needs of pride and physical passion, but, like the lovers of gratification in *Jane Eyre* and *The Mill on the Floss*, like Edward Rochester and Stephen Guest, his attractiveness accompanied a need to dominate. (Paul Emanuel is, of course, only an apparent tyrant: he bullies and liberates at the same time.) Webb was initially drawn to Chamberlain by the very qualities that made their marriage an impossibility. She confessed to being fascinated by the kind of courtship which 'almost asserts . . . that you yourself are without importance in the world except in so far as you might be related to him' (16 March 1884).

It is difficult to piece together the course and events of their

short-lived and idiosyncratic courtship, even from the evidence of
Webb's diary. But it seems clear that it ended in earnest almost as
soon as it had begun, in the winter of 1883–4, and continued to
sputter for some years afterward. There has been debate about
whether or not Chamberlain actually proposed marriage,
whether or not Webb ever had the opportunity of refusing his
offer, but the debate seems to be an academic one.[6] Chamberlain,
like Jane Austen's Mr Bingley, a man 'in want of a wife', obviously
saw Webb as a prospective mate, as an eminently eligible,
unmarried young woman, and came to visit her in her father's
house with the object of indicating his interest and evaluating her
wifely suitability. What is also obvious is that his failure to
propose and/or her decision to refuse had the same cause:
Chamberlain's desire for a quietly supportive wife – 'attractive,
docile and capable', Webb estimated – who would assent to his
opinions and be an asset to him in his political career, and Webb's
constitutional inability to be that kind of wife.

A diary entry of 12 January 1884, describing Chamberlain's
first visit to the Potter home, merits quotation in full because it
indicates so clearly why the relationship was doomed at the
outset, and because it reveals the novelistic quality and ironic
distance of some of Webb's finest diary writing. The days at
Standish began well: 'That evening and the next morning, till
lunch,' Webb writes, 'we are on "susceptible terms" '. But the
susceptibility was soon marred by disagreement:

> A dispute over state education breaks the charm. 'It is a
> question of authority with women, if you believe in Herbert
> Spencer you won't believe in me.' This opens the battle. By a
> silent arrangement we find ourselves in the garden. 'It pains me
> to hear any of my views controverted' and with this preface he
> begins with stern exactitude to lay down the articles of his
> political creed. I remain modestly silent; but noticing my
> silence he remarks that he requires 'intelligent sympathy' from
> women. 'Servility', Mr Chamberlain, think I, not sympathy
> but intelligent servility: what many women give men. . . .
>
> And so we wandered up and down the different paths of the
> Standish garden, the mist which had hid the chasm between us
> gradually clearing off. . . . He was simply determined to assert
> his conviction. I *think* both of us felt that all was over between
> us. . . . 'You don't allow division of opinion in your household,

Mr Chamberlain.' 'I can't help people *thinking* differently from me.' 'But you don't allow the expression of the difference?' 'No.' And that little word ended our intercourse. (12 January 1884)

It did not end there, and all was not over between them. They continued to see each other, and Webb continued to contemplate the idea of marriage to Chamberlain even as she dreaded it. Two months after the fiasco in the Standish gardens, she recalled with pleasure the excitement of feeling 'that susceptibility increasing' on the first night of his visit and, in the same diary entry, began to muse on the likely damage to her mental and emotional life that marriage to Chamberlain would do:

> I don't know how it will all end. Certainly not in *my happiness*. . . . [I]f the fates should unite us (against *my will*) all joy and lightheartedness will go from me. I shall be absorbed into the life of a man, whose aims are not my aims; who will refuse me all freedom of thought; . . . to those whose career I shall have to subordinate all my life. . . . If I married him I should become a cynic as regards my own mental life. (16 March 1884)

In marrying Chamberlain, either her 'intellectual individuality' – or independence – would be destroyed under the 'influence of strong feeling', or she would give up trying to make her own 'moral' decisions for the sake of agreement with her husband. If she married him, her intellect would surely die, could not co-exist with the married life, and she would become 'par excellence the mother and the woman of the world'. She saw her choice in terms of absolutes: marriage, motherhood and womanliness on one side and intellect, reason, the exercise of independent thought on the other.

In but another two months' time it had become clear to Webb that she would never marry Chamberlain and, despite her previous assessment that it would have meant the end of true happiness and self-respect to do so, she mourned the death of the relationship as the thwarted fulfilment of her 'woman's nature':

> I look hopelessly through the books on my table and neither understand nor care to understand what I read. My imagina-tion has fastened upon one form of feeling. The woman's nature

has been stirred to its depths; I have loved and lost; but possibly by my own willful mishandling, possibly also for my own happiness; but still lost.   (9 May 1884)[7]

The affair with Chamberlain helped to accentuate her sense of inner discord: 'Instantaneously he dominated my emotional nature,' she later wrote, 'and aroused my latent passion. But my intellect not only remained free but positively hostile to his influence' (1 January 1901). She had responded to him as a divided personality, and it was the 'womanly' side that had been drawn to him. Union with Chamberlain, she reasoned, would make her a woman, and love would add a 'soul' to her 'intellect and thought'. She would reach a state of 'maturity' in 'present satisfaction' of her romantic longings or in 'present renunciation' of them (29 January 1885). She was left with renunciation, with work, intellect and thought; she had seen, she believed, the possibility of fulfilling her 'woman's nature' pass her by.

In a section of *My Apprenticeship* entitled 'The Dead Point', Webb describes the depression and psychological crisis that followed the disintegration of her relationship with Chamberlain. She interprets her breakdown, her thoughts of suicide, her acute sense that life had ended, as the product of a divided self. One part of her was the 'normal woman seeking personal happiness in love given and taken within the framework of a successful marriage'; the other part 'claimed, in season and out of season, the right to the free activity of "a clear and analytic mind" '. 'For in those days,' Webb notes, 'of the customary subordination of the woman to the man . . . it would not have been practicable to unite the life of love and the life of reason' (p. 270). Again, Webb perceives her choices in absolute terms: she could lead either a life of love as a 'normal woman' or a life of reason as an unmarried one. 'Reason' suggested to her a certain freedom of thought which she saw to be necessarily inhibited by the subordination of the female to the male in marriage. 'Marriage is to me,' she once told R. B. Haldane on an occasion when the subject arose, 'another word for suicide – I cannot bring myself to face an act of felo de se for a speculation in personal happiness' (1 December 1890). This extreme reaction to the idea of marriage, reminiscent of the attitudes of Harriet Martineau and Florence Nightingale, was the result of an increasingly firm conviction that one kind of 'personal happiness'

– marriage – and another – an independent intellect – were not compatible.

Total dedication to a life of reason and work caused her regret and despair, as marriage to Chamberlain would also have done. She continually asked herself whether the 'extent of [her] brain power' *warranted* 'sacrificing happiness, and even risking a peaceful acceptance of life, through the insurgent spirit of a defiant intellect' (p. 270). '[D]ay and night,' she wrote of a trip to Bavaria she took with Margaret Harkness after the courtship had ended, 'I cried secretly over my past and regretted the form which my past life had given me. For who can undo the moulding work of years?' (p. 272). She could not eradicate her own need for activity and thought – for 'craft' and 'creed' – and she entered into her work in the East End of London with diligence and characteristic intellectual enthusiasm. But she also could not dispel the 'old craving for love and devotion' that returned to her in moments of discouragement and weariness:

> But at times a working life is weary work for a woman. The brain is worn and the heart unsatisfied – and in those intervals of exhaustion the old craving for love and devotion, given and taken, returns – and an idealised life of love and sympathy passes before one's eyes – little-ones too of flesh and blood.   (28 September 1886)

Even as she built her reputation as a social investigator, published her writings and became a recognized authority on the problems of labour in the East End, she longed for what she called the 'restfulness of an abiding love'. Work made her *weary*, but not *restful*, at least in part because her sexual longings went unsatisfied. 'God knows,' she declared in her diary, 'celibacy is as painful to a woman . . . as it is to a man' (7 March 1889).

She suffered from a constant seesawing of desires, from a frenzy of ambivalence; she cursed her own 'doublemindedness', her seeming inability to follow either aspect of her being 'to the bitter end', and she scrawled in her diary a desperate and circular disquisition on her 'duplex personality' (10 December 1886). She had, she notes, been slowly sinking into a 'slough of despond', and had fallen into the 'deepest and darkest pit' of all during her father's 'catastrophic illness' in the winter of 1885–6. In

November, Webb's father suffered a paralysing stroke, and she withdrew from the normal activities of her life to become his nurse and companion. Webb's acute crisis of identity, which I have discussed in Part I in the context of Victorian autobiography, followed this familial trauma: months of depression, of 'anxiety and gloom', of suicidal despair, followed. She now could neither marry nor work; her career 'looked as if it had come to a sudden and disastrous end'. Rent-collecting and social investigation had to be left aside: 'this abstinence', Webb writes, suggesting celibacy of a number of kinds, 'was tormenting'. She made up an informal will in January, in which, among other things, she advised her father to choose one of his married daughters – and not Rosy, the only other unmarried one – to tend him in his illness, for the 'position of unmarried daughter at home', she wrote, 'is an unhappy one even for a strong woman'.[8]

Her crisis of identity was in fact a crisis of sexual identity. She felt the utter hopelessness of a young woman who thought she had given up all chance of 'personal happiness' in order to be able to work and study and write, only then to be prevented from doing any of those things. She was neither wife, nor mother, nor professional, nor student. Her life began to seem to her a series of mistakes:

> I am never at peace with myself now; the whole of my life looks like an irretrievable blunder. I have mistaken the facts of human life as far as my own existence is concerned. I am not strong enough to live without happiness. . . . I struggle through each new day waking with suicidal thoughts early in the morning; I try by determined effort to force my thoughts on to the old lines of continuous enquiry, and to beat back Feeling into the narrow rut of duty. . . . Eight-and-twenty, and living without hope!   (pp. 272–3)

Virginia Woolf, some twenty-five years later, echoed these sentiments in the throes of a similar depression: 'I could not write,' Woolf declared in a letter to her sister Vanessa, 'and all the devils came out – hairy black ones. To be 29 & unmarried – to be a failure – childless – insane too, no writer.'[9]

Webb had been moving toward this 'dead point' for three or four years: since the days when she assumed the role of housekeeper for her father and became a young woman living three or four lives at once, since the time she encountered Joseph Chamberlain and realized that married life with him would exclude all other lives, certainly since she had let the opportunity of marrying Chamberlain pass her by. But all of the conflict that had been building finally reached a point of eruption when she was forced to give up all efforts at creating a career for herself in order to nurse her sick – she thought dying – father. We are reminded here of Lucy Snowe's breakdown during the Long Vacation, when her reined-in agony overwhelmed her as she was forced to care for a helpless, retarded child. We are reminded too of Jane Addams' collapse after the death of her father and of George Sand's suicidal mania, which developed as her grand-mother suffered her last illness and she, Sand, felt the stirrings of maternal tenderness for the first time.

Webb, like Addams and Sand, sensed that she was losing the parent who had in some way allowed her to feel that she had a right to ambition, achievement and the exercise of her mind. Richard Potter, though his dying wish was for Beatrice to marry, had treated her almost as a business partner, had sought her advice, trained her and challenged her to use her intellect. Like Sand, she felt herself a 'nurturer' for the first time; tending her sick father brought to the surface all of those longings she had been fighting to keep down, longings she associated with her womanliness and felt she had abandoned in her life of work. Had she not been struggling to resign herself to giving up the possibility of maternity? She suffered the horrible inaction of the bedside vigil, the frustrations of stagnating, the discomfort of feeling agony while having to keep still. She would lose the father who had encouraged her to use her abilities and, in the course of losing him, she would be deprived of the exercise of those abilities and would be called upon to tap new resources which would find no other object after his death.

RESOLUTION: FAITH, SERVICE AND SIDNEY WEBB

If plagues of vanity and daydreaming, the embracing of religious commitment, the plight of the unmarried daughter, rejections of marriage proposals and periods of emotional and physical collapse are familiar to the reader of nineteenth-century women's memoirs, the neat resolutions of life and literary structure of Webb's *My Apprenticeship* are not. When Webb informs her reader that she was almost magically 'helped over the "dead point" ' by the publication in the *Pall Mall Gazette* of her signed letter-to-the-editor on East End unemployment, she signals the commencement of the unfolding of this resolution. It begins with this 'recognition of [her] capacity as a writer' and ends with her marriage to Sidney Webb. She is even tempted at this point in her narrative to 'make the trite reflection' that when she looks back on 'that slough of despond into which I had been slowly sinking from 1884 onwards', she seems to see a 'guardian angel busily at work hardening my own purpose and perhaps another person's heart!' (p. 275). Even the 'compulsory withdrawal' from active social investigation in the 'field' of the East End gave her, she claims, the unlooked-for but much needed opportunity to improve her knowledge of history, constitutional law, industrial development and political and economic theory. There was purpose and design in this time of crisis, something working to keep her unmarried and tied to a course of study, some providence – divine or otherwise – that moved her toward the resolutions of Fabianism and marriage-as-partnership.

In the first phase of Webb's recovery from the 'dead point', she felt herself to be aided by a renewed spirit of religion. This spirit, which had left her during the affair with Chamberlain and its subsequent dissolution, enabled her to re-dedicate herself to her work and to accept with some equanimity her single state. It reincorporated that aspect of 'emotive thought' into her labours, and it offered her an alternative ideal of the female mission:

> It is strange that the spirit of religion always dwells on an unmarried life, devoted to work, rather than on the restful usefulness of wifehood and motherhood. . . . In those dark days of worldliness and sensual feeling it had died away; it rose again with the resigned fulfillment of my daily duties. Faith in my own capacity to do this work burns in communion with my faith in the Great Spirit, before whom all things are equally small: it brightens or darkens with this higher faith.   (p. 274)

She might not find her usefulness as a woman in marriage and maternity, but she would find it in a life combining faith and work, in a life of service. She had written to her father from the East End, just before he became ill, that the 'strong women' she met working there had a 'great future before them in the solution of social questions'. 'They are not just inferior men,' she wrote her father, '[though] they may have [a] masculine faculty, but they have the woman's temperament, and the stronger they are the most distinctively feminine they are' (pp. 266–7).[10] Webb now saw herself as one of these women, able to combine a 'woman's temperament' and a woman's faith with a 'masculine faculty' in the service of humanity. She was now what she liked to call a glorified spinster'.

The addition of faith to her determination to work at a 'craft' also served to eliminate from her ambitions the 'vanity motive' which had been so disquieting to Webb in the days before she met Chamberlain. The idea of service, of working for the good of others in the spirit of religious faith, seemed to her to solve the problem of egoism. Perhaps, she speculated, 'instead of cold observation and analysis, all done with the egotistical purpose of increasing knowledge', there would now be the 'interest which comes from feeling and from the desire humbly to serve those around me' (pp. 256–7). She continued to wonder, in the pages of her diary, if her desire to devote her life to the solving of social questions was presumptuous and vain. She fought the moments in which she fell prey to 'passion, self-consciousness and egoism' and prayed that her life might be a useful one, that she might 'dedicate herself] earnestly and without trembling to a search after the truths' that would help other people.

Marriage to Sidney Webb was to be but a continuation of this mission, a way of preserving aspirations and commitment to a public role while gaining a means to private happiness. This marriage was Beatrice Potter's attempt to reconcile the seemingly divergent aspects of her nature, to achieve an integration of self and to join the spheres of love and work. Sidney and she would be partners working at the same craft and believing in the same creed, as well as husband and wife. The split between the spiritual and physical needs of women, as it is so clearly depicted by Charlotte Brontë in *Jane Eyre* and George Eliot in *The Mill on the Floss*, is transcended in Brontë's *Villette* in its uniting of love and work, relationship and authenticity of self. In marrying Sidney Webb, Beatrice Potter was striving for that kind of transcendence.

In the last days of her unmarried life, Beatrice wrote to Sidney that she was about to throw off the doubleness of her existence: 'In

the future my life will be one life only – you and my work bound
together.'[11] Rather than living a public life as dutiful daughter
and a private life as student and worker, she would be able to take
up one life only, identical in public and private, as wife-and-
worker. The distinction between private and public spheres could
be safely eliminated. 'And now the old life is over,' Webb wrote in
her diary after her engagement had been made public,

> or rather the old *shell* is cast off. . . . Past are the surroundings of
> wealth, past the association with the upper middle class; past
> also the silent reserve and the hidden secret. Now I take my
> place as a worker and a help-mate of a worker – one of a very
> modest couple living in a small way. But in essentials I remain
> the same – the same woman who collected rents, studied the
> Docks, worked in the sweated dens, and dined with the Board
> of Directors of the Wholesale Society three times a week
> (1 January 1892)

Not only might two selves become one, but the unified self that
emerged would be the authentic, the essential one. Like Lucy
Snowe at the conclusion of *Villette*, Webb could abandon 'silent
reserve and the hidden secret'. Like M. Paul Emanuel, Sidney
Webb would enable her to break down the division between inner
and outward self, between private and public existence.

The hoped-for transcendence of inner division could be
achieved, however, only at a certain cost and under certain
anomalous conditions. One essential condition was Beatrice's
class superiority: the class difference between Sidney and Beatrice
was her means to liberation and to power. In marrying him she
freed herself from the social demands that would automatically
have been imposed upon her by marrying a man of her own social
class, a man like her father or brothers-in-law, or like Joseph
Chamberlain. She would not marry as her mother or sisters had
done; she would not tie herself to the duties of a large country
house, to the rigours of the London 'Season', to the dictates of a
husband with whom she might disagree. '[F]ar better to marry a
clerk in the Colonial Office,' she wrote to Sidney, 'than a leading
politician to whose career I should have to fit and to sacrifice my
own.'[12] She could be and act as she wished as the upper
middle-class wife of a lower middle-class Civil Servant: her
political beliefs, her desire to investigate poverty and her literary

ambition would not be stigmas in the context of such a marriage. The unconventionality of her desired role as a woman would create less strain within the framework of a socially unconventional match.[13] And, as Jane Eyre attained sexual equality with Rochester by bringing to her marriage newly-inherited wealth, so Webb was able to compensate for the powerlessness of her sex with the power of superior wealth and station.

But if 'marrying down' was in part a means to power within a sexual relationship, it was also, like Maggie Tulliver's attractions to Philip Wakem and Stephen Guest, an expression of anger at her family. It served that double purpose of freeing her from social convention and enabling her to thwart openly the family and friends who had upheld those conventions. Sidney Webb was not merely 'an ugly little man with no social position and less means', as Beatrice facetiously described him in her diary; he was also a socialist with a public reputation. The extent to which Beatrice Potter rebelled against her family and class in marrying Sidney Webb cannot be fully appreciated until one considers the vehement opposition of her friends and relations to this match, as it is reflected in the letters they wrote to her after hearing of her engagement.

Ella Pycroft, with whom Beatrice worked in the East End, wrote to beg her friend to think again before she married Sidney. She also reported that the Playnes, Beatrice's sister and brother-in-law, did not like the idea of the engagement at all but were willing to remain friendly 'if Mr Webb succeeds in life'. 'I can really feel very much for your family,' Pycroft admitted, 'it was bad enough for you to hold dreadful opinions and proclaim them, without marrying a man who will encourage and abet you.'[14] Mary Playne herself wrote to Beatrice, claiming that she intended to meet Sidney with an open mind, but warning that the course of their 'acquaintanceship' would depend on his attitude: 'If he thoroughly dislikes and disparages the class to which we belong and the traditions we think have a real value, it is not likely there will be much sympathy between us.'[15]

Beatrice's family neither approved of Sidney nor were they comfortable with what they were convinced would be his automatic disapproval of them. Her friends, like Ella Pycroft, who might have been expected to sympathize with Beatrice's needs, suspected that she was accepting Sidney for fear that no other man would present himself as a suitor. Why else, they wondered,

would she contemplate this marriage? Charles Booth, the cousin
by marriage with whom she had been working as a social
investigator, was honoured with the news of Sidney and Beatrice'
relationship long before any member of the immediate family. His
response, in a letter professing great love and concern for Beatrice
was simply: '*Don't do it I say*. Life has not yet by any means reached
its last chapter for you; turn another page and read on!'[16] Booth, a
confirmed Individualist despite his recognition of the need for
'socialistic' reform, regarded Sidney as a political opponent. A
great gap remained between the position of Beatrice Webb's
reformist friends and the Fabianism of Sidney Webb. Ultimately,
Charles and Mary Booth ceased to consider Beatrice an intimate
friend; this wounded her as greatly as did Herbert Spencer's
unequivocal decision to drop her as his literary executor after her
marriage.[17] Like Maggie Tulliver, she lashed out at those closest
to her, and mourned their consequent rejection of her.

Arabella Fisher, one of Beatrice's closest confidantes during
this period of her life and herself a writer and natural scientist who
had been an assistant to Sir Charles Lyell, wrote to question the
genuineness of her new political views, suggesting that she was
being subtly brainwashed by Sidney and drawn by him into
extremism. She wondered whether 'this friendship is giving you a
clear view of life, or narrowing its issues to class prejudices (I
mean working class prejudices)'.[18] She feared that Beatrice's
judgement as a scientific investigator might become clouded and
that she would become 'entangled in a web [sic] of Socialism'.[19]
Webb's friends perceived Sidney Webb's politics as an affront to
their way of living and believing. For many, the Fabians did
represent what Arabella Fisher called an 'extreme section of life',
and for those, Beatrice Potter's marriage to one of the Fabian
leaders was an act of social and familial defiance.

The greatest price Beatrice paid, however, for marrying a man
who would allow her to do and be what she liked, and who would
be her partner, was her admitted lack of passionate – or romantic
– feeling for Sidney. In the days when he first courted her and she
resisted him, she explained to him in letters that though she
admired him and felt the 'strength and calm' of his affection, she
did not love him. Frankly comparing her feelings for him to her
feelings for Chamberlain, she wrote: 'That other man I loved but
did not believe in. You I believe in but do not love.'[20] She was here
articulating the dichotomy that gives form to the autobiographi-

cal novels of Brontë and Eliot. 'You were personally unattractive to me', she bluntly admitted to Sidney, reminding him that she was not physically attracted to him and had been passionately attracted to Joseph Chamberlain.[21]

The problem for Beatrice, and for other women who attempted to break with convention and become the 'equals' of their husbands, was to overcome the social inhibitions that had become internal ones. Webb suffered from an attraction – a logical attraction, in light of the conventions that governed relations between the sexes – to a man who assumed superiority over her. She was first drawn to Chamberlain precisely because he treated her as insignificant, 'without importance except in so far as [she] might be related to him'. A man like Sidney Webb, to whom she might feel equal in many ways and superior in others, could not inspire her sexual or romantic feeling. Like Maggie Tulliver, her physical and her moral impulses were divided and at odds. Unlike Maggie, she did not end by giving up hope of integration of self; nor was she able to return to a diminished and chastened 'Rochester', like Jane Eyre. She strove, instead, to transcend inner division by marrying a man she believed in and *hoped* to love.

Beatrice translated her lack of sexual feeling for Sidney into a virtue, part of an ennobling renunciation and a rejection of egoism. Marriage to Sidney, she wrote in her diary when she was finally persuaded to marry him, would be 'an act of renunciation of self and not of indulgence of self' (22 May 1891). She convinced herself – and wrote to Sidney – that only commitment to public service mattered: 'Personal happiness to me is an utterly remote thing,' she wrote just before their wedding, 'and I am to that extent heartless that I regard everything from the point of view of making my own, or another's, life serve the community more effectively.'[22]

In *My Apprenticeship*, marriage to Sidney Webb is a resolution of the conflict of sexual identity, just as Fabian Socialism is a resolution of the conflict between the 'Ego that affirms' and the 'Ego that denies'. Fabianism allowed for a synthesis of Beatrice Webb's need for faith, which she thought a 'feminine' need, and her scientific scepticism, which she thought a 'masculine' faculty. So did her marriage to Sidney Webb allow for a synthesis of her 'feminine' desire for private fulfilment and her 'masculine' desire to analyse, write and work. Webb ends her autobiography with a conclusion appropriate to romance:

Here ends 'My Apprenticeship' and opens 'Our Partnership': a working comradeship founded in a common faith and made perfect by marriage; perhaps the most exquisite, certainly the most enduring of all varieties of happiness.   (p. 400)[23]

When Webb writes, in the final section of the autobiography, that meeting Sidney was the 'culminating event' of her life because it led to the end of apprenticeship and, therefore, 'to the ending of this book', she emphasizes the degree to which her life, like fiction, had a climax, a denouement and a resolution. Unlike the resolutions of *Jane Eyre* and *The Mill on the Floss*, this one involves no loss of limb or life; it suggests, on the contrary, a discovery of wholeness, like Lucy Snowe's. Whether the open-endedness and uncertainty of *Villette* would have been more appropriate to the story of Webb's life, whether the life resolved itself as the autobiography did, are questions to be taken up later in this study.

Part III
'Creed' and 'Craft':
Social and Political
Transformations, 1870–92

Introduction: a 'Field of Controversy'

I now turn from a consideration of Webb's autobiography as literary text to an examination of its biographical and historical content. *My Apprenticeship* belongs to the tradition of Victorian autobiography because of the nature of its content – because it places the phenomenon of conversion at its centre, because it traces the dialectic between faith and reason and because it treats the discovery of vocation as the essential moment of individual life. *My Apprenticeship* belongs to traditions of women's writing because it focuses on the resolution of female conflict and on the problematic reconciliation of private and public spheres. Webb was able to imagine her life according to a specific model of human growth, and to write a certain genre of autobiography because the facts of history allowed her to find vocation and achieve reconciliation. Political events, economic crises and intellectual movements form the subjects of *My Apprenticeship* and are the reasons for its very existence.

The last five chapters of *My Apprenticeship*, from 'The Choice of a Craft' through 'A Grand Inquest into the Condition of the People of London' to 'Why I Became a Socialist', describe Beatrice Webb's professional and political evolution in the decade of the 1880s. Webb began her active public life as a 'glorified spinster' engaged in social service, as an Individualist in the tradition of Herbert Spencer, and as a student of abstract economy theory. By the early years of the 1890s, she had left the ranks of unmarried female social workers and had become a social investigator, identified with a profession of 'brain-workers' rather than with a class of women. She had developed a critique of Individualism, become a proponent of Co-operation and Trade Unionism, and allied herself with Fabian Socialists. And she had abandoned abstract theory for a synthesis of empiricism and historical method. During this period of rapid and dramatic intellectual and professional development, Webb forged a personal identity that she felt would satisfy all of her conflicting needs.

Webb's evolution in the 1880s was shaped and directed by a number of historical phenomena that converged in the final decades of the nineteenth century to create what Webb called a 'field of controversy'. In her autobiography, she identifies two strands of the controversy that dominated periodicals and topical literature, and gave rise to 'perpetual arguments within my own circle of relations and acquaintances': 'on the one hand, the meaning of the poverty of masses of men; and, on the other, the practicability and desirability of political and industrial democracy . . . as a means of redressing the grievances of the majority of the people' (p. 167). What are the causes of poverty and what might be its remedy? The influx of large numbers of women into various areas of social service, into philanthropic work, the organization of charity and agitation for social reform, allowed Webb a convenient entry into the arena of controversy. Developments in British sociology, most particularly Charles Booth's mammoth undertaking of an analysis of poverty in London, provided her with an apprenticeship in social investigation and an opportunity to observe the lives of the poor. And the so-called 'Socialist Revival' of the 1880s, the appearance of groups like the Fabians and the Social Democratic Federation and the growing rejection of *laissez-faire* ideology, gave a focus to her own questioning of the efficacy of Individualist policies in the elimination of poverty.

5 Women's Work

Beatrice Webb began her apprenticeship for professional life in 1883 as a visitor for the Charity Organization Society under the supervision of Octavia Hill, and continued in 1885 as a rent-collector at Katherine Buildings, an East End working-class dwelling. When Webb began this volunteer work, she was one of a mass of upper middle-class women who spent time 'slumming' in the East End, benefiting, in this comparative freedom of activity, from the accepted notion that charity and social service were women's spheres. The participation of middle-class women in this kind of work, though apparently frivolous and benignly conventional, often led to more serious, more socially radical and incipiently professional involvement. Such was the case for Webb, for whom 'East-Ending' marked the beginning of a movement *away* from the individualist and paternalist ethic of the Charity Organisation Society, and of a commitment, not to professional social work, but to empirical social investigation.

As she evolved within this framework of women's work, her sense of herself as a woman changed: she moved from a personal identification with the circle of unmarried, service-oriented women she found working in London to a more clearly professional definition of herself as social investigator. She relinquished, to return to Webb's notion of sexual dichotomy, the need to stifle 'egoism' in 'feminine' service and self-subordination, and risked the desire to make a name for herself through the exercise of 'masculine' intellect and ambition. In so doing, she ceased to think of herself as a 'woman worker' and began to consider herself a social scientist – a 'brain-worker' – without special professional allegiance to other women. Her rejection of more traditional women's work and her ultimate dedication to the empirical sociology of Booth helped to determine Webb's peculiarly ambivalent relationship to late-nineteenth-century feminism. As COS worker and rent-collector, she happily entered the society of like-minded women; when she turned her back on these occupations, she rejected women's culture and resisted any overt identification with other women or with the work they might be expected to undertake.[1]

TOWARDS PROFESSIONALISM: WOMEN, THE PHILANTHROPIC TRADITION AND THE 'DISCOVERY' OF POVERTY

By the middle decades of the nineteenth century, large numbers of middle- and upper-class women had become active in the areas of social reform that involved poverty, health, and education. When Hippolyte Taine visited England in 1861–2, he was struck by the serious and sober preoccupations of the females of that nation, and impressed by the articles on social issues he found in *The English Women's Review* and in the publication of the National Association for the Promotion of Social Service.[2] Philanthropic work provided socially acceptable and useful activity for middle-class women, and posed no threat to the conventional separation between male and female spheres of labour; it involved women in public work, but only as an extension of private duties.

By the last decades of the century, however, it had become clear that the ethic of female charity had provided women with a legitimate entry into various professional fields: into areas of education that had previously remained closed to them, into medicine, local government, the civil service and policy-making. After 1880, women were able to train as physicians, after 1870 to sit on school boards, in 1875 to become Poor Law Guardians and in 1888 to be part of the new London County Council.[3] 'In a generation not less scientific than benevolent,' G. M. Young has remarked, 'the evolution of the ministering angel into the professional teacher, nurse or doctor was inevitable.'[4] That evolution, though it may seem in retrospect to have been inevitable, natural and unopposed, constituted a struggle for those women who began to demand, not merely to help, but to be trained, to be paid, to have the value of their experiences recognized and to be able to contribute to the creation of social policy.

In an article on women's participation in Social Science Congresses, written in 1861, Frances Power Cobbe observed that men had long relegated women to the nursery and the sick chamber. Now that women in large numbers seemed to be vigorously involved with the young, the poor and the ill, Cobbe complained, men instructed them not to meddle with this school or that hospital, not to testify before Parliament or 'write papers about paupers, and women's employment, and children's education'.[5] 'In a word,' Annie Besant later summarized the attitude Cobbe had been indicting, 'it is unfeminine to know how to do a thing, and to do it comprehendingly, wisely and well; it is feminine to do things of whose laws and principles we know absolutely nothing, and to do them ignorantly, foolishly and badly.'[6]

The years in which women fought to transcend this distinction between what was considered to be 'feminine' and what was considered to be 'unfeminine' work, from the 1870s to the 1890s, were what Ray Strachey has called the 'lean years of the suffrage movement'.[7] Women occupied with the professionalization of their work and with gaining a role in local administration of social services 'believed in but [did] not care for suffrage. Politics . . . seemed to them a remote and comparatively useless matter, . . . but for practical purposes their own work in a settlement, a school, or a philanthropic society, appeared more immediate and urgent.'[8] These women defined emancipation, not in terms of enfranchisement, but in terms of gaining the right to do officially, publicly and professionally what they had been doing in an unacknowledged and unpaid form.

The entry of women into the profession of social work depended, then, on what Viola Klein calls the 'loophole provided for them by the increasing awareness of social evils and of the need for effective remedies'.[9] The 'discovery' of poverty in the last decades of the century seems to have provided new and more numerous 'loopholes' as a result of the proliferation of organizations and institutions created in response to this 'discovery'. The Charity Organisation Society and the Salvation Army were organizations to which women gravitated, and which were particularly receptive to their participation. New local authorities formed during this period – School Boards and the London County Council have already been mentioned – provided women with the opportunity to fill administrative posts. Many women had developed expertise as volunteers in areas of social service, and some had begun to receive the benefit of higher education: the

University of London first granted degrees to women in 1878, Cambridge University in 1881 and Oxford in 1884. Their valuable training, well-developed skills and potential for being economically independent made them a new 'class' of women seeking the means to enter into an established social structure.

Historians of these last Victorian decades, particularly those interested in the connections between the creation of political ideology and the structure of class relationships, have remarked on the degree to which groups like the COS and the Fabians represented the efforts of new social groups to integrate themselves into a fairly rigid class structure. Gareth Stedman Jones observes that the COS, with its insistence that the 'practice of charity depended as much on knowledge as upon money', was engaged in trying to form a 'new urban gentry' which relied for its power not upon birth or wealth but upon expertise. The poor, the COS had concluded, suffered an utter separation from the salutary influence of the upper classes; they, the COS workers, would be able to re-inject that influence, not as a traditional aristocracy, but as a 'professional gentry'.[10] Thus, a segment of the middle class might promote and establish itself through knowledge and professional status.

Making a related argument in his essay 'The Fabians Reconsidered', Eric Hobsbawm analyses Fabianism as a socialism of the new, self-made, professional middle class, trying to find a 'firm place in the middle- and upper-class structure of late Victorian Britain'.[11] Fabianism developed out of a *nouvelle couche sociale* of 'trained, impartial and scientific administrators and expert advisers'. The socialism they created revolved, in part, around the kind of skills and expertise they themselves possessed; its institutionalization would be expected, then, to bring them material, social and intellectual rewards, and to integrate them into existing structures of power.

The fact that both the COS and the Fabian Society had large female memberships suggests that the analyses of Jones and Hobsbawm should be expanded to apply to what was, in effect, a new class of women created by the training of philanthropic work, newly-available higher education and increasing legal and economic autonomy. Not only were most of the COS 'visitors' female, but Octavia Hill's scheme for the middle-class supervision of working-class dwellings was constructed upon the very principle of female volunteers. Hobsbawn observes that in 1890, before the first wave of expansion of the Fabian Society, women formed more than a quarter of the total membership. These were 'emancipated and presumably middle-class women', writes Hobsbawn, 'independent women, often earning their livelihood as writers, teachers or even typists'.[12] (Only one addition was ever made to the original Fabian 'Basis', or statement of principles, and that was an amendment in favour of women's suffrage.) It is not surprising, then, that when one thinks of the literature of the turn of the century written about the 'New Woman', one thinks of the works of two Fabians – George Bernard Shaw and H. G. Wells. Shaw and Wells encountered these 'new' women in the Fabian Society, among other places, and female members of the Society served as models for a number of their heroines. Vivie Warren and Barbara Undershaft bear a striking resemblance to Beatrice Webb herself.[13]

WEBB AT THE EAST END: SUPERVISING THE POOR

Many young women who came of age in the last decades of the nineteenth century entered the field of social service under the tutelage of Octavia Hill. Hill was of the generation that formed a bridge between the untrained, upper-class women like Josephine Butler and Angela Burdett-Coutts, whose philanthropic work was of an unsalaried, self-instructed kind, and those women born in the 1850s and 1860s who worked in a trained, salaried and professional way. The kind of work that Hill did in the recruitment of female rent-collectors was pivotal in the transition to professional social service made by women in the nineteenth century: she brought women into a regular, systematic relationship with the people they were meant to serve, and she provided them with a form of training or apprenticeship in social work. Hill also represents the ideological and methodological point at which Beatrice Webb entered public life, and away from which Webb evolved after that initial entry.

Hill's attitudes toward poverty grew out of a Ruskinian critique of industrial society, and the Christian Socialism of F. D. Maurice (Maurice's son married one of Hill's sisters; another sister married the son of George Henry Lewes).[14] Both Ruskin and

Maurice had a strong personal influence on her: Maurice met Hill at the Ladies Co-operative Guild, where he taught Bible classes for the same Ragged School children she supervised in toy-making, and he appointed her secretary of Queen's College for women in 1856; Ruskin purchased for her, with a portion of his family inheritance, the first slum tenements she managed in 1865. Ruskin also aided in the founding, in 1868, of the London Association for the Prevention of Pauperization and Crime, later to be transformed into the Charity Organisation Society, which Hill joined in 1870. She shared with Ruskin the conviction that the lives of modern, urban workers sorely lacked art, amusement, imagination and beauty, and her emphasis on the establishment of recreation rooms, gardens and playgrounds in her working-class dwellings grew out of this Ruskinian belief. 'I have tried', Hill wrote,

> as far as opportunity has permitted, to develop the love of beauty among my tenants. The poor of London need joy and beauty in their lives. There is no more true and eternal law to be recognised about them than that which Mr Dickens shows in *Hard Times* – the fact that every man has an imagination which needs development and satisfaction. Mr Sleary's speech, 'People mutht be amoothed, Thquire', is often recalled to my mind in dealing with the poor.[15]

Another tenet of Hill's belief about the lives of the poor was that indiscriminate charity-giving had produced a demoralized, unenterprising, passive class of 'paupers'. The very purpose of the COS, of whose Central Council Hill became a member in 1875, was to organize centrally and to systematize charity so that alms-giving might be controlled and checked. If only those who 'deserved' charity received it and if those who used their wiles to get more than they needed were stopped, then 'the "clever pauper" would be forced to turn back from mendicancy to labour', as Gareth Jones has put it, 'and the demoralized poor would relearn the virtues of thrift and self-help'.[16] COS visitors would go to the homes of charity recipients to determine whether the individual or family in question needed and deserved assistance. This 'visiting' would serve not only to control the flow of charity, but to help bridge the demoralizing gap between rich and poor. The poor suffered from class separation, from the absence of middle- and upper-class influences. 'It is becoming clear to the public,' Hill wrote, 'that there is a right and a wrong, a wise and an unwise charity.' But, she went on to say, we must not rely on committees to make these distinctions but on individuals, thus bringing 'the rich and the poor, the educated and uneducated, more and more into communication'.[17] The poor must be dealt with *as* individuals *by* individuals.

These principles of supervision and a belief in 'guidance' to restore the virtues of labour, self-help and honesty formed the basis of Hill's scheme for managing working-class dwellings with the aid of female volunteers. Some tenements were first acquired by individuals – Hill and Ruskin among them – and eventually sold to companies that continued to depend on female workers, some of whom were paid minimal salaries, for rent-collection. The women also attempted to see to repairs and problems of overcrowding, and to evict tenants for non-payment of rents or for 'bad behaviour'. In an article for *Macmillan's Magazine* in 1869, Hill wrote:

> I think no one who has not experienced it can fully realise the almost awed sense of joy with which one enters upon such a possession [a series of London tenements] . . . , conscious of having the power to set it, even partially, in order. . . . As soon as I entered into possession, each family had an opportunity of doing better; those who would not pay, or who led clearly immoral lives, were ejected.[18]

She advised her volunteers to be strict about rent-payment, to offer work rather than money or goods, to 'strengthen by sympathy and counsel the energetic effort which shall bear fruit in time to come', and to coax each individual tenant to the 'spirit of judging rightly' rather than to judge him or her oneself.[19] To collect rents properly was quite simply to become a moral force in the lives of those from whom one collected.

Hill stood in opposition to many of the responses to urban poverty that her own activities seemed inadvertently to have produced. Women who came to volunteer with Hill often wanted to commit themselves in a regular, professional manner to social service, but Hill made it clear that only volunteers would suit her, only women for whom their own homes came first and their work second. 'The work amongst the poor,' she concluded, 'is better done by those who do less of it.'[20] She resisted the idea of social service as a full-time career for women, yet she gave them experience, training and a taste for the rewards of labour. The degradation of slum life that Hill's projects helped to expose to the public led many to the conclusion that the state should accept some responsibility for ameliorating the lives of the very poor, but Hill opposed any form of state intervention. If private alms-giving demoralized the poor, then anything the government doled out would do so as well. When, in 1898, the London County Council turned to Hill's example and proposed to build and supervise working-class dwellings in competition with commercial Building Societies, she thoroughly disapproved.[21] She maintained that the LCC would offer lower rents than private builders, but would then tax builders mercilessly to subsidize the cheaper LCC housing. When Charles Booth's volume on East London – prompted by the controversy over the nature of poverty to which Hill herself had contributed – was published, she thanked the friend who sent it to her with reservation:

> They are all reading it with interest. I believe I shall do so, some day, if we may keep it so long; but I prefer 'Old News', like a true disciple of Ruskin's, and would rather read it when the fuss is a little over. I know in my heart of hearts, what I think; and *that* is that all depends on the spiritual and personal power; and *that* we must measure if at all, in the courts, rather than in the book.[22]

Beatrice Webb was, of course, to be one of the principal contributors to Booth's volume, but she started on her career in public life as one of Octavia Hill's acolytes.

Webb's older sister Kate had worked with Hill at the COS, but vacated her post there upon marriage to Leonard Courtney. Beatrice agreed to replace her sister, not because of an urgent sympathy with the poor, but because poverty seemed to her a live and controversial issue, and because her reading of social thought – of Spencer, Comte and Mill – convinced her that the issue could not be solved in the realm of theory but in the observation of human beings in their daily, working lives. 'Why,' Webb asks in her autobiography, 'did I select the chronic destitution of whole sections of the people, whether illustrated by over-crowded homes, by the demoralized casual labor at the docks, or by the low wages, long hours and insanitary conditions of the sweated industries, as the subject for enquiry?' (p. 167). She was not, like sister Kate, 'led into the homes of the poor by the spirit of charity', but because of the 'state of mind in the most vital centres of business enterprise, of political agitation and of academic reasoning', because the problem was current, pressing and infinitely interesting to her (p. 167).

The purported methods of the COS appealed to her at first precisely because they seemed to be scientific and to depend upon the skills of observation that she wished to develop. 'In these years of my apprenticeship', Webb writes in the autobiography, 'the COS appeared to me as an honest though short-circuited attempt to apply the scientific method of observation and experiment, reasoning and verification, to the task of delivering the poor from their miseries' (p. 189). Webb also subscribed, at that time, to the belief on which COS policy was based, that 'spasmodic, indiscriminate and unconditional doles, whether in the form of alms or in that of Poor Law relief', was a major cause of the 'mass-misery' in the great cities (p. 193). Investigation of each individual charity case was necessary in order to weed out those whose state of poverty could be attributed to their own 'culpable negligence or misconduct' and thus to be able to concentrate on those whose poverty was out of their control. The aim of the COS visitor became, in other words, the differentiation between the 'deserving' and the 'undeserving' poor. Investigators were to determine, on a 'scientific' basis, the justification for any charitable gift.

A subtle shift in the criterion for aid, however, ultimately developed out of the limits of available charity funds, and this shift precipitated Webb's disenchantment with the COS. Eventually, the 'criterion of desert' was abandoned in favour of the criterion of practicability: ' "the test is not whether the applicant be deserving" ', Webb quotes the COS *Principles of Decision*, ' "but whether he is helpable" ' (p. 195). It was difficult and, in the majority of cases, arbitrary enough for the investigators to determine which families were guilty of any trace of 'patent vice or crime' and which were consistently sober, industrious, respectable and thrifty; but to reject charity applicants because they were too needy was an absurdity and an injustice at which Webb finally balked. 'The most deserving cases,' she notes,

often proved to be those whom it was plainly impossible to help effectively either by money or by philanthropic jobbery. . . . Most numerous were the cases of chronic sickness, or those needing prolonged and expensive medical treatment. Others, again, were hopeless without a complete change of environment. There were innumerable other varieties ruled out, in practice, because any adequate dealing with them involved an expense altogether beyond the means available. . . . All 'hopeless' cases – that is, persons whom there was no hopeful prospect of rendering permanently self-supporting – were, however blameless and morally deserving had been their lives, to be handed over to the semi-penal Poor Law. (pp. 195–6)

The visitor was made to feel a sham and a hypocrite, and those visited were faced with rejection if they either suffered from 'bad characters' – whatever that was determined to be – or were too desperately, chronically or permanently in need of assistance. 'Thus,' Webb writes, 'well-to-do men and women of goodwill who had gone out to offer personal service and friendship to the dwellers of the slums, found themselves transformed into a body of amateur detectives, . . . initiating prosecutions of persons they thought to be imposters, and arousing more suspicion than the recognized officers of the law' (p. 196). Webb concluded from her COS experience not that indiscriminate charity was insidious, but that all charity was useless in trying to remedy social inequities. 'By rudely tearing off the wrappings of medieval almsgiving,' Webb says of the COS, 'they had let loose the tragic truth that, wherever society is divided into a minority of "Haves" and a multitude of "Have Nots", charity is twice cursed, it curseth him that gives and him that takes' (pp. 196–7).

Webb had come to suspect that there were causes of poverty that had little to do with the individual characters of the poor, and much to do with the structures of labour and the economy. By the time she came to write *My Apprenticeship*, she was able to speak of the 'skeleton at the feast of capitalist civilization', to attribute social misery to 'unrestrained and unregulated capitalism and landlordism,' but in 1883 she had only the suspicion that it was necessary to investigate the way people worked, the way they were paid, the *reasons* they were not educated and *why* they lived in unsanitary tenements. She wrote with sorrow in her diary of a family she visited for the COS: the husband had been a dispenser of drugs and had become an opium addict, now unable to work;

the wife supported him and their three children on fifteen shillings a week. She wrote that the situation tempted her to 'righteous indignation against the man', but, she then challenged herself, 'did he make himself?' (20 May 1883). Was it the 'shortcomings of the destitute persons themselves, whether by delinquency, unwillingness to work, or a lack of practicable thrift' that caused chronic poverty, or were there in fact, as socialists had begun to claim, a 'mass of fellow-citizens . . . of all degrees of sobriety, honesty and capacity . . . who throughout their lives were shut out from all that makes civilization worth having?' (pp. 207–8).

She would surely not, she felt, find the answer to this fundamental question as a COS visitor, and the uncomfortable ironies of 'slumming', of doing volunteer work in the midst of the socializing of a London Season, began to rankle. 'I walk back down Piccadilly', she wrote of a Sunday afternoon's work in the London slums,

> meeting the well dressed young men and women who had been praying to Jesus of Nazareth that he should forgive them, having twirled and whirled and chattered through the last week – '*sensitively*' ignoring the huge misery around them. . . . Why do these hundreds and thousands of cultivated people go on boring themselves with unrealities when there is near to them this terrible reality of tortured life. (20 May 1883; 7 July 1883)

Another means of observing poverty and of fulfilling her mission to humanity would have to be discovered.

So, in the winter of 1884–5, Webb found herself 'casting about for some way of observing the life and labour of the people' and again took advantage of her sister Kate's conventional commitment to social service – and of her marriage – by replacing her in a scheme to supervise an East End working-class dwelling. Again Webb sought to exercise analytic powers while doing practical work, both because such work seemed the most readily available to her as an upper middle-class woman, and because she was determined to carry out her religious and purportedly 'feminine' mission to assist humanity. In January 1885, she became a rent-collector and manager of Katherine Buildings with Ella Pycroft, a Devonshire physician's daughter who had come to London in 1883 looking for work and was to spend five years at Katherine Buildings. The two women were assisted by Maurice

Eden Paul, medical student, sometime suitor to Ella Pycroft and son of the publisher Kegan Paul. He ran Boys' Clubs and reading groups in the Buildings, and left all 'managing' to his female colleagues (pp. 251, 260).[23]

The buildings, constructed by the East End Dwelling Company, were in Aldgate, very near to the St Katherine's Docks, and were inhabited by the 'poorest of the poor', the casual labourers, dock-workers, porters, hawkers and costermongers who, according to Webb, had been 'ousted from their homes by the Metropolitan Board of Works in its demolition of insanitary slum property' (p. 252). Webb describes the dwelling as a long, low tenement, the most distinctive feature of which was inadequate plumbing. The dwelling consisted of

> a long double-faced building in five tiers; on one side overlooking a street; on the other, looking on to a narrow yard hemmed in by a high blank brick wall forming the back of the premises of the Royal Mint. Right along the whole length of the building confronting the blank wall ran four open galleries, out of which led narrow passages, each passage to five rooms identical in size and shape, except that the one at the end of the passage was much smaller than the others. All the rooms were 'decorated' in the same dull, dead-red distemper, unpleasantly reminiscent of a butcher's shop. Within these uniform, cell-like apartments, there were no labor-saving appliances, not even a sink and water-tap! . . . on the landings between the galleries and the stairs were sinks and taps (three sinks and six taps to about sixty rooms); behind a tall wooden screen were placed sets of six [water] closets on the trough system, sluiced every three hours. . . . The sanitary arrangements, taken as a whole, had the drawback that the six sets of closets, used in common by a miscellaneous crowd of men, women and children, became the obtrusively dominant feature of the several staircases, up and down which trouped, morning, noon and night, the 600 or more inhabitants of the building.   (pp. 255–6)

In order to attract tenants, the East End Dwelling Company was obliged to keep rents low.[24] They could manage to make a profit, however, by spending minimal sums of money on facilities for convenience and sanitation. The women who collected rents accepted the absence of all amenities as an economically necessary feature of such an enterprise. Octavia Hill, testifying before a Royal Commission on the Housing of the Working Class, specified that running water in every flat was unnecessary for working people – 'It is no hardship to carry a pail of water along a flat surface' – and that no appliance ought to be given them that could be broken – 'These people are not at all accustomed to the use of appliances, and everything of that sort is a difficulty to them.'[25]

Webb and Pycroft had the charge of Katherine Buildings from the day of its opening, and were responsible not only for collecting rents, but for choosing the original tenants and replacing them when necessary. They kept accounts, prodded tenants not to fall behind in rents, threatened drunken tenants with eviction, and got rid of those who did not pay or did not behave. In 1885, seventeen tenants were ejected for 'bad conduct' and ten for non-payment of rent; but fifty-six left of their own accord, primarily because they 'objected to the arrangements.'[26] Webb, who at the time had no misgivings about the 'harmlessness of this intrusion of the relatively well-to-do into the homes of the very poor', expected the management of Katherine Buildings to be a far better apprenticeship for social investigation than COS visiting: here she would be watching not 'instances of failure in the way of adaptation to this world', but 'a group of families spontaneously associated in accordance with the social and economic circumstances of the particular district' (pp. 251–2). The COS visited those in need of assistance; the inhabitants of Katherine Buildings, Webb assumed, had adjusted smoothly to their social and economic conditions. Furthermore, she would be regarded by the tenants not as an investigator, or detective, of a superior social status, but as 'part of the normal machinery of their lives' (p. 252). The female rent-collector would become a familiar figure, like a 'school attendance officer or pawnbroker', and would arouse no suspicion or extraordinary sentiment on the part of the tenants.

Margaret Harkness, the second cousin with whom Webb had attended school at Bournemouth, had come to London to make her living, first as a nurse and then as a writer. She lived in Katherine Buildings for a time, and was in the unique position of being able to observe both the rent-collectors and the tenants' reactions to them. She described the phenomenon of the lady collectors in her first novel, *A City Girl*. The inhabitants of

'Charlotte Buildings' in Harkness' novel do not see their rent-collectors as detectives but as oddities, largely because of their sex:

> The outward and visible signs of government were manifest to the tenants in the form of lady-collectors. Several times in the week ladies arrived on the Buildings armed with master-keys, ink-pots and rent-books. A tap at the door was followed by the intrusion into a room of a neatly-clad female of masculine appearance. If the rent was promptly paid the lady made some gracious remarks, patted the heads of the children and went away. If the rent was not forthcoming the lady took stock of the room (or rooms), and said a few words about the broker. The Buildings were, in fact, under petticoat government, which like everything else in the world, has its advantages and its disadvantages.
>   'She takes the bread out of a man's mouth, and spends on one woman what would keep a little family,' grumbled a tenant to his neighbor. . . .
>   'I pity her husband,' responded the neighbor. 'She'll have the stick on him if he comes home a bit boosy.'
>   'Females like 'er don't marry,' mumbled a misanthropic old lady.[27]

Many of the tenants in *A City Girl* find that among the very few attractions of the Buildings, aside from low rents, are the 'female despots':

> Many a sick baby was cured, many a girl was sent to service, many a boy was started in life by the ladies who collected the rents. Some tenants grumbled against petticoat government, but others liked it; and all agreed that 'an eddicated female' was a phenomenon to be much watched, criticised and talked about.[28]

The female rent-collectors suffered the disadvantage of not being taken completely seriously, and enjoyed the advantage of not being wholly identified with the male landlords. Neither the fear nor the hostility was as great as it might have been had the rent-collectors been regular, salaried, male employees of the owners of the building.

GLORIFIED SPINSTERHOOD AND WOMAN'S MISSION TO WOMEN

The working-class tenants of Harkness' 'Charlotte Buildings' accept the stereotypic image of the 'New Woman': 'masculine' in appearance, unmarried and unlikely ever to be married, scrupulously serious and intolerant of moral weakness. Such an image does not differ radically from that subscribed to by the middle-class peers of women like Webb, Pycroft and Harkness, nor is it altogether dissimilar from the ways in which many such women were led by the pressures of social convention and limited choices to conceive of themselves.[29] When Webb went to work at Katherine Buildings, she was acutely sensitive to the grievances of her sex, having recently suffered through the failure of her relationship with Chamberlain; and she was in the process of dedicating herself to 'glorified spinsterhood'. That sense of absolute choice, of a radical split between the private contentments of marriage and the public rewards of work, imposed upon Webb and upon other ambitious women like her a set of seemingly irreconcilable options. If she was not to be the wife of Chamberlain *because* of her ideas, her independence of spirit and her ambition, then she would become a confirmed spinster dedicated to just those aspects of her nature that had apparently been rejected by 'eligible' men. Webb found sustenance in the alternative identity of an unmarried working woman, devoted to the public service of humanity rather than to the private service of husband and children. Other single women became important to her: she saw her own conflicts reflected in theirs, and she clung to the collective identity they together created.

The movement to bring women into various areas of social service, the agitation for increased employment of women, and even the early campaign for suffrage were tinged with a good deal of rhetoric about the problem of what was often called the 'superfluous woman'.[30] When those who fought for the rights of women wrote and spoke in support of the cause, they often used the issue of the unmarried woman, her need to support herself, to be represented politically and to give vent to those 'womanly' instincts traditionally expressed within the family. The problem of the 'superfluous woman' was raised because women did in fact outnumber men, and many women therefore needed employment in the most immediate and material way.[31] But the use of this issue

was also an attempt at political manipulation of the accepted idea
that if a woman was closed out of the sphere of marriage, she
would of necessity be forced to enter the sphere of work.

In 1869, Josephine Butler edited a collection of essays entitled
Woman's Work and Woman's Culture.[32] It included contributions on
careers for women in education, medicine and science, on family
life and the property disabilities of married women, and one piece
called "How to Provide for Superfluous Women', By Jessie
Boucherett. Butler herself, in the introduction to the volume,
called for an end to the doctrine 'that in marriage lies the only
possible salvation for women'. 'Our unmarried women', Butler
continued, 'will be the greatest blessing to the community when
they cease to be soured by disappointment or driven by destitution
to despair.'[33] Frances Cobbe, who published an article with the
calculatedly provocative title of 'What shall we do with our Old
Maids?', believed it logical to assume that a woman's place was in
the home only if she had one of her own. Those women who did
not were the focus of Cobbe's attention: 'There must needs be',
she wrote, 'a purpose for the lives of single women in the social
order of Providence.'[34] Unmarried Catholic women had always
had the alternative of the nunnery, but it was the 'Protestant "old
maid" ' who had been 'for centuries among the most wretched
and useless of human beings – all her nature dwindled by
restraint, and the affections . . . centred on a cat or a parrot'.[35]

Cobbe was suggesting the idea of a secular sisterhood, a life of
service as a Protestant alternative to marriage. Again we are
reminded of the imaginative force of the idea of the convent for
women who wished to give expression to ambition outside of
marriage but within a framework of humility and service to
humanity. George Gissing's novel *The Odd Women*, with its
ambiguous title suggesting both the peculiarity and the 'superflu-
ousness' of the women whom he describes, touches on the idea of
secular sisterhood for single women who wish to lead independent
lives. The central character of the novel, a woman of determined
individuality, observes that there are half a million more women
than men in Britain (the novel was published in 1893), and swears
that she will 'train the reserve' to be self-sufficient.[36] The
character's name is Rhoda Nunn; she dresses in black, with high
collar and long sleeves. Her mission is to prepare the 'odd women'
for a useful life, to 'propagate a new religion.'

When Webb settled at Katherine Buildings, she wrote to her

father of the women she had discovered working in London. She said that those she most admired were the 'unknown saints' who dedicated themselves willingly and religiously to the lives of the poor. But, she went on to say, it could not be denied that there was a growing number of women who were made 'superfluous' by the whims and contingencies of society, and who sought work and careers as a consequence. These women found a 'matrimonial career' shut to them, and were bent upon finding a 'masculine reward for masculine qualities':

> I would do anything to open careers to them in which their somewhat abnormal but useful qualities would get their own reward. They are a product of civilization, and civilization should use them for what they are fit, and be thankful. At the best, their lives are sad and without joy or light-heartedness; they are now beginning to be deeply interested and warmed with enthusiasm. I think these strong women have a great future before them in the solution of social questions. (pp. 266–7)

These women, she concluded, were not 'inferior men' but possessors of a 'masculine faculty' combined with the 'woman's temperament', and Webb hoped that rather than trying to 'ape men' they would 'carve out their own careers, and not be satisfied until they have found the careers in which their particular form of power will achieve most' (p. 267). Webb was writing here not only, of course, of the woman with whom she worked, but of herself as well. She had just begun to see herself as one of these 'superfluous' women, and her use of the third person belies some ambivalence about openly identifying herself with them. It must also be noted that she wrote these thoughts of her father, whose hope remained that all of his daughters, even Beatrice, his second-in-command, would marry, and whose respect for her independence and intelligence did not extend to an acceptance of the idea of a career for her or a permanent state of spinsterhood. Kate Potter had also dabbled in COS visiting and rent-collecting, but she had given up these pursuits upon marrying.

Beatrice's investment in the world of work and social service went somewhat deeper than Kate's, and was of an altogether different nature. During the years of work at Katherine Buildings and of social investigation with Charles Booth, she came to conceive of herself as an unmarried woman intent upon a career, her future tied to a community of women who had gravitated to London – and especially to its East End – to find work and companionship. Such women as Ella Pycroft, Margaret Harkness, Olive Schreiner, Amy Levy, Eleanor Marx, Rose Squire, Mary Ward, Emma Cons and Octavia Hill found a field for work in London's slums; and each was connected, in ways personal or professional, with Beatrice Potter in her first years of working life.

Webb's admiration for and sense of identification with Schreiner, Levy, Cons and Hill, and her camaraderie with Pycroft and Harkness, represent a peak of good feeling towards other women in her life. Her correspondence with Ella Pycroft during her absences from Katherine Buildings and in subsequent years is characterized by warmth, intimacy and respect: they wrote about the 'sad stories of K.B.', described the life histories of new tenants, expressed anxiety about their futures as single, working women and about their failed love affairs and, in the case of Pycroft's advice to Beatrice against marrying Sidney Webb, counselled one another 'like old widows' on the advisability of marriage.[37]

Webb was impressed by the intelligence and directorial skills of Octavia Hill, but what touched her most about this woman, she wrote in her diary, was the history of her frustrated relationship with Edward Bond:[38]

> I remember her well in the zenith of her fame, some 14 years ago. . . . At that time she was constantly attended by Edward Bond. Alas! for we poor women! Even our strong minds do not save us from tender feelings. Companionship, which meant to him intellectual and moral enlightenment, meant to her 'love'. This, one fatal day, she told him. Let us draw the curtain tenderly before that scene and enquire no further. She left England for two years' ill health. She came back a changed woman.   (28 May 1886)

Webb's somewhat sentimental account of what was a period of real crisis in the life of Octavia Hill does indicate the extent to which she saw herself and her own life mirrored in Hill's experience of failed 'personal happiness' and consequent psychological distress.

Hill's close friend Emma Cons was known to Webb as a rent-collector and manager of Surrey Buildings in South London.

But Cons left the supervision of dwellings to take over the Victoria Music Hall, which she ran until her death in 1912. Upon her death, she was succeeded by her niece, Lilian Baylis, who transformed the music hall into the British National Theatre, housed for so long in the 'Old Vic'.

Of a slightly younger generation than Hill and Cons were Rose Squire, who became one of the first women sanitary inspectors in 1893, and Mary Ward, who also took up the cause of factory reform, helped to found the settlement house University Hall, and published a novel – *Robert Elsmere* (1888) – whose hero collects rents and lectures to working men in East London.[39] Squire inspected the very London workshops that Webb frequented when she worked with Booth, and Webb later sponsored Squire's appointment to the Royal Commission on the Poor Law.[40] In 1901, Webb edited a book of essays by women called *The Case for the Factory Acts*, and asked Mary Ward to write its preface.

Margaret Harkness had come to London from her home in Salisbury to find some means of supporting herself after she had scrupulously refused to improve the family fortunes by marrying well.[41] While living at Katherine Buildings, she began to write a series of novels about the lives of the London poor under the pseudonym 'John Law'. Her first, *A City Girl* (1887), about a young, working-class woman living in an East End dwelling, inspired Engels' now-famous letter on socialist realism in which he praised Balzac over Zola. Her next novel, *Out of Work* (1888), follows the progress of a boy from the provinces who comes to find his fortune in London, only to be confronted with unemployment, casual labour at the East End Docks, Hyde Park Riots and starvation. *In Darkest London* (1891) describes the work of the Salvation Army among the poor of East London; and *George Eastmont, Wanderer* (1905) contains an account of Harkness' own experiences in the Labour Movement and in the Dock Strike of 1889, in which she played an undetermined but significant role in association with Tom Mann and Ben Tillett.[42]

Margaret Harkness – and, to a lesser extent, Beatrice Webb – knew three other young women who frequented the East End and whose lives were themselves intertwined. Olive Schreiner, born in South Africa in 1855, came to London in 1881 with the manuscript of her *Story of an African Farm*, which she proceeded to have published there under the name of 'Ralph Iron'. Schreiner made her home in the East End ('I live in the East End', she wrote,

'because the people don't wear masks'),[43] became involved with
W. T. Stead in his campaign against white slavery in the London
slums, and was associated with members of the Fellowship of the
New Life, a Fabian precursor. She formed a close friendship with
Havelock Ellis, and became acquainted with Eleanor Marx,
Margaret Harkness, Beatrice Webb and a young Jewish novelist,
Amy Levy. Webb recorded in her diary in October 1887 that
Schreiner was staying with her in London: 'she is a wonderfully
attractive little woman brimming over with sympathy' (p. 165).
In October 1889, Webb recorded the suicide of Amy Levy, the
woman whose novel *Reuben Sachs* (1888) Eleanor Marx was to
translate into German, and with whom Olive Schreiner had spent
her last days in England before returning to South Africa.[44] 'The
very demon of melancholy gripping me,' wrote Webb, 'my
imagination fastening on Amy Levy's story, a brilliant young
authoress of seven-and-twenty, in the hey-day of success, who has
chosen to die rather than stand up longer to live. We talk of
courage to meet death; alas, in these terrible days of mental
pressure it is courage to *live* we most lack, not courage to die'
(p. 385).

Webb had had experience of such suicidal despair herself, but
failed to recognize the marks of a similar despondency in Eleanor
Marx when they met in the refreshment room of the British
Museum in 1883. She thought Marx's 'fine eyes [were] full of life
and sympathy', but feared that her complexion showed the signs
of an 'unhealthy excited life, kept up with stimulants and
tempered by narcotics', and she was distressed by Marx's
inability to 'recognize the beauty of the Christian religion' (pp.
291–2).[45] The two women came from radically different worlds
but met, not only on the common ground of research at the British
Museum, but in the 'field of controversy' of the East End. Eleanor
Marx's active involvement in working-class politics in Britain
began when Margaret Harkness took her 'exploring' in the East
End in 1888. This exposure to the daily lives of the poor
contributed to her growing impatience with the 'ceaseless faction-
alism' of the Socialist League, of which she was a leading member,
and to her desire to engage in labour-organizing. She played an
active role in the rubber workers' strike at Silvertown in the
late-1880s, and she embarked on an attempt to organize the
Jewish workers of the East End, whom she addressed, remarkably
enough, in Yiddish.[46]

Webb and Margaret Harkness occasionally took a privileged rest from tenement life in the Leonard Courtneys' empty London flat. 'And then once back in that perfect house,' Webb recorded in her diary,

> Maggie Harkness fresh from her novel writing to greet me to chat on all subjects human and divine and to play snatches of good music on the parliamentary piano – I, lying on the sofa, watching the river and barges on it creeping by. Happy fellowship in work, rest and also in memories. 'Who would have thought it', we said constantly to one another, 'when we two as school girls stood on the moorland near Bournemouth; watching the sunset and the trees against it – discussed our religious difficulties and gave vent to all our world-sorrow and ended by prophesying we should in ten years be talking of cooks and baby-linen . . . and other matronly subjects, who would have thought of our real future' – one struggling for her livelihood with queer experiences of a workingwoman's life – of another with her cook and big establishment [Webb was still the female head of her father's house] but also absorbed in work outside home duty – both passed through the misery of strong and useless feeling, the baby-linen out of our reach. (15 September 1885)

Webb's positive sense of her new identity, her actual enthusiasm – tinged with a muted regret – for her new role as worker and for the 'fellowship [sic] of work' is evident from this description of her independent life. She declared in her diary that she could clearly envision her future as a worker, and saw loyalty to her sex as an integral part of that future:

> I see before me clearly the ideal life for work – I see it attainable in my present circumstances. Love and cheerfulness in my home-life; faithful friendship with a few – to those tied to me by past association, to those bracing me by moral genius, to those who will aid me to judge truthfully – and, lastly, charity and sympathy towards women of my own class who need it, whether they be struggling young girls, hard-pressed married women or disappointed spinsters. Every woman has a mission to other women – more especially to the women of her own class and circumstances. (pp. 307–8)

Webb's sense of woman's mission to women and her celebration of herself as a single, working female were short-lived and confined to those years of East End involvement when she was surrounded by others like herself. Her consciousness of herself as an anomalous woman, with all the consequent disadvantages and conflicts, preceded this period of her life and lingered long after it, but her positive enjoyment of her singularity reached a high point during these years, and with it increased her sense of solidarity with other women.

THE REJECTION OF SOCIAL SERVICE

The very phenomenon that gave Webb psychological sustenance during those years of East End work, the entry of women like herself into the professions of social service, was, paradoxically, a phenomenon that ultimately contributed to her rejection of a conscious identification with other women. Webb gradually grew disenchanted with the project of social service, with the professional slots for women that had been created over the last half of the nineteenth century, with what had come to be thought of as women's work. Her temperament and talents moved her away from social work and towards the social investigation she was finally able to do directly, rather than obliquely, with Booth. As she came to reject the intellectual, and ultimately political, constraints of rent-collecting and the supervision of working-class tenants, she also came to reject the mentality of the women with whom she worked. She ceased to conceive of herself as a 'glorified spinster' as she simultaneously ceased to believe in the legitimacy of the paternalist and Individualist premises of the work in which she was engaged. Webb wanted, she found, to do the kind of work that she did not see other women doing, the kind of work she began to do even as a rent-collector and which the women around her seemed not to understand or appreciate.

It was clear to Webb, after some ten months of work, that Katherine Buildings were an 'utter failure'. The rent-collectors had little or no salutary effect on the tenants, and the tenants who were employed, 'sober' and 'respectable' had little to do with, and therefore little influence upon, the tenants who were not. The existence of the people in the buildings had, to Webb's mind, a demoralizing and brutalizing effect: rowdy tenants disturbed peaceful ones, peaceful ones moved out, boys and girls were forced to socialize ('to gamble and flirt') at the toilets because the latrines occupied the only lighted places in the buildings, and drunken, out-of-work tenants continued to drink and to be unemployed. 'The lady collectors', Webb lamented in her diary, 'are an altogether superficial thing. Undoubtedly their gentleness and kindness brings light into many homes: but what are they in the face of this collective brutality?' (p. 268). She and Pycroft were superficial, indeed superfluous, because they had nothing, no hope of employment, economic improvement, better health or better life, to offer:

> And how can one raise these beings to better things without the hope of a better world, the faith in the usefulness of effort? Why resist the demon drink? A short life and a merry one, why not? A woman diseased with drink came up to me screaming, in her hand the quart pot, her face directed to the Public [House]. What could I say? Why dissuade her?   (p. 268)

If she had wished to dissuade the woman, she would have had no leverage with which to do so, no argument to offer on the preferability of sober degradation to drunken degradation.

Many of the immediate problems of Katherine Buildings were due to their ownership by a company of men who controlled the fate of the buildings while knowing little about them. The 'Directors', Webb wrote to her father, had no conception of who would or would not agree to live in such dwellings: the inadequacies of the buildings – their lack of convenience, privacy and minimum comfort – prevented many working-class people from living there or staying there, and many of those who consented to stay could not afford to do so or were evicted. The constant coming and going of tenants meant 'continual loss in bad debts and dirty rooms to the landlord', but the landlords seemed to remain indifferent to the root cause of these losses.[47] Ella Pycroft, in her year's-end report to the directors, stated politely that of eighty-three tenants who had left the buildings during 1885, fifty-six did so because 'they objected to the arrangements', and she humbly suggested that the problem of the 'constantly choked' sinks and badly arranged latrines might be remedied.[48]

If the rent-collectors had no impact on the lives of the tenants and the Directors refused to help, then, Webb concluded, the tenants would have to govern themselves. Her visit to Bacup in Lancashire between the time of her COS work and the beginning of her rent-collecting, a pivotal episode in her political evolution which I shall discuss in some detail in later chapters, had convinced her of the benefits to working-class life of self-rule, cooperation and 'corporate feeling'. She wrote to her father that she hoped the Reading Room club in the buildings might become a representative body, a 'council to consider questions of management and superintendence and any proposals for the improvement of the society as a whole'.[49] She saw no reason why the principle of representative government should not be introduced, why, indeed, 'corporate feeling' might not ultimately be achieved through 'corporate ownership'.

To collect rents and supervise tenants was clearly insufficient activity to satisfy Webb's interests and ambitions. She wanted to go beyond impotent supervision and casual observation to the analysis of problems of poverty and labour and housing. 'Practical work does not satisfy me', she noted in her diary, 'it seems like walking on shifting sand' (p. 267). She wrote to her father that she was not content to 'stick to her own little bit' of work, as Kate Potter had done, but that she was struck with the ambition to 'master the whole question of artizan dwellings'.[50] Webb wished not to manage the poor but to study poverty, to find some way of examining social classes and organizations. The limitations and constraints of social service frustrated her analytic curiosity and intelligence, but she saw no clear way of finding an outlet for them. She felt hampered by her sex and by what she thought to be her lack of ability:

> So I think, if I were a man, and had an intellect, I would leave political action and political theorizing to those with faith, and examine and try to describe correctly and proportionately what actually happened in the different strata of society; more especially the spontaneous growth of organization – to try and discover the laws governing its birth, life and death.   (p. 186)

She was student enough of Herbert Spencer's to be curious about the 'lives' of institutions, but she was sceptical enough of his theories to want to leave them in abeyance until the process of investigation was completed. Webb felt sure of her own 'audacity of mind', but she complained of her lack of method and her ignorance of history (pp. 262, 266). She planned to write an analysis of 'social diagnosis', and began a campaign of historical study (p. 278).[51]

She soon found herself out of sympathy with the women among whom she worked. While she appeared to be collecting rents and governing tenants, her authentic activity was cerebral and analytic. She kept thorough notes on the tenants in a ledger which I shall presently describe, and she believed this to be of central importance to her work. When she went to visit Emma Cons, who was then managing a similar working-class dwelling in South London, to do some comparative investigation, she found that not all rent-collectors shared her priorities. She described Cons in her diary:

> Certainly she is not a lover of fact or theory; she was not clear as to the total number of rooms, unlets or arrears. No description of tenants kept. Did not attempt to theorize about her work. Kept all particulars as to families in her head. To her people she spoke with that peculiar combination of sympathy and authority which characterizes the modern type of governing woman. I felt ashamed of the way I cross-questioned her. . . . A calm enthusiasm in her face, giving her all to others. 'Why withhold any of your time and strength?' seems to be her spirit. No desire to solve the general questions of the hour.   (p. 258)

Webb admired Cons' singular devotion to the practical and her commitment to individual service, but she did not share them. Nor did she conceive of her mission precisely as Octavia Hill did. She saw Hill one night at the home of Samuel and Henrietta Barnett, and they discussed, appropriately, artisan dwellings:

> I asked her [Webb recorded in her diary] whether she thought it necessary to keep accurate descriptions of the tenants. No, she did not see the use of it. 'Surely it was wise to write down observations so as to be able to give true information,' I suggested. She objected that there was already too much 'windy talk': what you wanted was action; for men and women to go and work day by day, among the less fortunate. And so there was a slight clash between us, and I felt penitent for my presumption. But not convinced.   (p. 269)

Hill, as I have mentioned earlier, was sceptical about the value of
Charles Booth's project to investigate the lives of the poor; she
doubted the good of measuring in a book what might more
appropriately be measured in the tenements in terms of the
'spiritual and personal power' of individuals. What was important for Hill was not the objective condition of the poor or the
reforms that might result from an inquiry into those conditions,
but the nature of the efforts made towards the poor by middle-class
individuals. Not only was Webb unconvinced of Hill's wisdom,
she was certain that for herself, the 'only peaceful and satisfactory
life lies in continuous enquiry' (p. 137).

THE REJECTION OF FICTION

Webb entered into professional life in the company of middle-
class Victorian women whose aim was service, but she had
authentic female ancestors among the women writers of the 1830s,
1840s and 1850s whose aim was 'continuous enquiry', investigation and instruction. These women, most of whom wrote about
Manchester and the smaller industrial towns of Lancashire,
attempted to describe the way working-class people lived and,
even more importantly, the way they worked. The nature of
occupations, the conditions of labour and the processes of
manufacturing attracted their interests and formed the subjects
for their novels, tales and articles.[52] Women like Jane Marcet,
Charlotte Tonna and Harriet Martineau combined an interest in
the dynamics of industrial life with a desire to educate the
middle-class public by translating the abstractions of political
economy into the concrete details of daily life and work. They
added a didactic temper to the study of Parliamentary Blue Books
and personal observation, and they formed a bridge between the
eighteenth-century women writers of moral tales – Hanna More,
Mrs Barbauld, Maria Edgeworth – and the novelists of industrial
life who dominated the middle decades of the nineteenth century –
Gaskell, Disraeli, Dickens, Kingsley.

A number of women writers – Caroline Norton, Frances
Trollope, Elizabeth Barrett Browning and Elizabeth Gaskell –
were moved to write on the subject of industrial life out of a desire
to expose the devastating conditions to which working people

were subjected, and to promote a spirit of middle-class sympathy. These women were, by talent or vocation, novelists and poets who devoted one or two of their numerous literary efforts to the plight of the industrial labourer. Charlotte Tonna and Harriet Martineau were, on the other hand, essentially prose-writers and publicists who employed fiction solely for the purposes of instruction. Tonna, though she considered most fiction to be sinful, wrote a novel, *Helen Fleetwood* (1839–40), about textile-workers and a series of fictional narratives, *The Wrongs of Women* (1834–44), about pin-makers, screw-manufacturers, lace-makers and mine-workers. Her most influential work, *The Perils of a Nation* (1843), was a plea for legislation on factory sanitation; it was a work of non-fiction and anonymously published.[53] Martineau, who found that she was working in the tradition established by Mrs Jane Marcet's *Conversations on Political Economy* (1816), published tales on machine-breaking, wages and strikes as *Illustrations of Political Economy* (1834) and later a series of articles on Birmingham manufacturing for *Household Words*.[54] It was largely the conventions of women's writing, rather than their own talents or aspirations, that led Tonna and Martineau – and, indeed, Martineau's precursor Jane Marcet – to fictionalize and transform into moral tales their inquiries into industrial life.

Beatrice Webb also believed in the salutary purposes of fiction, and she was periodically tempted, throughout the decade of the 1880s, to write a novel. Her first commitment was always to the revelation of man's social nature and to the investigation of his social relationships, but she believed that throughout the nineteenth century the writers of fiction had been among the only true social investigators. 'For any detailed description of the complexity of human nature,' she writes in *My Apprenticeship*, 'of the variety and mixture in human motive, of the insurgence of instinct in the garb of reason, of the multifarious play of the social environment on the individual and of the individual ego on the social environment, I had to turn to novelists and poets, to Fielding and Flaubert, to Thackeray and Goethe' (p. 133). She began to record 'realistic scenes of country and town life' in her diary in the early years of the 1880s, to write 'analytic portraits' of relations and friends, and to record social encounters in dramatic form.

Webb felt the impulse to find 'some way of bringing home to rich and poor those truths about social organisation that I may discover, illustrations of social laws in the terms of personal suffering', but she felt herself bound to find those laws before any other work could be done. 'But these must be delayed', she wrote of her proposed 'illustrations', 'until I have discovered my laws!' (p. 385). Like Tonna and Martineau, she wished first and foremost to investigate and instruct, but, unlike them, she came of age in a time that had begun to lose its faith in the socially regenerative powers of fiction and had put its faith instead in the possibilities of a 'science' of society. 'What have the whole lot of them', Webb asked, referring to the 'whole multitude' of novels, 'accomplished for the advancement of society on the one and only basis that can bring with it virtue and happiness – the scientific method?' (p. 385).

It was also a time, unlike the decades of the 1830s and 1840s, in which it seemed possible for women safely to abandon fiction and express themselves in other literary forms. The fictionalizing of social observation and the moralizing of economic and social laws were no longer absolutely required of women who wrote of the workings of a 'male' sphere. It was no longer taken for granted that women needed to publish non-fictional tracts anonymously; nor was it any longer assumed that only a female or juvenile audience would be likely to read the works of a woman on industrial subjects. In *A Room of One's Own*, Virginia Woolf remarks on just this shift in the literary sphere of women. She sees the possibility arising that women might be freed from the necessity of writing only novels. Of the four great English women novelists of the nineteenth century (Jane Austen, Emily Brontë, Charlotte Brontë and George Eliot), Woolf suggests, only two were 'by nature' novelists: 'Emily Brontë should have written poetic plays; the overflow of George Eliot's capacious mind should have spread itself when the creative impulse was spent upon history or biography'.[55] Like many of Woolf's assertions, this one has its mix of speculative flourish and critical acuteness. Novel-writing, and novel-writing of a circumscribed kind, was certainly the logical choice for a middle-class woman of the nineteenth century, much as social service was the likely and sanctioned choice for the middle-class Victorian woman who desired an active role in social issues.

FIRST EFFORTS OF A SOCIAL INVESTIGATOR

Webb would have to wait until her work with Booth to become
engaged in systematic and directed 'continuous enquiry', but she
worked at her apprenticeship for social investigation while
rent-collecting by studying the lives and work of her tenants. She
wrote two essays on method for the perusal of friends, the one on
social diagnosis and another on the limitations of a 'self-
contained, separate, abstract political economy' (p. 422). These
essays reflect her desire to approach social problems through a
'science of society' and to transcend both the economic theories of
men like Ricardo and Alfred Marshall and the sensation-
mongering exposés of the lives of the poor that were currently
appearing in books and journals. She also wrote the article on
unemployment that was published in the *Pall Mall Gazette* of 18
February 1886, in the month of the first Hyde Park Riot. As an
ongoing exercise in investigation, she kept a book on the
inhabitants of Katherine Buildings. The information she
gathered on the labour, salaries, histories and families of the
tenants formed part of the groundwork for both her article on
unemployment and her subsequent studies of dock-labour and
the sweating-system for Booth's volume on East London.

'A Lady's View of the Unemployed at the East', as Webb's brief
comment on the problem of unemployment was entitled, is
important for an understanding of Webb's personal evolution
because it reveals the degree of her initial resistance to the idea of
state intervention in social problems, and because it contains
within it certain tensions that are characteristic of her early,
pre-Fabian work. In this article she argues against the institution
of a system of public works for the unemployed because she
estimates that such a gesture would only attract more foreigners
and provincial Englishmen from the agriculturally-depressed
countryside to London, and create even more intense competition
in an already overcrowded labour market. Workers would suffer
the 'disappointment of false expectations' and come to believe –
falsely – in their right to demand work from the State.[56] Further,
those newcomers drawn to London by the promise of work would
expand the 'leisure and parasitic class' of workers corrupted and
demoralized by the evils of metropolitan life.[57]

The tensions, or contradictions, in her article are a result of her
desire to understand the structural reasons for unemployment in

the East End on the one hand and her expression of a conventional belief in the 'moral' causes of unemployment on the other. From her newly-undertaken readings in history and economics, and from her 'interviews' with the tenants of Katherine Buildings, she concluded that the problem of unemployment was so acute because of certain structural changes in the London economy:

> Half a century ago, sack-making, gun-making, and other handwork industries flourished in the waterside districts of London, employed thousands, and, if we may trust the memory of the inhabitants, paid them well. With the introduction of machinery, the cheapening of transit, the increase of metropolitan rates and taxes, and from other economic causes these industries moved into country and suburban districts.[58]

Industries had left the centre of London in order to lower the costs of production, and they had, quite simply, taken the jobs with them. As for the docks, the 'greatest of lower-class labour markets' in London, they appeared to be 'on the eve of their departure'.[59] After making these observations on the reasons for severe unemployment among the poor Londoners she knew, she went on to attribute their unemployed status to their unwillingness to work regularly and diligently at that which was offered them, and to their city-induced loss of morale and reliability. The article shifts from an analytic to a moralistic tone, and the emerging social investigator is undercut by the COS paternalist: if unemployment is the result of degeneracy and the dissipations of city life, then to what degree is it the result of the abandonment of the city by industry?

In the autumn of 1885, Webb began to keep a ledger on the inhabitants of Katherine Buildings: it was to be no mere account of payments and arrears, but a collection of brief case histories. The ledger, now in the library of the London School of Economics, is revealing as the work of a female rent-collector in an East End tenement and, more specifically, as the early efforts of a self-created empirical sociologist. Included in the notebook is a list of points of information Webb wished to gather on each family; the list indicates the nature of her interests, and suggests the systematic quality of her inquiries and interviews:

1. Number of family: alive, dead

2. Occupation of each member. Permanent. Casual.
3. Income: from work, charity, savings
4. Race. Englishborn? Foreign?
5. London born? London stock?
6. Reasons for Immigration
7. Previous residence in neighborhood
8. On site of Katherine Bldgs.?
9. Religion?
10. Attendance at place of worship
(Previous history and present characteristics. Cause of leaving or ejectment)[60]

Webb wanted to know how much the tenants earned, what they worked at and how they worked, where they had come from and what they believed; if they left or were removed, she would look for explanations in their 'histories'.

In addition to a description of the physical setting of the buildings, a list of rents, the results of questionnaires on such subjects as the reasons for evictions and the case histories of the tenants, Webb included a list of occupations, one for male and one for female inhabitants. The occupations themselves are of interest to the historian of labour, and that they were of interest to Webb should not surprise those who know her work with Booth or the histories she wrote with her husband in later years. Of the 161 male tenants listed, forty were dock-workers and, significantly, twenty-four of those forty were casually employed. In her subsequent researches on the dock-workers for Booth's study, Webb pursued the question of the structure of permanent, semi-permanent and casual labour, as well as the relationship of this structure to the problem of chronic poverty. The next largest group of male workers (thirteen) were porters, some at the docks and others at railways or shops. The rest of the 108 men were scattered among some forty-nine occupations, from scavengers to bookbinders to musicians.[61] Of the 106 women labourers, Webb noted that only forty-seven were married, the rest widowed, separated from husbands or never married. As opposed to a small number of males who worked at the tailoring trade, as many as twenty-four of the women were tailor hands, the largest concentration of women in a single occupation. Webb's decision to examine the sweating-system for Booth follows logically from the fact of this concentration. There were nearly as many women (twenty-three) employed as office cleaners and charwomen, and the rest, like the men, were scattered among a large number of occupations.[62]

Webb's case histories of the tenants, which fill the major part of the ledger, are a remarkable, and at once horrifying and colourful, set of descriptions. They reflect the same ambivalence that Webb displayed in her article on unemployment, for they combine an attitude of disapproval of laziness and immoral conduct with objective accounts of the reasons for the impoverishment of the individuals. The stories of these tenants are notable, in fact, for the variety of circumstantial explanations of poverty and unemployment they contain. The facts of these tenants' lives encouraged Webb's increasing curiosity about 'sociological' causes of poverty.

One set of rooms was shared by an Englishman and his French brother-in-law, Jean Lassarrade.[63] Lassarrade had been a successful cork-maker in the Champagne, the employer of twenty workmen, who lost his money in the Revolution of 1848, moved first to Paris, then to New York and finally to London looking for suitable and lucrative work. His bad legs prevented him from keeping steady employment, and he ultimately became semi-paralysed and was sent for treatment by the COS to a French hospital in London. Upon his return to Katherine Buildings, he was still barely able to crawl about his room, was abused by his brother-in-law and finally evicted for his inability to pay rent and for quarrelling with his neighbours, some of whom owed him money. Another tenant, Timothy Dee, was blind; he chose to make his living by playing the concertina on the street because the trade of brushmaking, taught to him at the Liverpool Catholic School of the Blind, did not provide him with a living wage. A third tenant, Matthew Daly, suffered from ill luck: 'he bought a van, and that broke down – a horse, and that failed – finally took to a barrow. Went into partnership with a man whom he "thought was an angel" . . . only to find himself swindled'.

William Mangle, a German ivory-turner by trade, had trouble finding the work for which he was trained, and was often ill as a result of wounds he suffered in the Franco-Prussian War. He could make 'good money' at his own trade, but was forced to work at sweated labour – slipper-making – and fell into arrears. Webb was warned, she does not say by whom, 'not to trust them [the Mangles] with arrears', and eventually saw them evicted.

Another tenant Webb was 'obliged' to evict for non-payment of rent was a widow, Ann Lester, who had once been in the workhouse and was determined not to return there. She did charring for a milliner and, though she was 'respectable and anxious to keep her room', she could not pay her rent because she herself was not paid regular wages, due to 'bad times'. Another woman, a Mrs O'Connor, was 'unwilling' to pay her rent because she claimed there was a ghost haunting her room; and yet another, an Irish Catholic woman, attributed her chronic drinking and tendency to quarrel loudly with her neighbours to the personal tragedy of having married a Protestant. The infirmities of the tenants of Katherine Buildings were not always of the body.

Still other tenants Webb described in her notebook died during her time of service at Katherine Buildings. Both Mr and Mrs John Taylor became seriously ill in January 1886, but they could afford for only one of them to enter the hospital at a time. John Taylor went to an infirmary and recovered, though he complained of the drunkenness and incompetence of the doctor who had treated him. When Taylor was released, Webb arranged for his wife to become an in-patient at London Hospital, but she was by then too ill to be helped, and she died in April. Michael and Alice Neal were two other casualties of what was physical infirmity compounded by inadequate medical attention. Michael had but one arm, and Alice was without legs; he was a sometime messenger and she a street-beggar. Neighbours objected to the couple because of their collection of dogs and cats, and circulated rumours about the 'impropriety of the woman's behaviour'. They paid rent regularly until Michael's death, at which point his wife got into arrears. Six months later she died, after one week's illness. Only a writer of Dickens' talent and temperament – and Webb had neither – could have written with both sympathy and irony of the plight of such individuals as the Neals, but the utter helplessness of these tenants and the complete futility of her involvement with them were not lost on Webb. 'Observation' of the inhabitants of Katherine Buildings contributed to her rejection of the project of social service, her questioning of the harsh paternalism of Octavia Hill, and her growing interest in an investigation of the social roots and structure of poverty.

PROFESSIONAL IDENTITY AND ANTI-FEMINISM

Webb deviated from the nineteenth-century conventions of women's work when she broke away from the task of social service, put fiction in abeyance and went to work with Charles Booth on his scientific and systematic investigation of the life and labour of the people of London. When she took on the work of social investigation, she left behind the community of women involved in the practical work of social service and embarked upon a kind of activity in which few women had previously been involved. What followed was a dissociation from other women workers and a rejection of the identity of woman *qua* woman. Webb did not at this time ally herself with alternative groups of women – either suffragists or socialists – principally because she was not in political sympathy with them. And her ambivalent ties to mother and sisters made Webb's relations with other women instinctively problematic, despite this brief period of dedication to female culture. She now felt angered at the pressure placed upon her to carry out work considered appropriate to her sex, and impatient with the vocation of social service.

The pressure from others to work *as a woman* persisted even after she had completed her work for Booth's first volume, and this pressure contributed to her growing sense of aloofness from the needs and conflicts specific to women working for economic independence and some measure of social equality. Booth wanted her to continue in the investigation with him and to undertake a study of 'Woman's Work at the East End', but for methodological and ideological reasons Webb wished to begin a study of the history of the Co-operative Movement in Britain. In March 1889, when Webb had firmly decided to go ahead with the Co-operative study, she encountered the economist Alfred Marshall on a visit to Cambridge, and was subjected to his criticism of her chosen project. The grounds for his objections were, quite simply, her sex: as a woman she was fitted to do a fine study of female labour and a mediocre study of Co-operation.

When she asked Marshall if he thought her unequal to the task she had set for herself, his reply was so provoking and disquieting as to have merited full transcription in her diary:

'Now, Miss Potter, I am going to be perfectly frank: of course I think you are equal to a history of Co-operation: but it is not what you can do best. There is one thing that *you* and only you can do – an enquiry into the unknown field of female labor. You have, unlike most women, a fairly trained intellect, and the courage and capacity for original work; and you have a woman's insight into a woman's life. There is no man in England who could undertake with any prospect of success an enquiry into female labor. There are any number of men who could write a history of Co-operation, and would bring to this study of a purely economic question far greater strength and knowledge than you possess. For instance, your views on the relative amount of profit in the different trades, and the reason of the success of Co-operation in cotton and its failure in the woollen industry might interest me; but I should read what you said with grave doubt as to whether you had really probed the matter. . . . To sum up with perfect frankness: if you devote yourself to the study of you own sex as an industrial factor, your name will be a household word two hundred years hence: if you write a history of Co-operation it will be superseded and ignored in a year or two. In the one case you will be using unique qualities which no one else possesses, and in the other you will be using faculties which are common to most men, and given to a great many among them in a much higher degree. *A book by you on the Co-operative Movement I may get my wife to read to me in the evening to while away the time, but I shan't pay any attention to it.'* (pp. 339–40)

Marshall's diatribe, though Webb accurately identified its tone as 'contempt sugared over with an absurdly kind appreciation for my talent for *one* particular type of investigation', succeeded in making her pause to question her own abilities. She quickly reassured herself, however, by remembering that in his forth-coming work on political economy, Marshall was supposed to quote a generalization of hers on the division of labour which was 'a purely intellectual one, unconnected with the special insight of a woman into the woman's life' (p. 341). She concluded the diary entry with the self-satirizing observation that her 'disagreeable masculine characteristic of persistent and well-defined purpose' would cause her to 'stick to my own way of climbing my own little tree' (p. 341).

What follows directly upon the account of her encounter with Marshall in *My Apprenticeship* is a section entitled 'A False Step', describing Webb's signing of a manifesto against women's suffrage that appeared in *Nineteenth Century* in the spring of 1889. As the title of this section suggests, Webb considered the gesture, in retrospect, to have been a mistake. She explains it, however, as a reflection of her simple lack of interest in the issue of suffrage, her irritation with the 'narrow outlook and exasperated tone of some of the pioneers of women's suffrage', her reaction against her father's paradoxical over-valuation of women, her dislike of Parliamentary politics and, what seems most perplexing to the reader of *My Apprenticeship*, her never having suffered the 'disabilities assumed to arise from my sex' (pp. 342–3).

Brian Harrison has done much to explain why 'antisuffragism was the obvious destination' for Liberal Unionist women like Mary Ward and for women of the political and social élite, but Webb's signing of the anti-suffrage Appeal had as much to do with her professional ambition as with her politics or her class.[64] She was moved to sign the petition, and thus risk gaining the label of anti-feminist, because of her resistance to being publicly classified *first* as a woman and only secondarily as a professional. If she were to advertise herself as a feminist or suffragist, she would, she feared, openly define herself *as a woman*, and she sought instead recognition as a social investigator, doing work not traditionally expected of a woman. She wished to remove herself from association with others of her sex, and to protest the kind of pigeon-holing in which Professor Marshall had engaged.

Webb's signing of the Appeal placed her within a female anti-suffragist tradition that had been established decades earlier by women like Harriet Martineau and Florence Nightingale, and was continued in her own time by Octavia Hill and Mary Ward, one of the authors of the petition. Nightingale had declined John Stuart Mill's invitation to become a member of the National Society for Women's Suffrage on the grounds that, though she believed in votes for women, she felt that there were other, more important things for which to fight.[65] Martineau wrote in her *Autobiography* that women would deserve rights when they became fit for whatever craft or action they chose and not merely out of some 'personal unhappiness'.[66]

Octavia Hill wrote to *The Times* to register her opposition to women's suffrage: women's time, she wrote, should not be wasted in Parliamentary politics but should be devoted to 'the care of the sick, the old, the young, and the erring, as guardians of the poor,

as nurses, as teachers, as visitors.[67] Mary Ward, ardent cam-
paigner for women's education and first secretary of Somerville
College, Oxford, cared not at all for the vote: 'We believed,' she
wrote in her memoirs, 'that growth through local government,
and perhaps through some special machinery for bringing the
wishes and influence of women of all classes to bear on Parliament, other than the Parliamentary vote, was the real line of
progress.'[68]

These women and other activists like them clung to the
importance of the work they had cut out for themselves, and
insisted on the supremacy of the inroads they had made into new
areas of activity. They were also, to a great extent, bearers of a
social ethic that relegated women to the sphere of service rather
than to that of direct political power.[69] Many mid-Victorian
women who helped to expand opportunities for others had been
loath to ally themselves with political feminists because they were
involved in creating new places for themselves, new occupations –
nursing, social work, teaching, writing – that demanded all of
their energies and set them, of necessity, apart from other women.
Octavia Hill refused even to sign an *anti*-suffrage letter to the
press, because she felt that it drew women into the political arena
and away from the pressing work that she offered them.[70] A
number of generations later, Webb rejected those very areas of
work pioneered by women like Nightingale and Hill, but she
shared their distrust of a public, political alignment with other
women.[71] It was as if in going forward into areas unpopulated by
women, they felt the need to deny the importance of their sex and
to shed the associations that would ostensibly have made them
unfit for the kinds of work in which they were engaged.

Webb later supported women's suffrage, although she
remained largely indifferent to it and, as a socialist, argued
against the suffragists' opposition to factory legislation and
objected to what she saw as the individualist tendencies of
feminism.[72] At this juncture in her career, however, she advertised
herself as an anti-feminist as a way of signalling her exodus from
the world of 'glorified spinsters', of service and of 'feminine'
self-subordination. She was ready to give vent to those 'masculine' qualities of ambition she had often lamented and had
tried, at times, to suppress. In her own mind, she conflated
suffragism and the atmosphere of secular sisterhood she found it
necessary to reject. She cut short her involvement in the issue of

suffrage when Frederic Harrison requested that she write a rebuttal to Millicent Fawcett's 'indignant retort' to the anti suffrage manifesto.[73] She declined to write the rebuttal because she wrote to Harrison, 'I have as yet accomplished no work which gives me the right to speak as a representative of the class Mr Fawcett would enfranchise: celibate women' (p. 342). Much of the early agitation for suffrage was on behalf of unmarried women: Webb wished to indicate, by her signing of the petition and by her remarks to Harrison, that she was no longer a member-in-good-standing of the community of single women, no longer a woman whose mission was to other women.

In the month that followed the appearance of the anti-suffrage manifesto in *Nineteenth Century* (June 1889), Webb attended a Co-operator's Conference in Ipswich, where she was cold shouldered by a number of the other women present. Enjoying the company of 'labor aristocracy' more than that of virtually anyone else at that time in her life, she engaged in animated discussion with Benjamin Jones, General Manager of the London Co operative Wholesale Society, John Burnett, Trade Union leader and J. J. Dent, secretary of the Working Men's Club and Institute Union. They were joined on one occasion by Professor Marshall also in attendance at the conference. Jones took the opportunity to challenge Webb gravely, but good-humouredly, on her position on women's suffrage, and accused her, with some justification, of being 'satisfied with her own position' because she was 'rich and strong' (p. 360). Professor Marshall chimed in to defend Webb thinking the two of them to be of the same opinion on the inherent inequality of men and women. Webb stopped him with: ' "Mr Marshall, I pity you deeply. You are obliged to come to the rescue of a woman who is the personification of emancipation in all ways who clings to her cigarette if she does not clutch at her vote." ' "That's just it," ' retorted Benjamin Jones, ' "that's why these women are so bitter against you. It is pure perversity on your side to say one thing and do another" ' (p. 360). It was indeed the curse of the anti-feminist 'feminist', the 'personification of emancipation' who refused to make emancipation her stated goal to be to all appearances a contradiction.

6   Social Investigation

> [C]an the investigator, coming from one social class, ever
> accurately analyse the dynamic force and the specific
> direction of the feelings of another social class?
>
> Sidney and Beatrice Webb, *Methods of Social Study*

In the spring of 1886, Beatrice Webb attended the first meeting of
Charles Booth's 'Board of Statistical Research', the team of
investigators that was to carry out his plan for an analysis of
poverty in London. By December of that year, Webb and Booth
had decided that she would undertake an investigation of East
End dock labour, to be followed by an inquiry into the 'sweating
system' of the East End tailoring trade (p. 286; 17 April 1886). So,
for the next two years, Webb worked on the investigative essays
that appeared in Booth's *East London* in 1889: in these years she
practised the 'craft' of social investigation, helped to create
methods of social inquiry, formed new opinions about political
solutions to social problems, and engaged in what must be called
experiments in identity.[1] For Webb it was a time of methodological and personal experimentation, a period of professional and
political transformation.

The methodological innovations of Booth's study, and of the
work Webb contributed to it, expressed an ideological deviation
from certain dominant middle-class attitudes towards poverty
and the poor. The work of Octavia Hill, the settlement house of
Samuel Barnett and the East End sojourn of Edward Denison all
implied that the correct relationship between rich and poor ought
to be one of close personal contact, in the interest of replacing the
relationship of the 'cash nexus' with one of human sympathy, and
of imbuing the 'lower' classes with middle-class knowledge,
habits and values.[2] Booth's work suggested a redefinition of the
ideal relationship between classes, a decision to find out about the
way working-class people lived, for the purpose of furthering
reform *without* having any direct, personal impact on the indi-

vidual poor. Scientific knowledge of a class, rather than persona
influence brought to bear on individuals, would bring abou
desired social change. In Booth's scheme, it was, in fact, th
middle-class observer who would be transformed through contac
with the working-class, and would then go on to promote reform
Statistical analysis and personal observation were the primary
elements of Booth's and Webb's methods for obtaining such
scientific knowledge, but the problem for them was to carry ou
observation without having any effect on those observed. This
was achieved by Webb through disguise and by Booth through
the anonymous occupancy of working-class lodgings during the
time of his investigations.

For Webb, the project of disguise was more than sound
methodology; it was also a form of psychological experiment.
Through it she could re-construct her relationship to the working
class and examine her own class identity. She could also express
parts of her personality that customarily lay dormant or were
hidden. During the years from 1883 to 1888, Webb's identity, as
we have seen, was in a state of flux: her sexual identity, her place
within her class and her ideological alliances were shifting and
undergoing rapid change. *My Apprenticeship*, as I have suggested
by placing it within a specific tradition of Victorian autobiography, is a work precisely about the problematic nature of identity,
about its crises and transformations. From what little we know of
Charles Booth's life and work, it seems clear that he, too,
experienced certain confusions about his place in the social
structure, his relationship to his family and his vocation. The
vulnerability of their uncertain identities and the ambivalence of
their social relationships predisposed Booth and Webb to
experimentation and to political, as well as methodological,
innovation.

They approached their study from a position close to orthodox
Individualism. The evidence that their investigations uncovered,
and the experience of investigation itself, worked gradual but
substantial political changes in both of them; but it is clear that
each evolved differently and ended by endorsing divergent political
solutions. For Webb, it was the breaking down of acquired
prejudice and class biases through the use of disguise and the
temporary redefinition of class identity that made ideological
change possible. As a result of investigation and an altered class
perspective, she arrived at political solutions that were heretical

within the context of her Individualist training. Private identification with working-class individuals, brought about because of personal and professional needs, led to the public espousal of methods for protecting that class.

BOOTH'S INQUIRY: PUBLIC DEBATE AND PRIVATE MOTIVE

Booth's decision to investigate poverty, to apply 'positivist' methods to a social problem, was a result of the political controversy and middle-class crisis of confidence that followed the onset of the 'Great Depression'.[3] It was in the wake of the 'hungry 'forties' that Henry Mayhew had undertaken his pioneering studies of the economic, social and cultural aspects of poverty. Booth and, later, Seebohm Rowntree were the first investigators since Mayhew to examine what one historian has called 'poverty in the round'.[4] The economic conditions of the late 1870s and 1880s, like the crisis of the 1840s, created great middle-class uneasiness and confusion about the causes of poverty and working-class unrest. Booth entered the controversy about the conditions of the poor out of mistrust of what he felt were the exaggerated claims of socialists and 'sensationalists'. People like Andrew Mearns were writing first-hand accounts of the gross inadequacies of working-class housing; the SDF had claimed, in 1885, that as many as 25 per cent of all Londoners were living in extreme poverty; and newspapers like the *Pall Mall Gazette* were defending and publicizing these findings. Booth set out to refute such claims and thereby discredit the socialist principles the SDF used them to justify. His motive was as much political as it was scientific: he wanted to bolster Individualist policies by proving that the condition of England was not so dire as it was currently assumed to be. 'It is curious,' Webb later said of the origins of Booth's study, 'that we [Booth and she] both entered upon it with a desire to explode the socialistic fallacies and sensational accounts of London misery.' 'But it had,' she concluded, 'rather the opposite effect.'[5]

Webb asserts in *My Apprenticeship* that Booth's great contribution was to show 'for the first time, how best to combine the qualitative with the quantitative examination of social structure'

(p. 238). The quantitative part of his analysis was derived from census reports, Householders' Schedules of rents and size of dwellings, and the reports of School Board Visitors on living conditions. The qualitative aspect consisted of what Webb calls the 'cross-verification of wholesale statistics by personal observation of individual cases' (p. 220). This was achieved through interviews conducted by Booth and his staff of assistants and through Booth's 'personal experience of working-class life'. Like Hill, Barnett and Denison, Booth sought personal contact with the poor but, unlike them, he lived among the poor anonymously.[6] Booth recorded tantalizingly little of his experience as an inhabitant of working-class lodging-houses. He wrote in *East London* that he lived in three different 'classes' of lodgings and 'became intimately connected with some of those [he] met'.[7] He had methodological and ideological reasons for taking up residence in poor neighbourhoods during his investigations, but he had other motives as well.[8]

Booth's first contact with the depressed working class, as an employer in Liverpool and an explorer of Liverpool streets, prompted him to make comparisons between the poor man's honest and direct way of facing life and his own coddled and arrogant middle-class way of doing so. One of his warehousemen informed Booth one day of the death of his son – his fourth to die – and requested half-a-day's leave to bury the boy. Booth wrote a letter to his future wife describing the incident and expressing contempt for his own class and admiration for his workers:

What a fuss we make about our losses by contrast. . . . The continual contact with the realities of life which the hand to mouth classes experience, the absence of the baize covered doors and well stuffed cushions of existence – these bring with them a train of consequences good and evil, of which the evil only are readily recognized by us.

We see and exclaim against the brutality and indecency of their life – and the callousness about death, the lotteries of the burial clubs; but there is something more which springs from this meeting with life as it is. They really feel of how little importance they and their sorrows are. They do not imagine themselves the central figures in a scheme of providence which is afflicting and chastening them for some mysterious purpose or other.[9]

The note of respect for another way of life in Booth's letter, and his near-disgust for the customs and 'baize covered . . . existence' of his own class recurred as themes of his investigations and of his life.[10]

During the first years of his marriage, Booth experienced severe psychological strain, the content of which is not clear from any of the biographical material left to us, and in 1873 he suffered a breakdown. Mary Booth took her infant daughter and incapacitated husband off to Switzerland for nearly two years, but this period of tranquillity and absence from the pressures of business did not cure him. It was not until the Booths returned to London in 1875 that he began to recover in earnest. At the point of recovery, he left for America on business, where he stayed for seven months. During the next two decades of his life, Booth spent long periods of time away from home, first on business and then to work on his investigations. Many Victorian businessmen travelled a good deal and were often absent from home; few left home to live in East End lodging-houses.

All of Booth's male assistants lived at Toynbee Hall during the investigation, but Booth chose to live in East End tenements, to the surprise of his colleagues and his family. Mary Booth wrote to her cousin Beatrice that she was beginning to suspect that Charles preferred the East End to 'Gracedieu', the manor house in Leicestershire that the Booths had newly acquired:

> I think it rests him more in some ways than even Gracedieu's quiet and beauty. At any rate it is plainly a second string to one's bow, looked on as a holiday relaxation – as one would not have expected beforehand. He likes the life and the people and the evening roaming – and the food! which he says agrees with him in kind and time of taking better than that of our class.[11]

Mary Booth's tone is light and matter-of-fact, but what she is saying here is that her husband considers East End working-class life a relief – culinary and otherwise – from his life with her and their children. In *East London*, he wrote in praise of the 'wholesome pleasant family life, very simple food, very regular habits, healthy bodies and healthy minds; affectionate relations of husbands and wives, mothers and sons, of elders with children, of friend with friend', that he found among working-class people.[12] He went on to venture the guess that the 'simple natural lives of working-class people tend to their own and their children's happiness more than the artificial complicated existence of the rich'.[13] When Booth wrote of the greater happiness of the poor, he was expressing some dissatisfaction with his own lot as much as, if not more than, he was recording an accurate observation of working-class life. He was signalling some discomfort within his own class and within his own skin.

There is a suggestion that Booth acted upon this discomfort even after he ceased to have investigation as an excuse for living away from his home and family. Six years after Booth observed the East End poor by living among them, and three years after the break with Beatrice Potter that followed her marriage to Sidney Webb, the Webbs invited the Booths to dine as a gesture at reconciliation. Beatrice recorded in her diary that evening that the Booths were not leading the same life: Mary was 'carrying on a great house in London and one in the country, entertaining the smart young friends of her children', while Charles was 'living most of the week in an artizan's house in a back street in Liverpool – not for the purposes of investigation but simply because he says "it suits him" ' (29 May 1885). Beatrice, as we shall see, was in a position perhaps better than anyone else's to appreciate the significance of Booth's peculiar pattern of living.

Beatrice Webb's description of Booth as he appeared during the period of his convalescence in the mid-1870s suggests a man who was out-of-the-ordinary within his class, and whose physical appearance made it impossible for an observer to guess his status, his profession or even his nationality:

> Charles Booth was an attractive but distinctly queer figure of a man. . . . [T]here was the additional interest of trying to place this strange individual in the general scheme of things. No longer young, he had neither failed nor succeeded in life, and one was left in doubt whether the striking unconventionality betokened an initiating brain or a futile eccentricity. Observed by a stranger, he might have passed for a self-educated idealistic compositor or engineering draughtsman; or as the wayward member of an aristocratic family of the Auberon Herbert type; or as a university professor; or, clean shaven and with the appropriate collar, as an ascetic priest, Roman or Anglican; with another change of attire, he would have 'made up' as an artist in the Quarter Latin. The one vocation which

seemed ruled out, alike by his appearance and by his idealistic temperament, was that of a great captain of industry pushing his way . . . into new countries, new processes and new business connections. (p. 212)

Webb's description emphasizes the ambiguities of Booth's identity, or at least of his outward manifestations, and suggests a connection between the fluidity of Booth's identity and the notion of physical disguise.

The personal and professional relationship that developed between Webb and Booth was based, in part, upon certain similarities of temperament and experience, some of which are touched upon by Webb in the passage just cited. She too had an ambiguous sense of identity, a penchant for disguise and a susceptibility to psychological breakdown.[14] Webb was drawn to him because he seemed to her to be a man who had overcome crisis: 'He interests me as a man who has his nature completely under control,' she wrote of him in the early 1880s, 'who has passed through a period of terrible illness and weakness, and who has risen out of it, uncynical, vigorous and energetic in mind, and without egotism' (pp. 214–15). Like Booth, she took peculiar pleasure in what she called the 'certain weird romance' of living among the poor (p. 256). The people of the East End seemed remarkable to her for their 'sociability and sharing of small means' and for the happiness and 'sights of love' she observed within their homes (pp. 268, 169). 'I enjoy the life of the people at the East End,' she wrote in her diary in the midst of her investigation of the tailoring trade, 'the reality of their efforts and aims; the simplicity of their sorrows and joys; I feel I can realize it and see the tragic and the comic side' (p. 309). Both Booth and Webb found burdensome the unrealities of their own homes, and the demands made upon them within those homes to live with all the customary conventions of upper-middle-class life.[15]

DOCK LIFE IN EAST LONDON

After spending the winter months of 1886–7 with her invalid father at Bournemouth, Webb returned to London, not to Katherine Buildings but to the Devonshire House Hotel in

Bishopsgate, where she set herself up to begin investigation of dock labour in the East End. Her inquiry began with a series of early morning visits to the docks to watch 'the struggle for work', the daily process by which casual labourers were taken on for an hour or a morning or a day. Her first reactions to the casuals she saw lined up at the docks smoking, scrapping, tossing halfpennies, and dropping off to sleep were harsh: she found them coarse, indifferent, 'low-looking' and 'content with their own condition' (p. 288). She began to soften her judgments after meeting and befriending working men who were thoughtful and articulate about their political opinions. She made the acquaintance of a man named Robinson, a socialist dock-worker whom she found 'superior and interesting-looking'. Robinson explained to her the injustices of the structure of employment at the docks: 'Gives deplorable account of lack of employment at Victoria Dock', she recorded of her 'interview' with him in St George's Yard, 'an average of two or three days for each man. Contract system spreading fast; eight men under contract system will do the work of thirty employed directly by the Company. Says he himself, when he is working for the Company, tries to do as little as he can' (p. 288). Webb respected the intelligence and the experience of this man, and she could not completely ignore his assessment of the state of dock labour or his dream of the 'complete reconstruction of society' so that the State might supply work for everyone.

Webb also befriended a Stepney School Board Visitor, a former seaman named Kerrigan, who explained to her the different 'classes' of dock-workers – permanent, preference and casual – and their various habits of eating, drinking, reading, working and marrying (p. 289). Kerrigan introduced her to Sunday afternoons in Victoria Park, the 'meeting-place of the enthusiasts and the odd-minded of the whole East End district' (p. 290). There they heard the harangues of 'The Elder Branch of Primitive Methodists'; the Young Men's Christian Association; two working-class disputants, one English and one Russian, on foreign emigration; a man from the 'Hall of Science' on the 'animalism of man'; and a social democrat, who drew the largest crowd (pp. 291–2). Webb was beginning to discover how working-class people perceived social reality, as well as how they worked. She was also engaged in sampling various political ideologies, all quite different from her own, as a way of exploring solutions to the real problems of unemployment and casual labour that she was confronting at the docks. She dined with Benjamin Jones, the secretary of the Wholesale Co-operative Society, and a Mr Hoffmann, a Christian Socialist. She found her 'East End experiences' to be far more stimulating than her 'West End dinner parties', which were 'easy and pleasant, but . . . all froth'; and she took pleasure in wondering what the 'conventional West End acquaintance' would say to her 'smoking and talking in the bed, sitting, smoking, working and bath room of an East End School Visitor' (p. 293).

Webb also prepared herself for writing the essay on dock labour by reading Mayhew's *London Labour and the London Poor*.[16] She found it to be 'good material spoilt by bad dressing'. 'It is a mine of information,' she wrote in her diary, 'both of personal observation and statistical enquiry – but there is no opening to it, nor any destination reached' (29 August 1887). Some modern critics would disagree with Webb – and some would agree[17] – but what she revealed in her evaluation of Mayhew was her own belief about the proper goals of investigation. She believed that the social investigator had an obligation to arrive at political or ideological conclusions, that he or she should work synthetically as well as empirically. Booth and Webb did, after all, embark upon investigation as a method to promote reform; Mayhew, though social change may have been an implicit goal of his work did not enter into his investigations with reform as an explicit aim. Booth believed that, in many cases, he could complete his role as investigator by placing 'facts' before the men of politics and power, but Webb felt a responsibility, and a desire, to reach a 'destination' and to present it to her audience. She tried to be descriptive, analytic and prescriptive, and Booth did not always agree with what she perceived to be the scope of her role as investigator.

Webb's essay on the docks, which first appeared in *Nineteenth Century* in October 1887 as 'The Dock Life of East London', marks a change from the strict Individualist perspective of her 'Lady's View of the Unemployed' and brings her at least a step closer to a collectivist solution to social problems. She was one of a number of observers at that time who were writing and talking about the crisis of the docks, the decline of the industry, the wild competition among employers and the oversupply of labour. She begins her essay, therefore, by distinguishing herself from the various sorts of critics who had commented on the problem heretofore: the 'economist' who deplores the 'attractions of low-class labour into

London' (this, of course, is precisely what she had done in 'A Lady's View of the Unemployed'); the 'philanthropist' whose heart bleeds while, at the same time, he sensationalizes the worker's plight; the 'indifferentist' who 'talks glibly of the inevitable tendency of inevitable competition in producing an inevitable irregularity of employment'.[18] Webb is a new kind of critic, who will employ facts to show things as they are and to describe the dock labourers neither as 'n'er-do-wells' nor as 'down-fallen angels' but as 'all sorts and conditions' of men.

She proceeds with a brief history of the London docks and of their decline over the last decades. Neither Booth nor Mayhew before him was interested in the evolution of trades, but for Webb the history and development of any social problem or institution was always essential. The phrase that concluded this brief history in her original article and that clearly betrays her Spencerian and Comtean inclinations – 'For all things are in the process of becoming, and the yesterday vies with the today as a foreteller of tomorrow'[19] – was, in fact, omitted from the essay when it appeared in Booth's volume. This is not the language of a scientific social investigator, and it is likely that Booth, rather than Webb, edited out the line.

Webb goes on to describe the operations of dock work – unloading, warehousing, stowing and preparing for sale – and remarks on the 'hidden irony' of the dock-worker's fate, 'touching all things and enjoying none'.[20] Conversely, she notes, the 'upper' classes do not realize that so many of their worldly goods have been handled, carried and sorted by dock labourers: 'The fine lady who sips her tea from a dainty cup, and talks sentimentally of the masses, is unaware that she is tangibly connected with them.'[21] 'One should come here,' Harriet Martineau wrote some three decades earlier of an electro-gilding and plating factory in Birmingham, 'to understand what pains are spent on the common articles we use every day.'[22] And George Orwell, four decades later, noted the peculiar material connections between the different social universes people inhabit:

> Down there where coal is dug it is a sort of world apart which one can quite easily go through life without ever hearing about. Probably a majority of people would even prefer not to hear about it. Yet it is the absolutely necessary counterpart of our world above. Practically everything we do, from eating an ice to

crossing the Atlantic, and from baking a loaf to writing a novel, involves the use of coal, directly or indirectly.[23]

Webb's contemplation of these ironies leads her to a more extreme bit of identification with the labourer's deprivation: the notorious petty thievery of the dock-workers, she explains, is a result of their anger at handling materials, particularly tobacco, which they crave, cannot touch and have to consign to the flames if marked 'undeclared' – 'To see it burning and not to be able to take so much as a pinch!'[24] This adoption of the worker's perspective is a consequence of Webb's friendship with Robinson, the socialist dock labourer who, Webb wrote in her diary, considered it 'a grievance that laborers are not allowed to take the tobacco that is being destroyed' and, therefore, 'made a point of secreting tobacco on his person in order to defy the rule' (pp. 288–9).

Webb then explains the structure of labour at the docks, and defines each of the three categories of workers: the 'Permanent' labourers who have regular employment and steady wages; the 'Preferred' labourers who work irregularly but have priority over others to be chosen for temporary employment if it is available; and the 'Casual' labourers who are taken on after the 'Preferred', and work only sporadically and at the lowest hourly wage. She estimates that there were *twice* as many irregularly employed as permanently employed dock-workers. The rigid hierarchy of labour, Webb argues, creates antagonism between the different 'classes' of employees, and breeds an isolation of workers that damages the social life of the East End community. The social dislocation that she observed in working-class London contributed, she believes, to the demoralization of this class, as did the irregularity of employment. Here Webb makes her contribution to an understanding of the 'culture' of poverty, a contribution that Mayhew also made, with little impact, thirty-five years before: 'where the means of subsistence occasionally rise to 15s a week, and occasionally sink to nothing,' Mayhew wrote in 'The Dock-Labourers', 'it is absurd to look for prudence, economy, or moderation.'[25] Webb puts it this way:

But a large wage one week and none the next, or . . . six months' work and six months' leisure, are not favourable conditions to thrift, temperance, and good management. Payment by the

hour, with the uncertainty as to whether a job will last two or
twenty-four hours, and the consequently incalculable nature of
even the daily income, encourages all the wasteful habits of
expenditure which have been noticed as characteristic of this
class.[26]

Unable and unwilling to pursue this kind of analysis of the
structural causes of 'demoralization' any further, Webb then
reverts to a 'moral' explanation, to a condemnation of the
'parasitic', 'semi-criminal' class that does not want to work,
prefers a hand-out and a life of 'leisure', and is 'eating the life out
of the working class, demoralizing and discrediting it'.[27] She shifts
from reasoned analysis, supported by observation, to moralizing
and condescension.

Webb summarizes her observations by saying that there are
two problems that plague the condition of dock labour: the
difficulty of living by regular work, and the ease of living without it.[28] The
question she must address in her conclusion, therefore, is whether
or not employment at the docks can be made to be more regular.
The decline in trade makes it impossible for employers to expand
their businesses, and shipowners and merchants force them into
rampant competition with one another. The trade – the employers and the employees – suffers from 'individualism run wild'
and the 'uncontrolled competition of metropolitan industry,
unchecked by public opinion or by any legislative regulation of
employment, such as the Factory Acts'.[29] Here Webb reaches a
conclusion that contradicts all of the Individualist teachings of
Herbert Spencer: uncontrolled 'individualism' and 'competition'
must be checked. The remedy she proposes, with timidity and
with a virtual disavowal ('which many of us would hesitate to
adopt'), is an amalgamation of the docks under a Public Trust in
which trader, consumer and labourer would be represented.[30] In
this way, trade could be organized, business coordinated and
employment regularized. Just three years after condemning
Joseph Chamberlain's politics as a barrier to a successful
relationship between them, she is using the phrase then most often
associated with his political career, 'municipal socialism'. She
continues her proposal with the plea, startling for the still
'unconverted' Beatrice Potter to make, that the adoption of a plan
for amalgamation not lead to the neglect of working-class interests

and the sacrifice of 'their economic and social condition . . . to the convenience of the trader and the dividend of the shareholder'.[31]

After making this proposal, rare, if not unique, in Booth's volume, Webb concludes her essay by reverting, once again, to older concerns and more conventional thinking. If, as she maintains, it is too easy for casual workers to live without regular work, it is the fault of 'other forces . . . encouraging and enabling the worker to cast off wage-earning capacity and deteriorate into the industrial parasite'. First among these forces is, of course, irresponsibly doled-out charity: 'Whole sections of the population are demoralized, men and women throwing down their work right and left in order to qualify for relief.'[32] 'A public opinion', she concludes, that is 'against worthful and persistent work', contributes to 'idleness varied by gambling and drink'.[33] Such an attitude toward charity would work against any plan to ameliorate the condition of dock labourers. These are words and sentiments that might just as easily have come from Octavia Hill or any other member of the Charity Organisation Society, as from Beatrice Potter, scientific social investigator. Her essay on dock labour is a hybrid of perspectives, an expression of her transitional and fluctuating point of view.

BACUP: FIRST USES OF DISGUISE

Webb was not wholly satisfied with her study of dock labour. She estimated that it was an 'inferior piece of work', not exhaustive enough and too quickly written (p. 298). When she began her research on the 'sweating system', she decided to go beyond the method of her first essay by performing an 'experiment' in the craft of social investigation. She would train as a trouser-hand, live among the 'actual workers' and thereby prepare herself to 'present a picture' of work and life in an East End tailor's shop (pp. 299–300). Webb believed that she had discovered more about dock-workers as an inconspicuous rent-collector in Katherine Buildings than she had as a recognizable investigator touring the docks or the labourers' houses. 'Observation,' she wrote, 'is, in fact, vitiated *if the persons observed know that they are being observed*' (p. 328). As a rent-collector, she was taken for granted; as a fellow labourer, she would be all but invisible. Besides, she had already used the technique of disguise when she visited Bacup, a small manufacturing town in Lancashire, in 1883. That experiment had proved a personal and professional success.[34]

In the autumn of 1883, Webb had completed her COS work, but had not yet taken up residence in Katherine Buildings. She was anxious to witness the daily lives of 'normal manual-working families . . . in their homes and in their workshops' without taking on the role of intruder or detective in the COS manner (pp. 146–7). In order to avoid the obstacles to observation created by the kind of class relationships on which the COS was founded, Webb visited Bacup disguised as one Miss Jones, a Welsh farmer's daughter. But Webb's 'first step as a social investigator' was also a 'sentimental journey': she chose Bacup because her Grandmother Heyworth's family – the Akeds – had come from this town, because many Aked relatives of hers still lived there and because Martha Jackson ('Dada'), who was a distant relation to the Akeds, visited there regularly and could serve as her escort and 'cover' (pp. 20, 147). Webb's maternal grandfather, Lawrence Heyworth, prosperous Liverpool merchant, had married Betsy Aked, the daughter of a power-loom weaver, who died when *her* daughter Laurencina was a young child. Webb never knew this grandmother and, at the time of her first visit to Bacup, she had never met any of this woman's family, all of whom, including 'Dada', were distinctly poor relations to the Heyworths and Potters.

Webb's first intimacy with wage-earning people was, therefore, also an inquiry into her own familial past and an examination of her heritage. The trip to Bacup and her disguise as the social equal of its inhabitants had a personal as well as a professional purpose: she was disguised with the aim of observation, but she was disguised as herself, or as *part* of herself. By calling upon her family's origins in Northern, Dissenting life to carry out her investigation, she was playing with her own identity. The journey to Bacup was also a gesture at reclaiming an intimate tie to her mother. A few weeks before Laurencina Potter died, she told Beatrice the story of a visit she had once made to Bacup as a child, with her father, to meet her own mother's relations. Eighteen months after Laurencina's death, Beatrice decided to make the 'sentimental journey'. She went a second time before she began her work with Booth in 1886, when she revealed her identity, and again in 1889 before she started to write her study of Co-operation.[35] Bacup became for her a kind of touchstone against which to measure all other working-class communities.

Webb might have investigated her mother's family *as herself*, but she chose instead to do so through the mediation of disguise. This provided her, in one respect, with distance – the people she met would not be able to involve themselves in the life of Beatrice Potter – and, in another respect, with the possibility of greater intimacy – those same people might truly accept her into their lives as an equal. She could shed simultaneously the vulnerability of personal identity and the inhibitions of class identity. The citizens of Bacup, her own relatives as well as numerous others, did accept her warmly and openly into their community, and she was in turn enchanted by the spirit of cooperation, of communal consciousness and of religious seriousness she encountered. In the letters she sent home to her father in Gloucestershire, she described their complete acceptance of her, the way they appointed her as 'reader' at evening prayers because of her distinct pronunciation, and the strange degree of comfort she felt within 'the charmed circle of artisan and small bourgeois life' (p. 150). 'Certainly the way to see industrial life,' she wrote, 'is to live amongst the workers, and I am surprised at the complete way they have adopted me as *one of their own class*' (p. 150). She was flattered by the readiness with which they would confide in her: 'It is curious . . . how they open their hearts to me and say that I'm "the sort of woman they can talk straight away with" ' (p. 152). She was impressed by what she called the 'religious socialism' of the Dissenting community and by the seeming lack of competitive spirit among its members, the apparent absence of any attempt 'to *seem* what they are not, or to struggle and strive to be better off than their neighbors'.[36] The Bacup community appeared to possess all of the virtues, the cohesiveness, warmth, collective spirit, selflessness, that Webb found lacking in her own immediate family and class.

Webb's discomfort within her own social class was inextricably connected to her discomfort with the conventions that governed the relations between the sexes within that class. Her letters from Bacup are full of praise for the way in which men and women could develop relationships casually and meet one another in the setting of work. Her own ambivalence about her sexual identity made her susceptible to a certain idealization of sexual relationships among working-class people. She was conscious of the contrast between the way members of her own class made matches and the way marriages came about among the textile workers of Lancashire: 'Young men and women mix freely,' she wrote to her father,

> they know each other as fellow-workers, members of the same or kindred chapels; they watch each other from childhood upwards, live always in each other's company. They pair naturally, according to well-tested affinity, physical and spiritual. (p. 159)

Webb was, in fact, convinced that the happiness she detected among the mill-workers resulted, at least in part, from certain kinds of equality between the sexes:

> They are a happy lot of people – quick workers and very sociable – men and women mixing together in a free and easy manner – but without any coarseness that I can see; the masculine sentiment about marriage being 'that a man's got no *friend* until he's a woman of his own'. Parties of young men and women go off together for a week to Blackpool, sometimes on cheap trips to London – and as the women earn as much or nearly as much as the men (except the skilled work) there is no assumption of masculine superiority! Certainly this regular mechanical work, with all the invigorating brightness of machinery and plenty of fellow workers of both sexes, seems about the happiest lot for a human being – so long as the hours are not too long.[37]

The split between love and work, between private and public existence, that Webb found so problematic in her own life did not seem to her to trouble the lives of factory operatives.

Webb enjoyed the casual communication she was able to have with the male workers of Bacup. She could speak and act more freely with them than could women of their own class because, in her case, the possibility of any involvement beyond the casual was eliminated, and because her knowledge and articulateness about matters of industrial organization enabled her to converse with them as an equal. Her cousin, John Aked, with whom she formed a lasting friendship, informed her that she was 'far more like a male than a female to talk wi' ' (p. 151). Having convinced the men that all Welsh women smoked (only the insularity of the Bacup community – and their ignorance of Wales – made Webb's disguise possible), she was able to pull out her cigarettes in 'mixed' company in order to promote camaraderie and discourse: 'You would have laughed, father,' she wrote, 'to see me sitting amongst four or five mill-hands smoking quietly, having been voted "good company", "interesting like" to talk wi' ' (p. 152). Webb would later reproduce this kind of scene with trade union officials, Co-operative Society members and other working-men she encountered in her investigations. She knew she had the ability to make others treat her as she chose to be treated, even if she preferred to be treated as their class equal rather than their class superior. If George Sand and Vita Sackville-West achieved some measure of social equality and freedom through male disguise, Webb achieved a kind of sexual equality – perhaps even sexual superiority – through class disguise. 'It is a daring thing in a young woman to drop "caste",' she wrote to her father of her incognito; but it was also, she might have added, a form of liberation.[38]

Although both observation with the use of disguise and scientific social investigation without it shared the virtue of not interfering with the lives of those observed or investigated, for Webb they differed in one essential characteristic: disguise allowed for – and expressed – a sympathetic identification with the people observed, while social investigation demanded the exercise of a critical spirit. One of the most revealing comments that Webb made on the use of disguise was a brief one in a letter to Richard Potter. She remarked that 'the only way to understand these people [the working-class inhabitants of Bacup] is, for the time, to adopt their faith and look at things in their light'. 'Then,' she continued, 'one gets a clear picture, *undisturbed by any critically antagonistic spirit*, of their life both material and mental.'[39] Webb suggests here that only through disguise can she become totally empathetic with the people she wants to investigate.

Clothed and represented as herself she would automatically assume a 'critically antagonistic' posture. For Webb, to be an investigator, to be analytic and scientific, was to be in opposition; objectivity meant to her the ability to be equally censorious and 'ideological' about everyone. Her remarks to her father imply that at first ('for the time') she wished to see things as her subjects saw them, and that only later would she translate her sympathetic apprehension of their lives into a critical analysis of them. The 'antagonistic' mentality characterized not only her role as social investigator but her class relationship to the people she wished to understand. Through disguise, she could transcend both what she saw to be the demands of scientific objectivity and the obstacles created by class division. In this, Webb anticipated George Orwell, who was more self-conscious than she about his class prejudices, but who also recognized that only 'in disguise' could he overcome them: 'To get rid of class-distinctions,' Orwell wrote, 'you have got to start by understanding how one class appears when seen through the eyes of another.'[40]

BEATRICE WEBB AND THE JEWS: PRIVATE IDENTIFICATION AND PUBLIC DEFENCE

'Sweating' and Anti-Semitism

Webb's investigation of the East End clothing trade yielded three pieces of writing: (i) an article on the trade itself for Booth's *East London*, first published in *Nineteenth Century*; (ii) 'Pages from a Work-girl's Diary', an account of her experiences as a hand in a tailor's shop, published only in *Nineteenth Century*; and (iii) another article for *East London* on the Jewish community of the East End, the only study of a religious or ethnic group in Booth's volume. Her reasons for conducting an extensive inquiry into the life and work of East End Jews were complex. The substantial Jewish population of Whitechapel and the large numbers of Jews in the tailoring trades were obvious features of the East End terrain; and the current controversy about 'sweating' – about the scandalous conditions of labour in East End workshops – was equally a controversy about the immigration into England of 'foreigners', that is, Jews, who were imagined to have created and made possible the very 'system' of 'sweating'. These immigrants were accused of bringing with them 'Jewish practices' of employment and labour, and of forcing English tailors out of work.[41]

Although Jews constituted a minority of masters and labourers in the so-called 'sweated' trades, they had long been associated with 'sweating' in the public imagination. In the earliest recorded use of the word, in 1843, a journalist referred to the 'Moses and Son principle of sweating'.[42] In *Alton Locke*, Charles Kingsley used recognizably Jewish names – 'Aaron', 'Levi', 'Isaacs' and 'Solomons' – to connote 'sweaters', and depicted all Jewish tailors as wealthy exploiters of the English poor.[43] One historian of Jewish immigration to England has observed that Jews became the very symbol of a new era in manufacturing in the 1840s and 1850s, of a 'new industry of cheap, mass-manufactured, ready-made apparel'.[44]

When the large wave of Russian emigration of the 1880s began to increase the numbers of Jews working in clothing industries, the East End tailoring trade came to be thought of as a province of labour dominated by Jews. British xenophobia, coupled with the growing concern of trade unionists and certain politicians about the miserable conditions in unregulated shops, led to a widespread tendency to blame Jewish immigration for the perpetuation of 'sweating' and for unemployment among English workers. One of the solutions offered to the problem of 'sweating' was the blocking of foreign immigration. Arnold White, one of the most widely-quoted authorities on the sweating-system, proposed repeatedly that foreign Jewish paupers be sent back to their homelands. The plight of their own working-class brethren had to be of greater concern to Englishmen than whatever persecutions awaited Jews of Poland or Russia.[45]

Webb's investigation of 'sweating' had also, therefore, to be an investigation of the East End Jewish community, at least according to the terms established by public controversy on the issue. But she had other motives as well, and they were of a more personal nature. It is striking that she does not discuss her work on the East End Jews in *My Apprenticeship*, and mentions her article on the subject only in a footnote (p. 300). The omission suggests embarrassment or ambivalence about her obvious interest in Jews and Jewish life in England, and this ambivalence was the result, at least in part, of her peculiar feelings of identification with Jews.[46] When she became a temporary part – through disguise – of the East End Jewish community, it was not precisely a 'sentimental journey', as her trip to Bacup had been, but it was another experiment in identity, an exploration of inheritance and a use of personal empathy to achieve a new political perspective.

Webb as a Jew: Another Case of Disguise

Beatrice Webb believed her paternal grandmother, Mary Seddon Potter, to have been Jewish, and described her as such in *My Apprenticeship* (p. 13).[47] This grandmother went mad when still a young woman, and was finally put into a lunatic asylum after she was apprehended in Paris on her way to redeem Jerusalem for the Jews. Webb felt a strong identification with this grandmother as well as with her Heyworth grandmother and, in fact, described herself and all of her sisters as 'unmistakably Potters, the descendants of the tall dark woman of Jewish type who read Hebrew and loved music' (p. 13). Like George Eliot in *Daniel Deronda*, Webb associated musicality with Jews, here, in her description of her grandmother, in her diary entry on the synagogue in Prague she visited as a child, and in her evocation of the small prayer-houses of the East End. She believed not just that she looked Jewish, but that she had certain 'Jewish' characteristics of personality.[48] When Webb estimated her own talents in *My Apprenticeship*, she emphasized 'tireless intellectual curiosity' and a 'double dose of will-power'. This will-power, she notes, was of the ' "overcoming by yielding" type . . . , inherited from my father, which, when I was living amid the Jews in East London, I thought I recognized as a racial characteristic' (pp. 59–60). She also mentions in *My Apprenticeship* that when she was working as a trouser-hand in a Jewish shop in the East End, she overheard the wife of the sub-contractor whisper to her husband that their new employee was a miserable seamstress but was 'fitted by nature or nurture' to supervise the outworkers as *they* did, ' "to give work out" ' and ' "to take work in" ' (p. 43). She thought she recognized herself in them and they in her.

Webb also neglects to mention in her autobiography that during her East End investigations she used her 'Jewish' appearance as another form of disguise. It is not clear whether the Jewish owners of the shops in which she worked took her to be a Jew, although their profession of fondness for her and their advice that she 'ought to get some respectable man to marry her', as their own daughters had done, suggests that they did.[49] It is clear, however, that other East End Jews did assume – and were allowed to assume – that she was Jewish. In her preliminary investigations of 'sweating', one of the tenants of Katherine Buildings, Mrs Levy, took Webb to see a 'sweater', a Mrs Cohen. In her notebook on the wholesale clothing trade Webb recorded: 'Mrs Cohen was at home; a small gentle Polish Jewess, with musical voice and pathetic accent. She claimed me as a compatriot, and to her my appearance was evidently "sympathique" '.[50]

In an interview in 1895, Webb recounted some of her investigative adventures, among them her greeting of Jewish immigrants while 'disguised' as a Jew. ' "When I was investigating the Jewish community," ' she told the interviewer, ' "I got hold of an agent who boarded the emigrant Jew ships. I used to go with him in the early morning to the vessels, and was supposed to be a Jewess in search of my relations. . . . I am considered to have rather a Jewish look about me, so the "make up" was not difficult." '[51] She became friendly with a Rabbi Adler, then the Chief Rabbi of England, and dined frequently at his home. Of a large dinner given by the Adlers for members of the English Jewish community of London to meet her, she wrote in her diary: 'The Jews have opened their arms to the dark-eyed christian [sic] who is studying their East End life – and at least two threatened me with "intentions" ' (26 April 1888). It is likely that, in the home of a Rabbi at least, these men would have made such 'intentions' clear only to a woman they assumed to be Jewish. A few days after the dinner at Rabbi Adler's, Webb wrote to her sister Mary Playne: 'The society I have been seeing most of is Jewish, of all classes – and on the whole I like and respect them – I almost think I have a *race-feeling* for them.'[52]

This respect and liking for individual Jews she encountered emerges clearly in her private writings and in 'Pages from a Work-girl's Diary', written, so to speak, from the point of view of a disguised Beatrice Webb. It is also present in her two investigative pieces, 'The Jewish Community' and 'The Tailoring Trade', but there it is mixed with the crude prejudice and racialist thinking that, considered in isolation, make Webb seem an anti-Semite rather than an admirer of Jews.[53] In 'The Jewish Community', for example, she writes with near rhapsodic admiration for the small immigrant associations – called *chevras* – that acted as places of worship, study and communal activity in the East End, and in the same breath condemns the lack of pride and covert desire to overcome that led Jewish workers to engage in competition 'unrestricted by the personal dignity of a definite standard of life, and unchecked by the social feelings of class loyalty and trade integrity'.[54] She praises the self-governing communities of East London Jews for the qualities they shared with the working-class community of Bacup; and she rationalizes British anti-Jewish feeling by pointing to the Ricardian 'Enlightened Selfishness' that she took to be a characteristic inherent in the Jewish 'race'.

All of her writing and thinking about Jews is characterized by strange extremes of sympathy and disgust and by the habit of attributing aspects of personality, intellect and behaviour to 'race'. Even her sympathetic statements about Jews *as a group* are tinged with a reliance upon racial stereotype. It was only when the use of disguise enabled her to respond directly and personally to individual East End Jews that she could abandon a racialist mode of thought; and it was through the experience of this direct contact that she was able to achieve what English Jews welcomed as a virtual exoneration of their immigrant co-religionists in the controversy about 'sweating'.[55]

'Pages from a Work-girl's Diary': a New Class Perspective

Disguise as a tailor-hand allowed Beatrice Webb to observe labour in a tailor's workshop without impinging on the behaviour of the people she investigated. It also enabled her to become one of those she was observing and thereby transcend the class divisions that usually separated her from the people she investigated. Her 'Pages from a Work-girl's Diary' is a clear example of the process of the suspension of judgment and instinctive prejudice, and of the adoption of an empathetic, rather than a critical, perspective. 'Pages' is essentially a transcription of Webb's diary entry of 11 April 1888, in which she described in narrative form her working days in a Jewish 'sweater's' shop. For the purposes of publication, she changed the names of the workers and shopowners, and expunged some of the female workers' dialogue that touched on the problem of incest (p. 310). The tone of this piece of writing is strikingly free of Webb's habitual harshness and critical edge; she writes with humour, sympathy and tolerance of people for whom she elsewhere expressed controlled but distinct contempt. She is able to drop the critical posture of the investigator and the expected responses of her class position by hiding behind disguise and what would appear to the unenlightened reader to be fiction.

At a number of points in the piece, she describes a sense of being two different people, one the trouser-hand, talking, working and commiserating with her mates, the other the investigator, silently weighing and questioning: ' "Coats evidently made out: I wonder where and at what price?" ponders the investigator as the work-girl loiters at the door.'[56] She listens to the mistress of the shop, 'Mrs Moses', talking about her business, and records:

> 'The name of a wholesale shipping firm; so she works for export as well as for retail and pays same price for both', inwardly notes the investigator as she glances at the shoddy garments (The work-girl meanwhile pushes her needle into her thumb-nail, and in her agony digs her elbow into her neighbor's half-turned back, which causes a cannonade all round the table).[57]

In the course of her day's work, as it is recorded in her diary and article, her role as labourer overwhelms her critical, investigative consciousness and, as a consequence, her impressions of those around her – particularly 'Mrs Moses' – are transformed. Because she is trying to appear a credible seamstress in the shop, she is made to feel vulnerable and subservient, nervous and unsure, just as the genuine shopgirl regularly feels. In this way, she gains insight into the position of the precariously employed labourer, and respect for the humane and generous way in which the mistress of the shop wields her power.

At the centre of 'Pages' is 'Mrs Moses', the mistress of the shop, who is first described crudely by Webb as a racial caricature:

> At this moment the 'missus' sweeps into the room. She is a big woman, enormously developed in the hips and thighs; she has strongly marked Jewish features, and, I see now, she is blind in one eye. The sardonic and enigmatical expression of her countenance puzzles me with its far-off associations, until I remember the caricatures, sold in City shops for portraits, of the great Disraeli. Her hair is crisp and oily – once jet black, now, in places, gray – it twists itself in scanty locks over her forehead. The same stamped cotton velvet, of a large flowery pattern, that she wore yesterday; a heavy watch-chain, plenti-ful supply of rings, and a spotlessly clean gown.[58]

In 'Pages', the husband and son-in-law of 'Mrs Moses' remain

stereotypes: they are described as vulgar, 'sensual' and addicted
to gambling – what Webb considered the only Jewish vice. 'Mrs
Moses' is first likened to Disraeli in appearance, then described as
having lines of anger above her mouth 'which must surely express
some race experience of the children of Israel'.[59] Rather than
attempting to describe her as an individual, Webb repeatedly
focuses attention on 'Mrs Moses' ' supposedly racial characteristics, the qualities that link her to other Jews. This habit of Webb's
not only suggests bigotry, but is consistent with her version of the
generalizing impulse of the social scientist.

It is Webb's experience of disgrace as a working-girl that works
the transformation of 'Mrs Moses' into an individual. By Friday
of the week Webb has started work in the shop, it is clear that her
performance as a seamstress has been poor and that she is on the
verge of dismissal. She is now at the mercy of her mistress, and her
nervousness is altogether genuine: 'I am "shaky all over",' she
writes, 'my fingers, worn in places into holes, refuse to push the
thick needle through the substance; damp hands (the more I rub
them in my apron the damper they become) stretch the thin
linings out of place; my whole energy is riveted on my work, with
the discouraging result that it becomes worse and worse.'[60] 'Mrs
Moses' inspects the garment in Webb's hands, declares that the
work 'will never do' and dismisses her with a 'wave of the
eyeglasses'. Webb arranges her trimmings and prepares to leave
without a word. She is, to her own surprise, overcome with
feelings of humiliation: 'Is it over-fatigue, or is it the perfect
realisation of my position as a disgraced work-girl? An ominous
lump rises in my throat, and my eyes fill with tears.'[61] At this
display of emotion, the other workers turn to Webb in sympathy,
and 'Mrs Moses' 'screws up her left eye' and looks at the failed
seamstress through her eyeglass. 'The deep furrows of inherited
experience,' Webb goes on to describe her mistress, 'relax in
favour of personal feeling. But this time it is human kindness.'[62]
'Mrs Moses' relents, and beckons Webb to her side to tell her that
she does not wish to be hard 'on any decent young person as is
trying to earn her living in a respectable way', and so will keep her
on to do even more rudimentary work. In fact, 'Mrs Moses'
admits, she has 'taken a fancy' to Webb and wants to encourage
her to 'improve' herself. 'Mrs Moses' becomes a benevolent
character, generous, maternal and good-humoured; she has

ceased to be a racial stereotype, and takes on an individual personality by virtue of Webb's experience of class inferiority.

Webb is reinstated among her fellow-workers, and now becomes a receptive and appreciative listener to their banter about music-halls and 'blokes'. She remarks on their 'warm hearts, . . . overflowing good nature, . . . intellects keenly alive to the varied sights of East London'. 'You cannot accuse them of immorality,' she writes in reaction to their stories of promiscuity, 'for they have no consciousness of sin. The veneer of morality, the hidden but secretly self-conscious vice of that little set that styles itself "London society" are unknown to them.'[63] A pale woman next to Webb observes that she has nothing to eat for tea, and places a thick slice of bread and butter in Webb's lap, then 'turns away to avoid thanks'. This gesture 'goes to the heart and brings tears into the eyes of the investigator'.[64] The workshop finally emerges in Webb's description as a congenial community of women, a matriarchy in which master and male workers are superfluous and the benevolent dictator 'Mrs Moses' reigns.

ON THE SWEATING-SYSTEM

Webb's article on the 'sweating-system', in its original version in *Nineteenth Century* (it was edited for *East London*), is not only a refutation of contemporary opinion on 'sweating' and Jewish immigration; it is also her first unequivocal statement of the need for regulation of trade and voluntary organization of labour. In this piece, more authoritative and more radical in tone than her work on dock labour, she redefines 'sweating', exonerates Jewish workers and points to solutions to problems that both Jewish and non-Jewish workers faced in the tailoring trade. That Webb ended as a public vindicator of Jewish immigrants and tailors, despite her instinctive prejudices against the Jewish 'race', is attributable, I think, to the sympathetic identification with Jews that she was able to express through disguise. The empathy with Jews and with workers that she expressed in 'Pages' and in the descriptive passages of 'The Jewish Community' are translated in 'The Tailoring Trade' into a denial of Jewish responsibility for 'sweating' and the espousal of decidedly anti-Individualist political solutions to problems of the condition of labour.

Webb's contribution to the controversy about 'sweating', the subject of heated debate in contemporary journals and in a specially appointed Select Committee of the House of Lords, was to explode some of the myths about the 'system' of 'sweating' and to dissent from the common wisdom that it was a phenomenon made possible by exploiting and exploited Jews *or* that its evils were systemic at all. Social commentators in the 1880s often wrote as if 'sweating' were an invention of that decade, but Webb knew from her reading of Mayhew that the problem was not a newly-created one. There is a startling continuity of concerns between Mayhew on the 'sweated' trades and Webb on East End tailoring, as there is between the two social investigators on dock labour; but a gap of almost forty years separates their writing, and in those years certain social problems seemed to have dropped out of the consciousness of the English public, only to reappear after the crisis of the Great Depression had set in. Webb's knowledge of Mayhew's work on 'sweating' in the 1840s helped her to be able to separate the problem of conditions of labour within certain trades from the question of mass Jewish migration to Britain in the 1880s.

In her work Webb tried to make clear that 'sweating' was not a condition that arose out of a struggle between alien and English workers, that it existed in places and trades where no foreigners – or Jews – worked, and that Jewish workers were confined to only a minority of the 'sweated' trades.[65] 'If the investigator,' she writes in *My Apprenticeship*,

> surveyed all the industries in which the evil conditions of sweating prevailed, whether in the metropolis or in the provinces, the Jewish workers were found to be but a fraction of the whole body of workers, and also, to a large extent, a non-competing group, confined to the manufacture of certain commodities, in many instances commodities which had not been produced before. In short, if every foreign Jew resident in England had been sent back to his birthplace, the bulk of the sweated workers would not have been affected, whether for better or for worse.   (pp. 319–20)

Webb here reversed her own conventional opinion – expressed by her in 'A Lady's View of the Unemployed' and shared by conservatives and trade unionists alike – that the influx of foreigners into London was responsible for the demoralization of English workers and of English habits of work.

If 'sweating' was not the result of foreign immigration, neither was it, Webb believed, merely a *system* or a means of organizing labour with the use of subcontractors, subdivision of labour, middlemen and certain kinds of machinery. These aspects of trade organization simply did not define *or* create the abuse of exploited labourers. Webb worked towards a redefinition of 'sweating', persuading the House of Lords Committee, before which she testified, that it was 'no particular method of remuneration, no peculiar form of industrial organization, but certain *conditions* of employment' (p. 318). Those conditions, unchecked either by legislation or by the organization for self-protection of workers, consisted of ' "earnings barely sufficient to sustain existence; hours of labor such as to make the lives of the workers periods of almost ceaseless toil; and sanitary conditions which are . . . injurious to the health of the persons employed" '.[66] She argued that villainous middlemen, the imagined 'series of parasites' sweating profits out of the workers, were a 'fact of the past' and but a 'fiction of the present'.[67] She noted that 'sweated' conditions did not predominate in Jewish workshops and that subdivision of labour did not necessarily indicate the existence of low pay and inadequate work facilities.

In most Jewish-owned shops, Webb asserted, there was 'no sweating, either in the price paid by retail shops to the contractor, or in the rate of wages the latter pays to his hands'.[68] The Jewish master did not, for the most part, exploit skilled labourers. Subdivision of labour existed primarily in a minority of large shops employing twenty or more hands. In these larger shops, both the employer and the employees were more prosperous and more comfortable in their places of work than were occupants of smaller shops with *less* subdivision of labour.[69] Subdivision went together, it seemed, with *better* treatment of workers and, though it was the 'fetish of the economist' and the 'bugbear of the trade-unionist', it was 'innocent alike of art or fraud' in the East End tailoring trade.[70] And though these few owners of larger shops did prosper, the average 'master' worked as hard as, if not harder than, his workers, and was not the affluent 'sweater' of the popular press, 'sauntering about his workshop with his hands in his pockets, . . . a cigar in his mouth, and . . . the East End equivalent to an orchid in his button-hole'.[71] Charles Kingsley's

'Shechem Isaacs, that sold penknives in the street six months ago, now a-riding in his own carriage, all along of turning sweater', was a myth created by sensationalist journalists and novelists.[72]

Webb ended her article on the tailoring trade in *East London* by stating that the 'soul' of sweating was the 'evil spirit of the age, unrestrained competition'.[73] In the article as it appeared in *Nineteenth Century*, however, she went on to analyse the problem further and to offer solutions. Again it seems likely that Booth thought it best to omit some of Webb's less 'scientific' conclusions. In her original version, she went on to say that the abuses of 'sweating' were made possible by (i) the supply of labour relative to demand, (ii) the 'indefinitely low standard of life peculiar to Jews and to women' and (iii) the 'absence of all regulation of employment either by voluntary combination among the workers or by legislative restrictions such as the Factory Acts'.[74]

The supposed 'love of profit' and lack of self-esteem of the Jewish worker, coupled with the spirit of 'unrestrained competition' among all wholesalers, retailers and landlords, could be controlled only by the introduction of 'standard earnings, a restriction of hours, and a regulation of workshop accommodation enforced by expanded Factory Acts and vigilant trade unionists'.[75] It was necessary, Webb believed, to extend factory legislation to apply to all workshops and to include all women, even those who worked at home. 'An inquiry into the so-called sweating system,' she concluded, 'must therefore be an inquiry into the condition of *all labour engaged in manufacture which has escaped regulation either by trade-union or by the Factory Acts*.'[76] Webb's recommendations here are more explicit, and her conviction about them surer, than in her article on the docks. Here she is certain about the validity of collective action and State intervention and regulation of industry. She has moved from a hesitant acknowledgement of the evil effects of 'individualism run wild' and an ambivalent, sceptically-offered suggestion about amalgamation of the docks to an explicitly and wholeheartedly anti-Individualist proposal for controlling absolute freedom of competition and protecting workers' rights.

CONCLUSIONS, CONTRIBUTIONS AND LIMITATIONS OF BOOTH'S STUDY

The Times described Booth's *Life and Labour of the People in London* as 'the grimmest book of our generation'.[77] It seemed so grim and was such 'a shock to the governing classes', Beatrice Webb tells us, because Booth demonstrated authoritatively and without sensationalism that 'as many as 30 per cent of the inhabitants of the richest as well as the largest city in the world lived actually at or beneath the level of bare subsistence' (p. 239). There were more impoverished Londoners, in other words, than even the SDF had calculated. If this were the truth about London, how had it come about: 'How had this mass of destitution and chronic poverty arisen during a period of unprecedented national prosperity?' (p. 240). Booth's work raised the question in the public mind, and offered limited but suggestive answers. Booth and his assistants had shown that 'among the circumstances or conditions found to be closely related to destitution and poverty were the character of occupations followed by the bread-winner; the unsatisfactory methods of remuneration, the irregularity of the hours of labor, the low degree of responsibility of landlord and employer for the sanitation and the cubic space of the work-place' (p. 241).[78] Webb, more than any other contributor to Booth's first volume of *Life and Labour*, analysed the relationship of occupation and conditions of labour to chronic poverty.

Booth's study also helped to explode certain commonly-accepted myths about the reasons for urban destitution. Such myths were propagated by the press and had, in fact, formed the basis for Webb's earliest writing on poverty. In her letter to the *Pall Mall Gazette* on unemployment, she had decried the influx of foreigners into London as one of the major causes of growing economic distress among English workers. The effect of her own work on the tailoring trade, and of Booth's volume as a whole, was to dispose of the 'sensational indictment of what was assumed to be a constant stream of aliens flooding the East End' (p. 242). Another misconception that Booth's study succeeded in under-cutting was the importance of charity as a constructive or destructive force in the lives of the poor. The giving of alms, discriminately or indiscriminately, neither helped nor hindered the recipient. Charity did not 'debase' the population, as the COS claimed, nor did the control of charity-giving according to COS

principles have any effect 'either on the poverty or on the misery o
the poor' (p. 243). At the conclusion of Webb's first contribution
to *East London*, she herself lamented the influence o
irresponsibly-distributed charity, and warned against the
demoralizing power of the reckless gift. By the time she wrote her
second article, charity seemed to her irrelevant to the problem o
'sweating' or to her analysis of its causes. Webb's and Booth's
experiences of working and living in the East End – and their
personal attractions to working-class life – enabled them to make
one other myth-destroying observation: at least 50 per cent of the
East End population lived in 'relative comfort and security', and
the majority of East End inhabitants were decent, ordinary
people, with their own communities, culture and pleasures. 'I see
nothing impossible,' Booth wrote in *East London*, 'in the general
view that the simple natural lives of working-class people tend to
their own and their children's happiness more than the artificial
complicated existence of the rich.'[79]

Webb concluded that the 'net effect' of Charles Booth's work
was 'to give an entirely fresh impetus to the general adoption, by
the British people, of . . . the policy of securing to every individual
. . . a prescribed national minimum of the requisites for efficient
parenthood and citizenship' (p. 248). 'This policy,' Webb con
tinued, 'may, or may not, be Socialism, but it is assuredly a
decisive denial of the economic individualism of the 'eighties.' Now
this was not Socialism, but it did represent a recognition that
collective action was necessary, and that the State would have to
intervene in people's lives and work: this in itself was a departure
from the 'economic individualism' to which Charles Booth and
Beatrice Webb both subscribed before undertaking their in
vestigations of the East End.

Booth's and Webb's newly-discovered anti-Individualism did
however, take different forms and led, ultimately, in two very
different directions. Booth proposed State aid in areas of health
and education, and he recommended that 'Class B', the 'very
poor' ($11\frac{1}{4}$ per cent of the population), be sent to State-run
settlements outside London where they would live and work away
from the rest of the working class as 'servants of the State'. These
settlements would constitute a 'Socialistic community living in
the midst of an Individualist nation'.[80] '[I]nterference on the part
of the State with the lives of a small fraction of the population,' he
argued, 'would tend to make it possible, ultimately, to dispense

with any Socialistic interference in the lives of all the rest.'[81]
Booth's 'Socialism' was a way of trying to preserve a non-Socialist
society.

Webb's anti-Individualist suggestions were both more practical than Booth's and more directly aimed at the problem that had
been uncovered at the base of poverty: the conditions of labour.
Modern critics have pointed out that among Booth's failures was
his inability to apply the idea of State intervention to the area of
employment and to make recommendations that could be taken
seriously by politicians and the press.[82] Webb's proposals, on the
other hand, for a possible amalgamation of the London docks
under a Public Trust, for increased organization of workers and
for the extension of factory legislation to cover unregulated
workplaces and unprotected workers were specifically directed at
problems of employment and were eminently practicable. Booth
wanted to apply 'Socialistic' measures only to those who could
not, apparently, fend for themselves, and whose inability to do so
supposedly contributed to the demoralization of other workers
around them. Webb wanted to apply such measures to the
conditions that affected all workers. Booth seemed more anxious
to attack the effects of poverty and Webb its causes.

Webb deviated from Booth's notions of investigation and
reform in one other essential respect. She found his method
'static', and effective only in determining the nature of present
reality; it was inadequate, however, in revealing cause and *process*:

> We may admit that the static method has well-defined limits to
> its power of discovery. When not repeated at intervals,
> according to strictly analogous schemes of classification, it
> seldom discovers what has happened in the past, or what is
> likely to happen in the future. And even when repeated, these
> statements of contemporaneous facts . . . do not reveal the
> actual process of birth, growth, decay and death. . . . The
> experienced investigator knows that . . . the *historical method* is
> imperative. . . . Only by watching the *processes* of growth and
> decay during a period of time, can we understand even the
> contemporary facts at whatever their stage of development; and
> only by such a comprehension of the past and present processes
> can we get an insight into the means of change. (pp. 237–8)

The Spencerian in her, interested in process, laws of change and evolution, sought a kind of social analysis that transcended mere empiricism. But the Boothian reformer and investigator in her insisted upon observation and the need for analysis to yield solutions to social problems.[83] *The Co-operative Movement in Great Britain* would combine explorations of political solutions with social investigation and the 'historical method'.

7 Fabian Socialism

> Providentialism was in the spirit of the age. Belief in the
> necessity of progress anyhow, was almost universal. Even
> Atheists believed in a sort of Providence.
> > H. G. Wells, *Experiment in Autobiography*

Beatrice Webb first declared herself a socialist in the privacy of
her diary in February 1890. In this entry, she was commenting on
the political ferment in London at that time – on the 'New Trade
Unionism', the success of the London Dock Strike and the
influence of socialist groups – and she was beginning to be able to
imagine a reconstructed social world emerging from this chaos of
political and labour activity:

> And the whole seems a whirl of contending actions, aspirations
> and aims out of which I dimly see the tendency towards a
> socialist community in which there will be individual freedom
> and public property in the stead of class-slavery and private
> possession of the means of subsistence of the whole People. At
> last I am a Socialist!   (p. 394; 1 February 1890)

Between the writing of her last essays for Booth in 1888 and the
making of this declaration in 1890, Webb's 'conversion' to
socialism had been completed. What had happened during those
intervening years to precipitate her final break with the Individualism of Spencer, the *'laissez-faire* bias' of her upbringing?
What enabled her to make the transition from the 'new Liberalism' of her days with Booth to the Fabianism she had all but
embraced in the early months of 1890? How had her vision of the
responsibilities and powers of the State changed so radically, and
how had the spirit of collectivism and cooperation of Bacup
become translated into a political and economic ideal?

FIRST STAGES OF CONVERSION

In the final chapter of *My Apprenticeship*, entitled 'Why I Became a Socialist', Webb describes the successive stages of her 'progress towards Socialism'. By the time her studies of East End life had been completed, she had passed through the first two stages: firstly, she had come to believe in the necessity of an 'all-pervading control, in the interest of the community, of the economic activities of the landlord and the capitalist', to be achieved through state regulation (legislation) and trade union pressure; and secondly, she had begun to favour a ' "national minimum" of civilized existence, to be legally ensured for every citizen' in the form of public education, public health, public parks and provision for the 'aged and infirm' (p. 378). She had also come to recognize what she called the 'psychological evil' of the proverbial 'two nations', of 'a community permanently divided into a nation of the rich and a nation of the poor, into a minority always giving orders and a vast majority always obeying orders' (p. 378). It was in the nature of *laissez-faire* capitalism, she realized, to give rise to a small class of wealthy and powerful men, who succeeded only in augmenting their personal fortunes and not in distributing any increased 'yield of rent and interest' among employees. Capitalism, as she observed it, was 'far from promoting economic equality'. She could not, however, at this stage of her 'progress', envisage any 'alternative to the authority of the profit-making employer' or any form of cooperative ownership, and so it was at this stage that she remained for some years (p. 379).

As I have suggested in the previous chapter, investigation revealed to Webb the inadequacies of the free marketplace. At the London docks, she had seen the disastrous results of 'individualism run wild', the chronic unemployment, physical misery and social disintegration that appeared to be the result of 'uncontrolled competition'. She attributed the low wages, unsanitary conditions and long hours of labour in East End 'sweat shops' to inadequate workshop legislation and a lack of organization for self-protection among workers. Landlords and capitalists, the evidence of her empirical observations told her, had to be checked and controlled. She was now willing, she told a dinner partner at a gathering in Cornwall after her investigations were completed, to 'sacrifice the individual to the community', to put limits on individual freedom for the ultimate good of the group (15 March 1887).

If investigation of East End labour convinced Webb of the destructive side of Individualism, her experience of Bacup provided her with an illuminating contrast to the misery and anomie of urban working-class life and with ideas for minimizing the liabilities of *laissez-faire* capitalism:

> the contrast between the sweated workers of East London and the Lancashire textile operatives made me realize how the very concentration of wage-earners in the factory, the ironworks and the mine had made possible, in their cases, what the sweater's workshop, the independent craftsman's forge and the out-workers home had evaded, namely, a collective regulation of the conditions of employment. (pp. 335–6)

Even before she had witnessed the consequences of the *absence* of regulation in the East End, Webb recognized that only Factory Acts kept the women and children of Bacup from working long overtime hours. '*Laissez-faire* breaks down', she wrote to her father in 1886 from the North, 'when one watches these things from the inside' (p. 159).

'Collective regulation' had an impact, Webb believed, that extended far beyond the physical well-being and comfortable subsistence of the Bacup workers: it was also responsible for the personal and civil morality of Bacup citizens. Collective activity 'raised' the workers 'into an effective democracy' and fostered in them the capacity for 'self-government' (p. 336). The social and, indeed, moral life of the community depended on two institutions, the Chapel and the 'Co-op', which served as general store, mutual insurance company and centre of entertainment. Through these institutions, this Dissenting community had learned to govern itself and to exist as a self-censoring body, as a ' "law unto itself" '. Religion and collectivism enabled the people of Bacup to be mutually supporting and mutually inhibiting: social equality and strong moral sanctions on individual behaviour were aspects of communal life which Webb admired. She believed that the inhabitants of the East End could benefit both physically and spiritually from the experience of collective regulation, collective bargaining, and the collective consumerism of the 'Co-op'.

What Webb feared, however, was that there would ultimately

be a split in Bacup between Chapel and 'Co-op', between the
religious and secular aspects of life:

> One wonders what will happen when the religious feeling of the
> people is undermined by advancing scientific culture; for
> though the 'Co-op' and the Chapel at present work together
> the secularism of the 'Co-op' is half unconsciously recognized
> by earnest chapel-goers as a rival attraction to the prayer-
> meeting and the Bible-class. One wonders where all the *feeling*
> will go, and all the capacity for *moral* self-government. . . . It
> saddens me to think that the religious faith that has united them
> together with a strong bond of spiritual effort and sustained
> them individually . . . is destined to pass away.   (pp. 161, 164)

The only possible 'safeguard' against the disintegration of what
Webb liked to call this 'religious socialism' would be 'a strong
local government' that would regulate individual behaviour and
yet allow for collective participation (p. 161). It was towards a
form of local secular socialism, or municipalism, that Webb was
looking.

FROM INDIVIDUALISM TO COLLECTIVISM: THEORETICAL TRANSITIONS

Beatrice Webb was schooled in an intellectual tradition that,
despite its insistence on *laissez-faire* politics and economics,
enabled her to be receptive to collectivist notions of business and
government. She was able to absorb and assimilate the implications of her investigations of East End labour and of Bacup
communal life, at least in part, because of certain aspects of
Spencerian philosophy. Boothian empiricism and reformism
together with Spencerian social theory eased Webb's 'conversion'
to Fabian Socialism. Intellectual historians of nineteenth-century
Britain have tried to explain the philosophical shift within
dominant liberal political values, away from Philosophic Radicalism, Benthamite Utilitarianism and *laissez-faire* ideologies, and
towards Collectivism, Socialism and the control of individual
welfare by the State. What accounted for this transition from the
'old' Liberalism of James Mill to the 'new' Liberalism of the John

Stuart Mill of the 1860s and 1870s, from an emphasis on Benthamite 'hedonism' to an interest in Comtean 'altruism'? The Philosophic Radicals wanted to prevent the State from abridging individual rights, while the Radicals of the 1880s wanted to involve the State in maintaining those rights. For the Individualist, free enterprise was the very source of progress; for the Collectivist, it was something that needed to be checked in order that real progress might take place. If there is some continuity between Utilitarianism and early English Socialism, if Sidney Webb was a legitimate heir to Jeremy Bentham, what ideas or nexus of ideas allowed for the transformations that clearly took place within nineteenth-century liberalism? A brief explanation of these mechanisms of transformation will also help to suggest why Beatrice Webb, a protégée of Herbert Spencer's, became a prime candidate for 'conversion' to Fabianism.

Comtean Positivism, particularly as it was understood in England, provided individualist Radicals with one 'bridge' to socialism. Royden Harrison, in his study of labour and politics in the years between Chartism and Fabianism, explains the English Positivists as a 'middle ground' between Utilitarianism and Fabian Socialism.[1] Comtean Positivism supplied Liberal Individualists with notions of collective life, altruism and the spirit of community. The aspect of 'secular religion' that English socialists discovered in Comte helped to fill the void left by loss of orthodox Christian faith. Liberals earlier in the century – like Webb's grandfathers and the Bacup workers – had Nonconformity to act for them as a necessary spiritual companion to political Radicalism, but for 'those whose faith was undermined by the strong currents of nineteenth-century skepticism', as Willard Wolfe has phrased it in his book on early Fabianism, 'the old Radical creed might, thereafter, seem inadequate either to make up for the loss or to function independently'.[2] Positivism, as a religion that was not a religion, suggested the possibility of a social philosophy with powers of moral and spiritual regeneration.

Beatrice Webb came under the influence of Comte's Positivism at a very early age. She found that Comte's appeal for her and for other English disciples lay in his 'union of the "religion of humanity" with a glorification of science'. That union, she maintained in *My Apprenticeship*, epitomized the 'mid-Victorian Time Spirit' (p. 139).[3] Comte, as he was interpreted in England, promoted the marriage of science and religion, and enlisted both in the service of humanity. Webb might have said that he allowed for a reconciliation of the 'two Egos', the sceptical, scientistic 'ego' and the believing, devout 'ego'. She first came to Comte through the writings of those considered to be his most important English disciples and admirers – George Henry Lewes, John Stuart Mill and George Eliot – and she ordered all of Comte's own works from the London Library (p. 139). She was reading Comte in November 1884 and, though she made notes on his 'positive method' of classification, it was a passage from Comte on altruism that she copied out in full as a preface to a new volume of her diary:

'Our harmony as moral beings is impossible on any other foundation but altruism. Nay more, altruism alone can enable us to live in the highest and truest sense. To live for others is the only means of developing the whole existence of man.

Towards humanity, who is the only true great Being, we, the conscious elements of whom She is compound, shall henceforth direct every aspect of our life, individual and collective. Our thoughts will be devoted to the knowledge of Humanity, our affections to the love, our actions to her service.' (p. 144)

Frederic Harrison, Webb's friend from youth, alerted her to the importance of altruism and collective spirit as they were expressed in trade organizations, in modern unions and in medieval craft guilds (p. 140).

The altruism of Comte and the collectivism of Harrison were influences not in harmony with Webb's Individualist, secularist education. In *My Apprenticeship*, she records a discussion with her sister Maggie on the supposed virtues of Comtean philosophy, about which Maggie, as a representative Potter, was extremely sceptical. ' "That spiritual power," ' Maggie declared, ' "I hate it. Having kicked religion out of the front door of the human intellect, why should it sneak in through the servants' hall?" ' (p. 141). ' "The root question raised by Comte," ' Maggie continued,

'the only one that concerns you and me, is whether we are all of us, here and now, to tumble over each other and get in each other's way by trying to better the world, or whether we are each of us to pursue his or her own interest according to common sense. I'm for each of us looking after our own affairs.

... As for the service of man, the religion of humanity; Heavens, Beatrice, what *does* it mean?' (p. 143)

Webb recalls this exchange, with its perhaps limited accuracy (it is not a transcription from her diary), not to reveal Maggie's opinions *per se*, but to suggest how alien were altruistic or collectivist beliefs within her own familial experience. Webb remarks that Maggie's was the voice of 'the Ego that denies', a voice of 'enlightened selfishness' heard often in the Potter home.

What Maggie did find congenial in Comte was his tendency to 'put the working man in his place' and to encourage working-class obedience to those in power. Comte's notions might lead to the establishment of order and to the suppression of strikes, and that, Maggie reckoned, was a 'jolly good thing too' (p. 142). It is probable that at the time of this discussion on Comte, in 1879, Beatrice agreed with Maggie on this particular point; but it is also likely that, even when she achieved a different perspective on working-class politics, Webb continued to find attractive what Gertrud Lenzer has called Comte's 'anticipatory conservatism'.[4] His preoccupation with *orderly* progress, with the need to resist anarchic change with 'stable' change, appealed to Webb as it did to so many ambivalent English proponents of social reconstruction. 'His entire work,' Lenzer asserts, 'was dedicated to the development and elaboration of a system that would resolve, once and for all, the disruptive and anarchic tendencies in the society of his time and the societies of the future.'[5] Webb found virtues in Comte similar to those she found in the Dissenting circles of Bacup: communal concern, a spirit of religion and the preservation of stability and moral order.

J. W. Burrow, in his excellent book *Evolution and Society*, offers the thesis that tensions in British thought between 'romantic-historical' and 'rationalist' approaches to society were resolved by evolutionary theory.[6] Those trained in a rationalist, utilitarian tradition had to find ways of understanding non-rational modes of thought and behaviour, and they turned to theories of evolution and history in order to make sense of institutions, ideas, even groups of people, that were not accounted for in the utilitarian calculus. Herbert Spencer, the major social evolutionary theorist of Victorian Britain, posited the universality of natural causation and the existence of certain discernible laws that govern social change. Like biological and geological evolutionists, he was 'concerned to present the relation of past and present as a steady growth, a chain of cause and effect.'[7] And for Spencer, evolution – or process – was also progress. Like his French colleague Auguste Comte, Spencer helped many Victorians to accept the idea of social change and to be scientific, or positivistic, while recognizing a form of limited relativism. As was characteristic of many 'evolutionary positivists', Spencer remained a *laissez-faire* Radical in regard to immediate, local political issues while he applied theories of evolutionary process to *humanity* as a species in history.

Spencer, the man who dropped Beatrice Webb as his literary executor after she became publicly allied with the Fabians, himself paved the way for her 'conversion' to Fabianism. It can be said that Webb used Spencer against Spencer – and she was not alone among collectivists in doing this – or that she turned him on his head. Spencer was the major intellectual influence on her life: he taught her the 'relevance of facts', even if he failed to use them honestly and accurately himself, and he urged her to view social institutions as organisms to be studied. He also served as a model for her when she was very young, for he was the first person she knew who dedicated himself 'to a task which he believed would further human progress' and who had 'an heroic disregard of material prosperity and physical comfort' (p. 29). But his most important legacy to Webb, and to other Individualists-turned-Collectivists, was his conviction that society evolved and that, as it evolved, it progressed.

Neither Webb nor Spencer found 'utilitarian ethics' to be an adequate guide for estimating the value of any action. Spencer began *Social Statics* with a critique of the Benthamite calculus: the 'expedience philosophy' might tell us what makes individuals happy but it does not tell us what is good. 'We seek a system,' Spencer wrote, 'that can return a definite answer when we ask, "Is this act good?"' [8] 'We cannot do,' he concluded, 'without a compass.'[9] Similarly, Webb declared her 'distaste for all varieties of utilitarian ethics, all attempts to apply the scientific method to the *Purpose* as distinguished from the *Process* of existence'.[10] In 1885, a number of years before she considered herself a socialist, she wrote in her diary that 'scientific socialists' seemed to start with the question of 'what *should* be a man's duty' rather than with the question of 'what duty can be enforced' (6 October 1885). Socialists first tried to answer the problem of 'Purpose' or, as Spencer would have it, the problem of finding a 'compass'.

Inasmuch as Spencer did not accept a conventional notion of God or religious belief as compass, his answer to the problem lay in the 'laws' of evolution, in the idea of process-as-progress. Spencer began with the idea of human perfectibility and of the universality of the 'impulse toward right conduct'.[11] Although humanity is not *naturally* adapted to a social state, and though 'all evil results from the non-adaptation of constitution to conditions', humankind, because imbued with a moral sense, will gradually adapt to the conditions of social existence. '[T]he belief in perfectibility,' Spencer asserts, 'merely amounts to the belief that in virtue of this process man will eventually become completely suited to his mode of life. . . . Progress, therefore, is not an accident, but a necessity.'[12] Evolution was, as many have said, Spencer's faith, his replacement for Christian orthodoxy, his cosmic philosophy.

From the principles of perfectibility and 'functional adaptation', Spencer drew the implication that the political apparatus of the State would disappear as humankind progressed: 'as civilization advances, does government decay. To the bad it is essential; to the good, not. . . . Its continuance is proof of a still-existing barbarism.'[13] As human beings become 'better', as they grow more socially integrated and mutually dependent, government will become unnecessary because, to Spencer's mind, government is made necessary only by the 'bad' in humanity. Government cannot really promote good, nor can it even prevent evil; all it can accomplish is the equalization of evil and the protection of individuals from it.[14] Assuming this attitude toward the role of the State and its relationship to ever-improving human nature, Spencer could only conclude that the least possible amount of government was the best amount. So, as Spencer indicates in *Social Statics*, he disapproved of factory legislation, poor laws, state education and a public Board of Health; he found control of currency and postal arrangements monopolistic; and he considered trade restrictions, the original bugbear of all *laissez-faire* Radicals, the equivalent of slavery.[15] Belief in free trade was the hallmark of the 'old' Liberalism, which had landlords and aristocratic control of property as its enemies, and which, for Spencer, was the only true Liberalism. 'New' Liberalism, finding its opponents in capitalists and rentiers, was only a 'modern perversion' of Liberalism, as Spencer wrote in his *Autobiography*, 'busily decreasing . . . liberties . . . by the multiplication of

restraints and commands'.[16] Spencer believed that the greates
amount of individual liberty and the highest degree of individua
tion could be joined with the greatest degree of mutual depen
dence.[17]

Beatrice Webb always held to Spencer's equation of proces
with progress (though, as we shall see in the next chapter, he
confidence was shaken a good deal by the First World War), but
while the equation pointed Spencer in the direction of *laissez*
faire, it brought Webb to the door of collectivism. Sh
accepted the notion of infinite perfectibility, of humanity's ability
to adapt to its social state, but the political conclusions she
ultimately drew from this notion were opposite to Spencer's own
Webb came to believe in the validity of State intervention in the
lives of individuals because she saw collective action as a way of
increasing mutual dependence. Rather than impeding progress
towards the perfection of social existence, Webb believed tha
collectivism would express and accelerate that progress. In
writing of Spencer's influence on her in *My Apprenticeship*, Webb
asserted that 'the importance of functional adaptation was . . . a
the basis of a good deal of the faith in collective regulation that I
afterwards developed' (p. 37). At first glance, this seems a highly
paradoxical statement: how did she use Spencer's principle of
'functional adaptation' to reject *laissez-faire* Individualism? She
simply reasoned that if humanity was in the process of adapting to
a social – or collective – state, then why not organize society more
collectively so that the progress towards complete adaptation
might be expedited? For Webb, legislation that controlled trade
and conditions of labour, that provided citizens with health and
education, would be an impetus, and not an impediment, to social
progress, mutual dependence and even greater individuation.

Not only did Webb wish to accelerate the process of social
evolution through State activity, but she also came to see State
intervention as part of the 'inevitability' in which Spencer
believed. By the decade of the 1880s, it was clear that legislation
governing industry, business and conditions of work had been
increasing over the century and was likely to continue to increase.
Such legislation, then, must be an inevitable expression of human
progress and perfectibility, a part of evolution. Whereas Spencer,
writing his autobiography in the 1890s, saw this trend as a
perversion of the true Liberalism, Webb embraced it as necessity.
The evolutionary stage of *laissez-faire* had passed; a new evolu-

ionary stage of collectivism was imminent. Spencer's own *social*
heory provided Webb with a framework within which to reject
Spencer's *political* theory. By the time she finished social investiga-
ion with Booth, she had gone beyond *laissez-faire* and arrived at a
orm of 'new' Liberalism, but she had not yet become an
unredeemed heretic in Spencer's eyes. Her next project, however,
a study of the Co-operative Movement, helped her to make the
leap from a belief in 'collective regulation' to a vision of State
Socialism and an 'alternative to the authority of the profit-making
employer'.

CO-OPERATION

In 1889, Webb left her work with Charles Booth and undertook a
study of the Co-operative Movement in Britain, because she had
reservations about Booth's method and because she wanted to use
investigation to explore political and economic solutions to the
kinds of social problems that she and Booth had uncovered.[18]
Webb wanted to discover whether, as some social critics claimed,
there was any 'practicable alternative to the dictatorship of the
capitalist in industry'. Socialists who made these claims, many of
them SDF members whom she had met in the East End, were
alien to her; they seemed to her to be preaching a 'catastrophic
overturning of the existing order' only to replace it with 'the
vaguest of incomprehensible utopias' (p. 336). The Fabians were
unknown to her, and she had not yet read *Fabian Essays*; and, what
is more, she was still, in her own words, 'biassed against socialist
solutions of political and economic problems' (p. 390). As a result,
she sought 'enlightenment', not from 'socialist lecturers and
theoretical pamphlets', but from a study of the co-operative
organization of production and consumption as it had evolved in
Britain in the nineteenth century.

The ideal of self-employment, as embodied in Co-operation,
seemed to be a possible answer to conventional capitalist
enterprise; it might lead to the abolition of the profit-maker, to an
increase in the security of livelihood for workers and to the
possibility of equal opportunity for all citizens. If, as Webb was
beginning to suspect, profit-making were really 'unlawful gain'
and a 'demoralizing force', and if a system of standard wages and

salaries were a 'higher form of industrial organization', then
perhaps the Co-operative stores of Bacup could serve as a model
for the re-organization of industry on a large scale (p. 362). The
concept of Co-operation appealed to a variety of people, for many
different reasons, as Webb noted in *My Apprenticeship*, and a good
deal of interest in it had already been generated among those
dissatisfied with standard business practices:

> To the workman it gave the feeling that he would be his own
> master; to the Conservative it seemed a reversion to the
> healthier conditions of a former time; to the Christian it seemed
> to substitute in industry the spirit of fellowship and mutual
> assistance for that of competitive selfishness. Even to the
> mid-Victorian orthodox political economist, with his
> apotheosis of pecuniary self-interest and his unbending faith in
> the struggle for existence, the self-governing workshop seemed
> the only practicable way of extending to all those who were
> co-operating in production the blessed incentive of 'profit on
> price' and thus broadening the basis and strengthening the
> defense of an acquisitive society.   (p. 364)

Co-operation suggested a way out of the traditional industrial
structure of *laissez-faire* capitalism without advertising itself as
socialism, and that in itself accounted for much of its appeal for
Webb, as well as for others.

It is clear from Webb's concise volume on the Co-operative
Movement that she was drawn to the idea of Co-operation for the
very reasons that she was drawn to Bacup, for reasons, that is,
that involved the moral and spiritual, as well as the economic, life
of the community. Co-operatives, by their very existence, assured
the supremacy of the group over the individual, and they
embodied a 'spirit of association' and faith in collective life. The
value of co-operation, Webb claimed, did not consist exclusively,
or even primarily, in 'a more equitable diffusion of the necessaries
and comforts of life', or in any material advancement for
individuals; it was to be found, instead, in 'the ancient doctrine of
human fellowship, . . . [in] the new spirit of social service, . . . [in]
a firm faith that the day would come when each man and woman
would work, not for personal subsistence or personal gain, but for
the whole community'.[19] Its value was, in fact, religious: only a
'fully-developed industrial democracy', as in Co-operation, could

provide 'the economic basis for the future religion of humanity'.[20] The Co-operative Movement would stand, like Bacup, as a moral ideal, and might even serve as a 'vanguard of human progress' because, on a small scale, Co-operation had been able to 'root up and extirpate the very foundations of the art of wealth-gaining *apart from rendering services to the community*'.[21] Co-operation, like Bacup, seemed to put social and economic checks on greed, selfishness and 'egoism', and it had replaced the competitive ideal of industrial capitalism with a co-operative and communal ideal.

In reading the history of the Movement, Webb discovered the importance of Robert Owen, as so many other neophyte socialists and Fabians did at the turn of the century, and made him the subject of her first chapter, 'The Co-operative Idea'.[22] It was Owen who first promoted the co-operative ideal and who was, to Webb's mind, the father of a distinctly British socialism. Owen's was not the revolutionary socialism of the Continent, of which she wholeheartedly disapproved, but the socialism that had been gradually unfolding throughout the nineteenth century and which had 'silently embodied itself in . . . all that mass of beneficent legislation forcing the individual into the service, and under the protection of the State'.[23] Owen's socialism grew out of a rejection of the law of 'Universal Competition' and out of adherence to a version of the theory that Webb had learned from Spencer: the 'modification of structure brought about by the modification of function', or the *law of functional adaptation*'.[24] Owen believed, with Spencer, that humankind would adapt to its environment and that human character would ultimately be determined by external conditions. The oppressed factory worker could be physically and mentally reduced by the circumstances of his or her labour and, conversely, the factory worker's child could undergo a rejuvenation of spirit and health if transported to clean, comfortable and humane surroundings.[25]

According to Webb, Owen, like Spencer, applied a 'biological principle . . . to the collective character of the race', but he extrapolated from that application a set of political principles altogether different from Spencer's. Owen believed simply that material conditions had to be altered in order to promote the well-being and felicitous evolution of the human spirit, and he was of the opinion that such alteration was the responsibility of the State. He did not believe that man 'should be left to suffer the consequences of his own action'.[26] For this reason, Owen was an early proponent of using legislation to limit the hours of factory labour, to provide free and compulsory education for all children, to establish free libraries, to build housing for the poor and to organize labourers with municipalities or counties.[27] The co-operative organization of industry – the scheme for the 'equitable exchange of commodities according to the cost of production' and for the abolition of individual profit-making – was but another Owenite idea for the re-creation of human character through the re-fashioning of social conditions. Although Webb criticized Owen's inability to grasp the 'significance of *Democracy*' as a way of enabling 'the *whole body* of people' to acquire a collective life, she did find in him a clear precedent for the use of the 'law of functional adaptation' as a basis for collectivist, rather than individualist, social policies.

Webb could, therefore, fit the Co-operative Movement into a framework of social evolution, and she could understand and appreciate the moral power of the co-operative ideal, but she was not, at first, able to account for the practical success of what seemed to her an impractical way of organizing business:

> How could I explain, by the canons of capitalist economics, the continuous growth of a business enterprise [the Consumers' Co-operative Movement], which was not making the private fortunes of any man or group of men, but was increasing the individual incomes, accumulated wealth and also the economic freedom of a whole self-governing community, to-day comprising a quarter or even a third of all the families of Great Britain; wielding a working capital approaching a hundred million pounds; doing a trade of nearly two hundred millions sterling annually; and still, as at all times, effectively open to any newcomer to join and participate in its benefits on equal terms with the original promoters?   (p. 367)

She discovered the answer to this question while investigating the history of the Rochdale Pioneers, the founders of the modern Consumers' Co-operative Movement, and, in discovering it, she stumbled on a kind of economic theory that was to prove important both for her own socialist ideas and for Fabianism.

The Rochdale Pioneers started a small co-operative grocery store with twenty-eight original members in 1844. They attracted customers by urging each one to become a member of their society and thus to share in the management and the accumulated capital of the store. Their co-operative system revolved around 'dividend on purchase', a scheme to return the margin between the actual cost and the selling price of articles to the customer in the form of a quarterly rebate or, more precisely, a share of the store's dividends at a certain rate per pound expended by the customer.[28] The Pioneers' store grew from a one-room grocery to a department store, and by 1851 there were some 130 co-op stores in the North of England and the Midlands of Scotland.[29]

Webb concluded that the reason for the success of these stores lay in their automatic policy of supplying a specific demand: the customers of the store were also its managers, and they sold in the store only what they needed or wanted to buy. 'To organize industry from the consumption end,' Webb wrote in *My Apprenticeship*, 'and to place it, from the start, upon the basis of "production for use" instead of "production for profit", under the control and direction, not of the workers as producers, but of themselves as consumers, was the outstanding discovery and practical achievement of the Rochdale Pioneers' (p. 370). The Rochdale Pioneers, Webb claimed, had discovered that 'the essential element in the successful conduct of production is the *correspondence* of the application of labor with some actually felt specific desire' (pp. 367–8).

Just as successful industrial production would result from the coordination of labour and use, so would a true industrial democracy come about through co-operation between producer (labourer) and consumer (user). Because Webb saw the necessity of a partnership between labourer and consumer, she stressed the importance of the Trade Union movement in her book on Co-operation. She recognized that it was difficult for Co-operators in the midst of 'an individualist and competitive society' to increase wages or lower prices while improving the quality of production.[30] An understanding of the complementary nature of the Trade Union and Co-operative movements, however, would act to promote better conditions for workers as well as better and cheaper products for the consumer:

> If the Co-operative workshop is to be made into a powerful lever for raising the condition of the workers, Trade Unionists must become energetic Co-operators; they must insist . . . on the responsibilities of the consumers, as well as on the rights of

the worker. The rank and file of the Store-members (most of whom are themselves Trade Unionists . . .) must banish the 'sweated' product from the store counter. The great mass of working-class consumers must resolutely boycott the private traders, and adhere to the store through good and bad repute, steadfastly insisting that democratic control shall supersede competition in lowering price and raising quality.[31]

Active unions and collective bargaining would prevent Co-operators' 'absent-mindedness' about conditions of labour in stores and workshops, while membership in a Co-operative would make the trade unionist part of 'the struggle toward the democratic control of industry'.[32]

In her conclusion to the book, however, Webb warned that the 'marriage' of trade unionism and co-operation, even if both movements should continue to expand, was insufficient to bring about the ideal state of society. As of 1891, four-fifths of the wage-earning class was outside of both the Co-op and Trade Union movements. Webb concluded that voluntary association would not succeed among those workers who lived in isolation, moved often or changed occupations, or among those too poor and too irregularly employed to be able to concern themselves with democratic association and self-government. She also noted that most of the middle and upper class would not stoop to participate in consumer co-operation. 'Propaganda among the rich,' she claimed, 'is as futile as propaganda among the very poor.'[33] Other remedies, measures more drastic than many co-operators or trade unionists proposed, were necessary in order to 'complete the social changes prophetically described [by] Robert Owen'.[34]

To surpass the good achieved by the organization of consumers and producers, she concluded, English democracy would have to accept more radical taxation and limited nationalization:

if they are determined to add to the social production of wealth (brought about by the new industry), to the communal administration and control (introduced by the Co-operative and trade union movements), the communal ownership of land and the means of production, they must use deliberately the instrument forged by political democracy, taxation in all its forms on unearned wealth and surplus incomes, and compulsory acquisition, not necessarily without personal compensation, of those portions of the national wealth ripe for democratic administration.[35]

Here Webb was forging beyond the 'new' Liberalism of her days with Booth, and beyond the acceptance of co-operation and unionism within a *laissez-faire* capitalist state. She counted herself, in her final chapter, among those who desired and believed in a 'socialist state'.[36] A year after the publication of her book, she was asked to speak at a conference of, Trade Union officials and Co-operators at Tynemouth. To them she spoke bluntly of the need for 'State or municipal socialism' where the voluntary association of producers and consumers failed to fulfil the ideal of the 'Co-operative State'.[37]

A further step had been taken in her 'conversion' to State socialism: she had reached the so-called 'third stage' in her 'progress towards Socialism' by examining Co-operation, by discovering an 'alternative to the authority of the profit-making employer' and, most importantly, by accepting a role for government that radically reversed the Spencerian notion of a State that might equalize evil but could not promote good. This last transition was the most difficult for Webb, and it was achieved only through her ability to expand the idea of consumer co-operation to encompass first the municipality and then the State. When she wrote her chapter on the Co-operative Union, the central organization of co-operators, she called it 'A State Within a State'. The Union included 1300 different Co-op Societies, and its magnitude made it seem state-like in its reach and power. The size and coordination of this organization, coupled with her discovery of the importance, both economic and moral, of consumer control, prompted Webb to imagine that the relationship between citizen and government might follow a co-operative model.

She came to believe that 'the municipality, and even the state itself, in so far as they undertook the provision of commodities and services for their citizens, were, from the economic standpoint, also associations of consumers, based upon an obligatory instead of upon a voluntary membership' (p. 380). The Co-operative Ideal could, therefore, be 'extended from merely voluntary groupings, associated for the purchase of household requisites, to the obligatory association of all residents of a city, for every civic purpose'. Jay Winter, writing of the Webbs' concept of industrial society as a conflict of interest between producers and consumers – rather than a struggle between classes – is correct in saying that the Co-operative Society was the Webbs' model for the future socialist state.[38] And, he might have added, it was Beatrice Webb who first showed an interest in Co-operation and in its applicability to the organization of government.

The concept of municipalism became important to Beatrice Webb as a kind of intermediary socialist step between consumer co-operation and state socialism. It was after working on the Co-operative Movement, she wrote, that she 'saw a new meaning in the steady growth of municipal enterprise and other forms of Local Government' (p. 380). She saw the possibility of transforming the municipality into one large co-operative unit, of extending the communal control of Bacup and the collective enterprise of the Rochdale Pioneers to entire towns and cities. Here was a collectivism founded upon evolutionary theory and the principle of 'functional adaptation', on a *gradual* absorption of the society into a co-operative framework. She was encouraged to think of the municipality as a large-scale consumer co-operative by her encounter with Sidney Webb in January 1890, while completing the research for her book. She had been referred to him by Margaret Harkness, then active in socialist circles in London, for help with the history of working-class associations. 'Sidney Webb, one of the Fabian essayists,' Harkness told Beatrice, 'is your man' (p. 392). Beatrice's discussions with this 'leading member of the Fabian Society' were instrumental in helping her to imagine the future direction of Co-operation, for it was Municipalism that was then at the very centre of the Fabian programme.

FABIANISM

The history of Fabian Socialism has been written a number of times, from a number of different points of view, and I do not intend to give a thorough account here of the origins of Fabianism or of its development.[39] I wish, instead, to discuss Fabianism with particular emphasis on those aspects that paralleled Beatrice Webb's own political evolution and attracted her to its ranks. Her joining with the Fabians was no accident, no mere result of her engagement to Sidney Webb; it was a step that followed logically and organically from the 'stage' of socialist thinking she had reached in 1889. It was not at all surprising that she was drawn to Fabianism; it was perhaps surprising that she was not drawn to it sooner. The Fabians could offer answers to her questions about the direction that a collectivist society might take, and they formed their answers in the language of an intellectual and political tradition that she shared.

Recent historians of the early Fabians have made it clear that Fabianism changed direction a number of times in the 1880s and absorbed many different influences while groping toward an orthodoxy of some kind.[40] Like Beatrice Webb's 'progress towards Socialism', Fabianism can be described as having undergone a succession of stages. Its origins were quasi-religious and utopian: the Fabian Society was a group that, in 1884, splintered off from The Fellowship of the New Life, a collection of young freethinkers looking for spiritual and social regeneration under the leadership of Thomas Davidson, a Scots Evangelical who preached Comteism and Transcendentalism.[41] The Fellowship of the New Life was one of many discussion groups, debating societies, secular faiths and political organizations that proliferated in London during the early 1880s and were made up of young, middle-class men and women who found Liberalism and Christianity to be inadequate guides to life, individual or communal. The Society for Psychical Research, the Progressive Association, the Dialectical Society, the Zetetical Society, the Land Reform Union, the Karl Marx Club (later the Hampstead Historic Society) and the Social Democratic Federation were all established within a period of five years, and among the membership of each group were future or current Fabians.[42]

Willard Wolfe has noted that very few of the original Fabians had been directly involved in conventional Radical politics or had taken an active role in specific political issues. 'Instead,' Wolfe writes, 'the Founding Fabians formed perhaps the purest example of the 1880s of the religious approach to Socialism – or, more specifically, of ethical Freethought reaching out to Socialism as a more complete and satisfactory form of substitute faith.'[43] They were influenced by the 'religious Socialists', by Owen, Ruskin, Morris, the Christian Socialists and the Christian Humanists of the 1880s, by Comte even more than by John Stuart Mill.[44] Sydney Olivier and Graham Wallas, both sons of Evangelical clergymen, began as disciples of Arnold Toynbee's Christian Humanitarianism; both were active in the university settlement house movement – they had been friends at Oxford – and both worked at Canon Barnett's Toynbee Hall. Edward Pease, the first secretary of the Fabian Society, entered Socialism as a follower of Ruskin and Morris; before becoming a Fabian, he worked as assistant to another disciple of Ruskin's, Octavia Hill, in her work of 'beautifying old graveyards'.[45]

As a young man in London, George Bernard Shaw started out as a member of the Zetetical Society, where he enjoyed 'complete freedom of discussion, political, religious and sexual'; joined the New Shakespeare Society, the Browning Society and the Shelley Society (where he proclaimed himself 'like Shelley, a Socialist, Atheist and Vegetarian'); became a convert to Henry George's land nationalization and single tax theories, and applied for membership in the SDF; then withdrew his application when he discovered the Fabians, who were of his own class and sensibility and not 'manual-working pseudo-Marxists'.[46] Annie Besant came to Fabianism from a 'religious' devotion to Bradlaugh's Secularist campaigns; and William Clarke, originally a member of The Fellowship of the New Life, was an Emersonian and a student of the neo-Hegelianism of the Oxford Idealists.[47]

The initial utopianism of the first Fabians, the amorphous faith in spiritual and social rebirth, passed into a phase of interest in abstract economic theory. It was primarily the American 'single tax' proponent, Henry George, who alerted the Fabians to the importance of an economic base for social equality. George's *Progress and Poverty* was published in England in 1881, and George himself appeared there on a speaking tour in 1883–4. Shaw heard him one night at the Nonconformist Memorial Hall and was, in his words, 'converted to economics': 'He struck me dumb and shunted me from barren agnostic controversy to economics.'[48] George argued that social inequality was caused by the monopolization of land, the source of all wealth, by a very few men. The remedy for such inequality, therefore, would be the imposition of a single tax on the value of all land and the consequent collecting of enough revenue to provide for the needs of all the people. The Fabian 'Manifesto' of 1884, drafted by Bernard Shaw, shows the influence of George, as does the later Fabian 'Basis'. In both of these documents there is an emphasis on land, taxation and rents. 'Our Manifesto,' Edward Pease wrote in his history of Fabianism, 'covered a wide field, but it nowhere touches Co-operation or Trade Unionism, wages or hours of labour. We are still playing with abstractions, Land and Capital, Industry and Competition, the Individual and the State.'[49]

The first Fabians' interest in abstract economic theory led them to form the Karl Marx Club along with Belfort Bax, John Burns and other SDF members, in order to read *Capital*, then available only in French translation.[50] Whether they could fully grasp Marxian theory in this manner is questionable, but they did form their own opinions of Marx based on this reading. Shaw found Marx's theory of surplus value unacceptable, Webb disapproved of his methodology, and Sydney Olivier was frankly surprised at his total neglect of matters *not* economic. According to Shaw, however, reading Marx did help to propel the Fabians into their next stage of evolution, the stage at which the ongoing character of the Fabian Society was formed. 'Marx . . . convinced me,' Shaw wrote in his autobiographical sketches, 'that what the movement needed was not Hegelian theorizing but an unveiling of the official facts of Capitalist civilization.'[51]

After 1886, the Fabians became interested in history, research and the gathering of social 'facts'. Sidney Webb began to dominate the formation of Fabian policy, and he coaxed the Society away from a preoccupation with theory and the idea of agitation. He convinced his fellow Fabians, as two recent critics have stated it, that the Society's 'primary aim was research and education, rather than action'.[52] Just as Beatrice Potter had done in 1886, the Fabians, under Sidney Webb's guidance, turned their backs on abstract economics, read English history, studied the Poor Law and embarked on a kind of 'social investigation'. In 1887, Sidney's *Facts for Socialists* was published as a Fabian Tract. In it, he combined statistics and 'facts' gleaned from traditional political economists with the rent theories of Henry George to suggest that a small fraction of the community – landowners and capitalists, to be precise – controlled the entire national wealth and thereby fostered the poverty of the majority.

As the Fabians became historians and investigators, they also became municipalists, and this too was largely due to the interests and influence of Sidney Webb. His preoccupation with the city was encouraged by the formation of the London County Council, by the election of three Fabians to the London School Board in 1888, and by the appearance of Charles Booth's *East London* in

1889. Just three months after Sidney Webb presented a Fabian lecture on Booth's work, he produced Fabian Tract no. 8, *Facts for Londoners*, in which he established the basis for a form of municipal socialism.[53] Municipalism was the Fabians' proposal for a Collectivism that could stop short of State Socialism. 'What the Fabian Society did,' wrote Pease, 'was to point out that Socialism did not necessarily mean the control of all industry by a centralised State.'[54] The idea of the collective regulation of local services, as had already been promoted in the municipalism of Joseph Chamberlain, provided the Fabians with a way into nationalization.[55] By the end of the 1880s, official Fabian policy included the nationalization of railways, canals and coal mines; municipalization of gas and water supplies, docks, tramways and markets; provision for the unemployed by County Councils; and municipal ownership of all land.[56] The founding Fabians had never privately relinquished their vision of moral regeneration, but by the time of the publication of *Fabian Essays* in 1889, they had begun to formulate publicly a strategy for regeneration that was 'scientific' and practical.

FABIAN ESSAYS

Fabian Essays in Socialism, edited by Bernard Shaw with a cover designed by William Morris' daughter, May, had a widespread appeal that surprised even the Fabians themselves (over 26,000 copies were sold within two years of publication).[57] A. M. McBriar has remarked that the Fabians 'supplied a doctrine which would enable a church warden, or an English trade unionist, to call himself a Socialist', and Edward Pease claimed that the popularity of *Fabian Essays* 'arose as much from what it left out as from what it contained'.[58] Fabianism did not embrace revolutionary zeal, offer a theory of 'the conspiracy of repression' or seem to call for radical change; and it defined socialism as 'but the next step in the development of society'.[59] The Fabians offered a socialism without Marx, without a vision of social apocalypse or a notion of class struggle. They did not at first seem opposed to capitalism *per se*, as E. J. Hobsbawm has noted, but only *laissez-faire* capitalism.[60] They separated socialism from the idea of a working-class movement, and thereby enabled middle-class intellectuals to create their 'own' socialism, a socialism stripped of many of the aspects of Marxism that middle-class readers would have found disquieting.

The Fabian theorists even adopted an economic theory of value, summarized by Shaw in his essay on the 'Economic Basis of Socialism', to oppose the Marxian one. The Marxian labour theory of value was challenged in English socialist circles by Revd Philip Wicksteed, a disciple of Stanley Jevons.[61] Wicksteed argued that Marx had been wrong in *Capital* when he excluded everything except abstract human labour as the measure of value. According to Jevonian theory, Marx had been in error particularly in ignoring the element of 'abstract utility', and this error called into question Marx's whole theory of surplus value. Shaw, who first defended Marx against Wicksteed's attack, eventually was 'converted' to certain aspects of Jevonian economic theory, and made them central to his discussion of Fabian economics in *Fabian Essays*. 'For some years,' Shaw wrote,

> I hammered away at the subject [of abstract economics], sitting under Wicksteed at a private society to which he lectured on the Jevonian theory. When I had thoroughly mastered what was left valid of Capitalist political economy I found that neither Marx nor anyone else in the Socialist movement understood it, and that as to abstract value theory Marx was wrong and Wicksteed right.[62]

It was in the Fabians' interest to repudiate Marx: they wished to distinguish themselves from the Social Democractic Federation and to attract Radical and middle-class followers.[63] Their adoption of a utility theory of value – and the creation of their own 'theory of rents' to replace the standard theory of surplus value – lent added logic and force to this repudiation. It also served as a point of congruence between the early Fabians and Beatrice Potter, whose study of consumer co-operation had convinced her of the central importance of utility in establishing exchange value.

The Fabianism of *Fabian Essays* was familiar and optimistic. It was a 'new' philosophy based on certain aspects of traditional Victorian thought, and it promised change as a matter of evolutionary inevitability. Beatrice Potter analysed the reasons for the book's success in her diary in February 1890:

The Fabian Essays on Socialism are making way: it is curious how many persons wake up to the fact that they have always been 'Socialists'. The *delicious positivism* of the authors, their optimistic conclusion that the world is most assuredly going their way, the plausible proof they bring in favor of their confidence, the good temper and the moderation – all impress the ordinary English reader. (15 February 1890)

The *Essays* succeeded in convincing many, and Beatrice Potter was among them, that what they *already* believed was Socialism. The essay that most impressed her when she first read the volume in 1889 was that written by her future husband, then unknown to her: in passing the book on to a co-operator friend, she wrote that 'by far the most significant and interesting essay is the one by Sidney Webb; *he has the historic sense*' (p. 390).[64] Shaw wrote on the 'Economic Basis' of Socialism, William Clarke on the 'Industrial' and Sydney Olivier on the 'Moral', but it was Sidney Webb's 'Historic Basis' that spoke most directly to her own Spencerian notion of history and social evolution. 'What interested me in this particular Fabian essay,' she recalls in *My Apprenticeship*, 'was an early presentation of "the inevitability of gradualness" ' (p. 391).

She recognized that Sidney's teachers were her own, that he claimed an intellectual tradition no different from hers. Willard Wolfe has concluded that the young Sidney Webb was neither the orthodox follower of John Stuart Mill nor the hard-nosed, unphilosophical Civil Servant that he is often assumed to have been. 'The evidence in Webb's letters, essays and lecture drafts,' Wolfe writes, 'makes it clear that he fitted neither of these stereotypes in his early life. Instead, his early intellectual work, including his social theories, was coloured by intense social and religious feeling and by keen interest in philosophy, and his strongest intellectual tendency was toward the Positivism of Comte and Spencer – not toward Mill.'[65] Spencer provided him with a 'social science', a way of understanding the evolution of society, and Comte offered the ideals of altruism and communal solidarity as the means to social regeneration. Speaking of George Eliot's novels in a lecture he delivered in the early 1880s, probably to the Zetetical Society, Sidney Webb said: 'We are at home . . . we have met all the characters.'[66] In his comments on Eliot he revealed both his social class – 'the world consists chiefly of that vast and undefined middle class to which nearly all George Eliot's characters belong' – and the intellectual and philosophical discourse with which he felt comfortable – 'in George Eliot's mind, and in the minds of those who surrounded her, this psychological and ethical phraseology was as familiar, and as constantly on their lips, as household words'.[67] Eliot, like Sidney Webb and Beatrice Potter, learned much of this 'phraseology' from Spencer and from Comte.

At the centre of Sidney Webb's essay on the 'Historic Basis of Socialism' is the idea of the constantly evolving state. In a passage which Beatrice, not surprisingly, included in her autobiography, he attributes the widespread acceptance of this idea to the three central nineteenth-century theorists of biological and social evolution:

> Owing mainly to the efforts of Comte, Darwin and Herbert Spencer, we can no longer think of the ideal society as an unchanging State. The social ideal from being static has become dynamic. The necessity of the constant growth and development of the social organism has become axiomatic. No philosopher now looks for anything but the gradual evolution of the new order from the old, without breach of continuity or abrupt change of the entire social tissue at any point during the process. The new becomes itself old, often before it is consciously recognized as new.[68]

Sidney uses Spencerian biologistic language to describe the social state throughout the essay, and he imagines society as an organism. This enables him to establish a framework for the organic, non-revolutionary transformation of society with which his readers can assimilate change and accept the leap from Radicalism to Fabianism. His essay is directed, in large part, to a Radical audience and to those, like Beatrice Potter, who were reared in Individualism and according to the tenets of orthodox political economy. By offering Radicals and other non-Socialists the notion of change *with* 'continuity' and by suggesting that 'new' and 'old' are often indistinguishable, he provides them with the theoretical tools for breaking away from Radicalism.

'The economic history of the century,' Sidney wrote, 'is an almost continuous record of the progress of Socialism.'[69] English society has been gradually evolving towards socialism, unwittingly and unselfconsciously, and complete 'industrial individualism' had, in any case, been a failure since its very inception. The force that has moved society away from Individualism and towards Socialism in the nineteenth century is Democracy: all that Socialism is, he argued, is the wedding of Democracy with Progress. All 'important organic changes', as everyone – 'Socialists as well as Individualists' – must realize, have to be (i) democratic, and so acceptable to the majority, (ii) gradual, and the cause of no dislocation, (iii) regarded as moral by the 'mass of the people' and (iv) constitutional and, therefore, peaceful.[70] There was little in Sidney's definition of socialist evolution with which Radicals – or Individualists – could argue, and this was precisely his intention.

He called upon the nineteenth-century sages and artists who opposed the creed of 'Philosophical Radicalism' ('essentially a creed of Murdstones and Gradgrinds') to show that the movement toward 'socialism' had been started long ago by many of the greatest of Englishmen:

> The 'nest of singing birds' at the Lakes would have none of it . . . Coleridge did his best to drown it in German Transcendentalism. Robert Owen and his following of enthusiastic communistic co-operators steadfastly held up a loftier ideal. . . . Carlyle managed to keep alive the faith in nobler ends than making a fortune in this world and saving one's soul in the next. Then came Maurice, Kingsley, Ruskin, and others who dared to impeach the current middle class cult.[71]

This artistic and philosophic push away from economic Individualism was mirrored in the actions of the 'practical men' who passed laws to protect labourers and regulate work conditions from the very beginning of the nineteenth century. But it was finally, Webb asserts, 'Comte and John Stuart Mill, Darwin and Herbert Spencer', who forced the concept of the 'Social Organism' to penetrate the minds of even 'our professors of Political Economy'.[72] It was evolutionary theory, Webb believes, that finally gave so many Individualists a rationale for adopting Collectivism, a way of bridging the gap from 'Philosophic Radicalism' to State Socialism. 'The steady increase of the government regulation of private enterprise,' he concluded, 'the growth of municipal administration, and the rapid shifting of the burden of taxation directly to rent and interest, mark in treble lines the statesman's unconscious abandonment of the old Individualism, and our irresistible glide into collectivist Socialism.'[73] In Sidney Webb's essay, history provides the justification for change.

AT LAST SHE IS A SOCIALIST

1899 was the decisive year in Beatrice Webb's own progress towards socialism: she began to write her book on the Co-operative Movement, read *Fabian Essays* and was witness to the London Dock Strike. Her investigations with Booth had convinced her that the dock-workers were fragmented and demoralized, and that they had been rendered incapable of collective action for the purposes of self-protection by the structure of life and labour at the docks. The Dock Strike altered her estimation of these workers because it suggested that the spirit of community and co-operation that was found in Bacup also might exist among the irregularly-employed slum dwellers of London. 'The Dock Strike becoming more and more exciting,' she wrote in her diary in August 1889,

> even watched at a distance. Originally 500 casuals marched out of the W. and E. India Docks – in another day the strike spread to the neighbouring Docks – in a week half East London was out. For the first time a *general strike of labour*, not on account of the vast majority of strikers, but to enforce the claims to a decent livelihood of some 3000 men. . . . Certainly the 'solidarity of labour' at the East End is a new thought to me. (29 August 1889)

The strike made it appear that the evolution of society toward a collectivist state might be occurring at a pace more rapid than she had imagined. Not only had the casuals at the docks shown initiative and the ability to organize, but their fellow-workers had proven to be altruistic and capable of unselfish, collective action.

In the first months of 1890, she began to meet the Fabians: in January, Margaret Harkness introduced her to Sidney Webb, and in the months that followed he in turn introduced her to Wallas, Olivier and Bernard Shaw. Before she joined with the

Fabians, however, she declared herself a socialist in the diary passage with which this chapter begins. She found herself during those first months of 1890 in a privileged position, 'in the midst of all parties': she knew Trade Union leaders, Co-operators of all kinds, dock-workers and London socialists, as well as 'those respectable and highly successful men' – her brothers-in-law – who were 'typical of the old reign of private property and self-interested action' (1 February 1890). She frequented the homes of the rich, the streets of the East End and the debating societies of working men, and she inhabited a 'true vantage ground for impartial observation of the forces at work'. From this position she could 'dimly see the tendency towards a socialist community' and, though maintaining the stance of an impartial social investigator, she felt that she had truly become a Socialist: 'And this is where observation and study have led me, in spite of training [and] class bias' (1 February 1890). She gave up her public non-partisanship unwillingly because she thought that political affiliation would inhibit her as an investigator and alienate family and friends. In 1891, she paid dues to the Fabian Society for the first time, but would allow only her initials to be entered on the list of Fabian subscribers.[74] Her 'conversion', though it had an internal logic, had an external incongruity about it of which she was nervously aware.

A spirit of community was what Beatrice Webb considered to have been the 'one thing needful' of her childhood. In a passage from *My Apprenticeship*, quoted earlier in this work, she describes what she understood as the fragmented and rootless nature of her young life:

> The world of human intercourse in which I was brought up was in fact an endless series of human beings, unrelated one to the other, and only casually connected with the family group – a miscellaneous crowd who came and went out of our lives rapidly and unexpectedly. Servants came and went; governesses and tutors came and went; businessmen of all sorts . . came and went; perpetually changing circles of 'London Society' acquaintances came and went. . . . Our social relation

had no roots in neighbourhood, in vocation, in creed, or for that matter in race. (pp. 40–1)

She thought that she had discovered what was lacking in her own family life – a life she associated with Individualism and *laissez-faire* capitalism – in the cohesive working-class community of Bacup, in the Consumer Co-operatives of the North and, finally, in the ideal of the collective governing of cities and States. The political and economic biases of her class and education were subverted by personal need. Fabian philosophy seemed to address itself to those needs without undermining completely the intellectual traditions within which Beatrice Webb was raised. By building on those very traditions, Fabianism could attract those, like Webb, who would not break irrevocably with their own intellectual and political pasts, but who clung to a vision of individual and social rebirth.

Part IV
Authorship

8 The Writing of *My Apprenticeship*

There was a Webb legend already flourishing when I first came to London as a boy: I have no doubt it still flourishes. But it is quite false. For it is a grim, inhuman legend – a legend of blue-stocking and blue-book – a legend of statistics, economics, infallibility, research, omniscience, lectures, pamphlets, dossiers, calculations, permeation and pedantry.

Possibly this false legend will flourish forever. Possibly, on the other hand, it is now dead, killed by the publication of Mrs Webb's autobiography. For it is the most human document you can imagine.

Gerald Gould, from a review of *My Apprenticeship*,
Daily Chronicle, 26 February 1926.

In January 1917, Beatrice Webb, then approaching her sixtieth birthday, began to type out and edit her manuscript diaries with the idea in mind of writing a 'Book of My Life' (3 January 1917). Over the next nine years, she wrote an autobiography based upon her diaries and, in so doing, performed the most revealing public act of her life. *My Apprenticeship* is revealing, not only in its content, but by its very existence: Webb's decision to write an autobiography signalled, however indirectly, a crisis in her private and public lives, in her dedication to Fabianism, in her political beliefs, in her career as a social scientist and in her role as Sidney's wife. In a paradoxical manner, which I shall elucidate here, the writing of *My Apprenticeship* called into question the very syntheses proposed within it, the syntheses of love and work in marriage-as-partnership and of science and faith in Fabianism. In order to discover the private motives for the writing of autobiography, it will be necessary to go beyond the framework of *My Apprenticeship* and to consult Webb's post-1892 diaries.

THE LIMITS OF PARTNERSHIP

As I have discussed earlier in this study, Beatrice Potter's
marriage to Sidney Webb enabled her to escape the rigid division
between her private life as student and ambitious intellectual and
her public life as dutiful daughter and mistress of a large
bourgeois household. 'In the future,' she wrote to Sidney, 'my life
will be one life only – you and my work bound together.'[1]
Marriage to Sidney would allow her to make public part of her
private self, to express openly her aspirations, political opinions
and intellectual interests. No longer, she hoped, would there be
need for a fragmented Beatrice Potter, leading two or three
separate lives at once. She soon discovered, however, that there
were aspects of her own personality, temperament and ideas that
found no expression within her marriage, and that there was a
deeper level of private existence that had to remain insulated from
public scrutiny. There were differences between Beatrice and
Sidney Webb that, while not preventing a long, affectionate and
productive partnership, did occasion Beatrice's suppression of
much that seemed vital to her own existence. The suppression, it
must be emphasized, was not altogether involuntary, for those
aspects of Beatrice with which Sidney was out of sympathy were
those aspects that she herself did not wholly trust.

The place for expression of that 'other self' remained, of course,
Webb's diary, which took on a new and perhaps more important
role in her life after her marriage. Samuel Hynes has remarked
that some of Webb's finest diary writing is to be found during the
years when the team of Webb was most prolific: 'with one side of
her nature she faced towards Sidney and "the work"; but with the
other self went on living in the prose that she addressed to
herself'.[2] Whenever the Webbs returned from a holiday, during
which time they either kept a joint travel diary or were too much
together for Beatrice to write in hers at all, she always remarked
on her pleasure at getting back her own voice. 'One cannot run on
into self-analysis, family gossip, or indiscreet and hasty descriptions of current happenings,' she wrote in her diary after their
return from America and Australia in 1899, 'if some one else,
however dear, is solemnly to read one's chatter then and there' (5
February 1899). She mused on the 'kindly indulgence or tolerant
boredom' with which Sidney might read her entries, and the
thought of this made it impossible for her to write 'whatever came

into my head'. Five years later, after a trip to Scotland, she welcomed back 'the old self, who knew me and whom I have known, for that long period before Sidney entered into my life – who seems to be that which is *permanent* in me' (16 October 1904).

During the twenty odd years between the Webbs' wedding and the outbreak of the First World War, they wrote *The History of Trade Unionism* and *Industrial Democracy*; campaigned for acceptance of the Minority Report of the Poor Law Commission, on which Beatrice served for three years; helped to establish the London School of Economics; started publication of the *New Statesman*; and took a year's trip to the Far East. These were years full of accomplishment, years in which the Webbs discovered their own brilliantly productive partnership. Beatrice blessed her 'luck in life' and the 'true comradeship with my beloved workmate' (12 June 1904). Her diaries of those years contain declarations of her happiness and of her love for Sidney, of her pride in her work and in her modest, 'brain-working' life, but they also contain recurring themes of discontent, yearnings for something not yet attained and questionings of the crucial choices she had made. These diaries give voice to that part of herself she once referred to as her 'Mr Hyde', and provide a clue to the crisis that precipitated her decision to write an autobiography.

When Beatrice married Sidney Webb, she estimated one of the strengths of their union to be its basis in a 'common faith'.[3] She believed her marriage to be founded upon a shared spiritual commitment to the idea of community, to Socialism and to social regeneration. It encouraged her to think that she and Sidney had a 'religious' bond between them, for the need for faith had long been a central part of her private mental and emotional life. But she soon found that Sidney and she had radically different attitudes towards religious belief, and that the 'faith' of Socialism, as they lived it, did not meet her spiritual needs. One year after their wedding, in the month of their first anniversary, Beatrice was again searching for 'the great want in my life – . . . "spirituality" '. For a brief time, she had been distracted by the discovery of Fabianism and by marriage to Sidney, but she soon returned to the preoccupations of her spinster days. 'I need prayer,' she proclaimed, 'or the substitute for prayer. . . . This spirit – this yearning for personal holiness I must again attain' (30 July 1893). Once again, as she had done in her days of 'glorified spinsterhood', she associated this need for spirituality with her femaleness. Men – and here she meant Sidney – did not seem to her to need the spiritual life. Men had work to occupy their intellectual faculties and women as a focus for their emotions; man's nature seemed 'more fully satisfied and absorbed in his work and his human affections'. Women, on the other hand, seemed to possess excess, undirected energies that needed the discipline of religious faith: 'spiritual life alone fills her being with the inspiration needful' (30 July 1893).

In the first years of the twentieth century, she began a campaign of reading on religious matters: theology, Theosophy, saints' lives and William James' works on belief, psychology and scientific method. James quickly became for her 'the truest of all metaphysicians' (16 July 1921).[4] Enlightened, intellectual and not immune from doubt, he believed in the need for faith and in the bankruptcy of scepticism. 'His main position,' she wrote in her diary, 'is that those who experience some kind of communion with a Higher Being and feel helped by it to lead a higher life, are as much entitled to believe it is reality as they are to believe in the evidence of other senses' (21 July 1902). James took the risk of faith in a supreme spiritual force while acknowledging that rational proof of its actual existence was an impossibility. Certitude was not necessary to the continued quest for an absolute truth. Beatrice found that James also believed in the 'practice of prayer as a means of personal salvation' and that he too regarded science as a failure at answering moral questions. 'Science can tell us what exists,' James wrote in a passage that is echoed throughout Beatrice Webb's personal writings,

> but to compare the *worths*, both of what exists and what does not exist, we must consult not science, but what Pascal calls our heart. Science herself consults her heart when she lays down that the infinite ascertainment of fact and correction of false belief are the supreme goods for man.[5]

She had discovered a kindred mind and spirit, she believed, in William James. During the years in which she read his work, she found herself 'slipping back into conformity with the Church of England'; she explained that those 'religious minded agnostics' like herself felt the need 'for days and hours set apart for prayer' (20 February 1905).

Sidney Webb felt no such need, and Beatrice suspected that he found her attitude towards prayer and religious faith something of an anomaly. 'Sidney,' she wrote at the end of a diary treatise on religion, 'does not sympathise with my faith in prayer, and perhaps, in his heart of hearts, regards it as "neurotic" ' (21 July 1902). Never having experienced the 'prayerful or religious attitude', he found William James' position in *The Will to Believe* 'tenable' but 'irrelevant'. Sidney, perhaps thinking his wife's habit of prayer 'neurotic', largely ignored it, but those friends of the Webbs who were allowed to know of this predilection of hers often argued with her, questioned her and badgered her about it. She recorded one such incident in her diary: in June 1909, the Haldanes, Richard and his sister Elizabeth, had invited the Webbs for dinner, and during the meal they all 'drifted on to' the subject of religious education. Beatrice remarked that she favoured a 'religious atmosphere and the practice of prayer as part of the school life':

> 'Nonsense – Mrs Webb,' blurted out the usually calm Elizabeth, with a sort of insinuation in her voice, that I was not sincere. I fired up and maintained my ground, and in a moment of intimacy, asserted that prayer was a big part of my own life. Whereupon, both the Haldanes turned round and openly scoffed at me – Haldane beginning a queer kind of cross-examination in law-court fashion . . . and Elizabeth scornfully remarking that prayer was mere superstition. It was a strange outburst met by another vehement assertion on my part that the two big forces for good in the world were the scientific method applied to the process of life, and the use of prayer in directing the purpose of life.   (18 June 1909)

The argument ended abruptly, as both sides realized the mistake of Beatrice's 'too great intimacy' and of the Haldanes' scoffing tone. She went away, however, with 'hurt feelings' and the conviction that discussion of her private thoughts and habits were better kept confined to her diary and to her communion with William James.

If spiritual questions were not solved by marriage to Sidney, neither were questions of sexuality, and for Beatrice, as we have seen, the two problems were inextricably linked. During the first decade of her marriage, she puzzled over the issue of motherhood and continued to be periodically obsessed by thoughts of Joseph

Chamberlain. She had not resolved the tensions of sexual identity that had so plagued her in the years before her marriage and that she had hoped to ease by choosing Sidney. The Webbs had decided against having children because of Beatrice's age (she was thirty-four when they married), their desire to use their time and energy for work, and her conviction that childbearing would destroy, at least for a time, the intellect that she had 'laboriously and with many sacrifices transformed . . . into an instrument for research' (1 January 1901). She had thoroughly accepted the notion of a rigid dichotomy between 'masculine' intellect and 'feminine' nurturing, and she could not imagine the reconciliation of the two qualities within herself. She felt the existence of a radical split between mind and body, and she judged herself unfit for motherhood after so many years of celibacy and intellectual endeavour: 'I had passed the age when it is easy and natural for a woman to become a child-bearer – my physical nature was to some extent dried up at 35 after ten years stress and strain of a purely brain-working and sexless life' (28 July 1894).

Although she had initially resolved to remain childless, she soon began to doubt the wisdom of the decision. In July 1894, in the month of their second wedding anniversary, Sidney was away and Beatrice was 'meditating on motherhood'. She recorded her meditations in an extraordinary diary entry that might stand as a paradigm for the musings of an intellectual woman who feels overwhelming confusion about the choices she has made. The entry does not bring to mind the familiar Beatrice Webb, nor does it fully represent her thoughts; it does, however, reflect her doubts about the seemingly irrevocable decisions that she had made for the sake of her ambitions, her mind and her freedom. 'First and foremost,' she began, contemplating what a perfect woman might be,

> I should wish a woman I loved to be a mother. To this end I would educate her. . . . From the first I would impress on her the holiness of motherhood – its infinite superiority over any other occupation that a woman might take to. But for the sake of that very motherhood I would teach her that she must be an intellectual being. . . . It pains me to see a fine intelligent girl, directly she marries, putting aside intellectual things as no longer pertinent to her daily life. And yet the other alternative – so often nowadays chosen by intellectual women – of deliber-

ately forgoing motherhood seems to me to thwart all the purposes of their nature. I myself – or rather we – chose this course in our marriage. . . . If I were young again and had the choice between a brain-working profession and motherhood, I would not hesitate to choose (as it is I sometimes wonder whether I had better not have risked it and taken my chance). . . . It is . . . overabundance of affection which the woman who is simply a brain-worker, even though she be also a loving comrade to her husband, deliberately wastes by forgoing motherhood.

'But what will be the solution of the woman's question?' she continued, still in confusion:

No thoughtful person wishes to see the old regime of economic and personal dependence preserved from the attacks of the modern woman's movement for complete freedom and emancipation. But . . . surely we need some human beings who will watch and pray, who will observe and aspire, and above all, who will guard and love all who are weak, unfit and distressed? (28 July 1894)

She had clearly not solved the 'woman's question' for herself, and it would continue to confound her.

The next time she returned to the question of motherhood in her diary was during a period of emotional crisis at the turn of the century. Years later, she wrote about the 'nervous breakdowns', as she called them, that she had suffered throughout her life and recalled 'one of the worst . . . in the summer and autumn of 1900 [when] I used to go out on the Yorkshire Moors and cry from depression' (14 April 1927). Already, in June 1899, she recorded a serious lapse into her old, 'cursed habit of sentimental castle-building', which caused her to dwell on the past: 'Scenes the vividness of which seem to make them real dominate my mind and I lose my self-control' (15 June 1899). It was Joseph Chamberlain she was daydreaming about, she later wrote in a codicil to the diary entry of 15 June, and it was the thought of Chamberlain that had contributed to her 'breakdown'. In the autumn of 1900, Beatrice had heard that his wife had left him, and she began to struggle with a 'terrible depression' (19 October 1900). The dreams about Chamberlain took on a new and more disturbing significance in the light of his presumed 'freedom': just as the news of his marriage to an American woman in 1888 had 'concluded the romance of four volumes of [Webb's] life', so did the possibility of his being wifeless stimulate her fantasies and cause her consequent agonies of conscience.[6] She passed a 'month of miserable suspense' until she discovered the rumour to be false and the Chamberlains to be living together as usual (16 November 1900).

Two months after the close of this episode, she was again contemplating the childlessness of her marriage. Had she made the right decision? Was it not, perhaps, her duty to the community to have children? Had she lost a 'safety valve for feeling and a valuable experience?' (1 January 1901). On the whole, she concluded, she did not regret their decision, and Sidney regretted it still less. Three months later, however, she was at the question again: 'Are the books we have written together,' she wondered, 'worth the babies we might have had?' Then again, she added in a characteristic afterthought, would one 'marry the same man in order to have babies, that one would select as joint author?' (24 April 1901). If this last question suggests an interest in biological planning, it also implies the acceptance of a mind/body split that Webb could not seem to escape. If Sidney Webb was the man with whom to write books, then perhaps Joseph Chamberlain, for whom her feelings were explicitly sexual, would have been the right man with whom to conceive a child.

During these months of pondering the value of parenthood, she continued in the state of agitation brought on by the news of Chamberlain's alleged separation. By the summer of 1901, her sister and brother-in-law, the Playnes, thought it best to take her to the Isle of Wight for recuperation while Sidney stayed in London to work. It had been a trying year for her, she recorded in the final month of 1901, although the full extent of its painfulness had largely been hidden from those around her. In a diary passage that she never allowed her secretary to type out in later years,[7] she summed up the year's unhappiness:

This year has been the most unsatisfactory year of my life since I married. How far I must apportion the blame between a bad state of physical health and a hollow state of mind, I cannot tell. But [in] the egotism, self-consciousness, vanity and a total incapacity for a really good day's work, I have excelled all my previous [illegible]. No one has been aware of this but myself: I have kept a brave face; I have seemed to be fully occupied by other thoughts. . . . This year has found me far more emotional than I have ever been before; I longed for music, I desired to be religious, I allowed my mind to dwell on all sorts of sentimental relations.   (9 December 1901)

It had been the year of her discovery of William James and of her renewed interest in religion. The themes of her adolescence and young womanhood – 'vanity', 'egotism', self-consciousness, day-dreaming, sexual longing and religious devotion – seemed to have re-entered her life in full force, apparently unaltered by marriage to Sidney.

'For long years,' Beatrice wrote in 1918, 'I have constrained my intellect, forced it to concentrate on one subject after another; on some of the dullest and least illuminating details of social organisation' (22 December 1918). This is the voice of the Beatrice Webb who felt that her mind, her talents and even her mode of expression were cramped and confined within the work of the partnership. As others have noted, the language and style of the Webb's books are clearly different from those of Beatrice's diary or of *My Apprenticeship*. 'In writing,' she confessed, 'I am parasitic on Sidney; I never write, except in the diary, in my own style, always in a hybrid of his and mine' (8 December 1913). And the 'hybrid' style of the work, one might add, had more in it of Sidney than of Beatrice. When they worked on their first book together, *The History of Trade Unionism*, she discovered that working in Sidney's mode was a strain for her: 'It is a horrid grind, this analysis – one sentence exactly like another, the same words, the same construction – no relief in narrative' (10 July 1894).

It was not merely Sidney's manner of writing that Beatrice at times found tedious: the kinds of projects they chose to undertake were of necessity laborious. 'I recall, for instance', she wrote, continuing to describe the long years of 'constrained intellect',

the weeks of grinding toil spent on disentangling the various methods of recovering the cost of public maintenance from different classes of recipients of relief and their relatives. I vividly remember the nausea with which, day after day, I went on with this task.   (22 December 1918)

No wonder, then, that she found herself once again longing to write fiction, as she had done in earlier, pre-partnership days:[8]

for the last three months an idea has haunted me that after we have ended our stiff work on Trade Unions I would try my hand at pure 'Fiction'. . . . The truth is, I want to have my 'fling'! I want to imagine anything I damn please without regard to facts as they are – . . . I want to try my hand at artist's work instead of mechanics. *I am sick to death of trying to put hideous facts, multitudinous details, exasperating qualifications, into a readable form.* (1 February 1895)

Included in this plan to write fiction was an idea for the imagined novel's two main themes: collectivism and the presentation of a 'fully fledged woman engaged in a great career'. The issue of sexual identity was never far from Beatrice Webb's expressions of discontent, either before or after her marriage. The novel she had in mind was to take place '60 years hence', and its heroine would be 'pictured just as we should *now* picture a man'. This novelistic plan suggests that Webb regarded equality between the sexes as an as yet unfulfilled fantasy, the stuff of a utopia or a society of the future. After all, she had achieved partnership with a man, but she had not been able to avoid a kind of intellectual domination by him.

THE CRISIS OF THE FIRST WORLD WAR

After the difficult first decade of marriage, Beatrice Webb's sense of personal frustration was eased somewhat by serving on the Royal Commission on the Poor Law, and by her subsequent campaigning on behalf of the reforms proposed in her Minority Report to the Commission. From 1905 until 1911, her energies were absorbed in research, public service and propaganda. Part of the result of the Webbs' involvement in agitation for radical Poor Law reform, however, was a loss of influence among moderate politicians, both Liberals and conservatives, and among Cabinet Ministers and civil servants alike.[9] By the time they returned from the Far East in 1913, in fact, they were out of favour both with established political parties and with the socialist left – particularly the syndicalists – and had reached a low ebb in their popularity. 'We are extraordinarily unpopular today,' Beatrice confided in her diary in the winter of 1913–14, 'more disliked, by a larger body of persons, than ever before. The propertied class look upon us as their most insidious enemies; the revolutionary Socialist or fanatical sentimentalist see in us, and our philosophy, the main obstacle to what they call enthusiasm and we call hysteria' (8 December 1913). By the time the War broke out, the Webbs had lost a good deal of the influence they had carefully cultivated by 'permeating' all parties and all classes: the surge of personal power Beatrice had felt as Poor Law Commissioner dissipated as the War approached, and by the spring of 1914 she was in a 'wicked state of mind'.

The War had an immediate and acutely debilitating effect on Beatrice Webb.[10] In August 1914, she began to feel 'distracted with depression and anxiety' and lost her capacity for work. 'It is almost impossible,' she wrote in her diary, 'to keep one's mind off that horrible Hell a few hundred miles away' (6 and 25 August 1914). In October, she was in 'the depth of gloom', obsessed by the 'consciousness of the mad horror of these battlefields, where the quick and the dead rot together', and by November she was suffering from 'mental and physical depression' (21 October 1914; 3 November 1914). As the War continued, she was unable to work: her life seemed to revolve around the newspapers and their reports of battles and casualties. 'The horror and terror of the war,' she recorded, 'eats into one's vitality, and I exist in a state of chronic weakness brought about by continuous sleeplessness' (12 October 1915). She wondered how she could go on, 'eating and drinking, walking and sleeping, reading and dictating, apparently unmoved by the world's misery' (2 July 1916). Her physical decline, a result of sleeplessness and psychological strain, convinced her, by July 1916, that she was gravely ill, that she had 'an internal growth . . . that would necessitate an operation' and that she would likely die undergoing surgery (24 July 1916). A physician in London assured her that 'there was no sign of any organic trouble', and she felt humiliated by her own lack of courage and by her obsessiveness. She had always, she wrote, been 'the prey to fear': 'These occasional and temporary obsessions or fancies are my "Mr Hyde" ' (24 July 1916). Sidney and Beatrice left for a summer in the country in the hope that she might relax and recover there, but the six weeks' holiday had little effect on her psychological state (16 August 1916).

By the end of the summer, she began to refer to her condition as a 'nervous breakdown', and then, in October, she got her 'first push upwards' by reading an article in the *Lancet* which described all of the possible symptoms of 'neurasthenia'.[11] She promptly recognized the symptoms as her own, and this alleviated her fears about suffering from a serious physical illness. The piece in the *Lancet* that she read was most probably a lead article entitled 'Neurasthenia and Shell Shock', about cases of 'war nerves' among soldiers who were not insane, or malingering, or acutely ill.[12] 'Shell shock' was a new term, used to describe the insidious psychological and physical effects of war on otherwise healthy young Englishmen; it was considered, in this article, to be a specific form of neurasthenia. The notion of neurasthenia had first been made popular in the 1880s by George Miller Beard, an American physician who defined it as a weakness of the nervous system, brought on by the stresses of modern life and likely to produce a host of different and varying physical complaints.[13] The *Lancet* article included defects of memory, vision, smell and taste, and 'disorders of cutaneous sensibility' as possible symptoms of the condition. Women's ills were particularly likely to be described as neurasthenic in the decades surrounding the turn of the century; and Virginia Woolf's episodes of mental disturbance, one of which occurred during the First War, were described as 'neurasthenia' by her doctors as well.[14]

Webb's 'neurasthenic' breakdown lasted in an acute form for six months and lingered in an attenuated form for over two years. In a diary note written in 1919, she attributed this breakdown to 'war neurosis', to a too-persistent effort to keep working so as not to brood over the horrors of war, and to a sense of 'general discouragement' at being out of favour in 'all sections of political and official worlds' (note to 24 July 1916, dated June 1919). This period of anxiety, depression, sleeplessness and ill-health marked a personal and public crisis in Beatrice Webb's life. She felt politically superfluous and intellectually inadequate: she was not wanted by the body politic nor was she, she knew, capable of solving the kinds of problems that the War had revealed to her and to the entire world.

'The great war will raise issues,' she wrote during the first year of the hostilities, 'which I have no longer the strength and elasticity to understand' (3 November 1914). 'The root of my trouble,' she continued, 'is of course a bad conscience.' Her conscience troubled her because all of her plans for the construction of a Socialist State seemed utterly irrelevant in the face of the dynamics, motives and mechanics of war. Her vision of the world could neither explain nor account for the existence and nature of that 'horrible Hell a few hundred miles away'. Everything that she had ever worked for seemed useless, pointless, and even misguided. 'It adds to my depression that the problems involved in its settlement,' she wrote towards the end of the War, 'are wholly outside my grasp' (5 October 1917). Leonard Woolf, whom Sidney Webb asked to write a book for the Fabian Society on ways of averting war (Woolf was the Fabian 'expert' on international issues), remarked that the Webbs' methods for understanding the structure and function of governments and institutions could never be applied to the passion for power, the ideals of nationalism, to national fears or hatreds. Much of international politics was, therefore, beyond their ken.[15] Woolf believed that the Webbs' thought was limited in this respect, that too much had been left out of it, just as John Stuart Mill had believed that certain essential things, a comprehension of certain parts of 'human nature', had been left out of the Benthamite calculus.

Closely connected to Beatrice's feelings of uselessness was her growing conviction that she, Sidney, the Fabians, and even Herbert Spencer, had been wrong about social progress. The War seemed irrefutable proof that humanity was not evolving towards some perfect state or towards greater social integration, that the 'inevitability of gradualness' had broken down, that Process might not be Progress after all.[16] A constant theme of her diary entries during and directly after the War was her questioning of the very premise of Fabian theory: man's gradual evolution toward social regeneration. Was the 'Human Being' 'groping his way toward the light', or was the War merely a 'hallmark of the race's idiocy'? 'Are we becoming God,' she asked during the worst phase of her breakdown, 'or are we merely on the way to sink back into chaos – without beginning and without end?' (18 August 1916).

Sidney refused to be discouraged, however, and his reaction to the War revealed the spirit of a stubborn optimist. Both Sidney and Beatrice adhered to an optimistic political and social philosophy, but she, unlike her husband, was by nature a pessimist. She recorded with respectful scepticism Sidney's pronouncements on the unseen value of the War:

He is far more philosophical about the war than I am. 'It is a sag back, but presently there will be a sag forward, and Humanity will move forward to a greater knowledge and greater goodwill: the Great War will seem to future generations a landmark of progress.' I wonder: the evil let loose seems too stupendous. (25 September 1915)

Sidney could assimilate even the War and its destruction into the great scheme of progress. He counselled sleep and food for Beatrice when she felt ill, and work when she was depressed: ' "Let us do our own work," he says, "like the French peasant cultivates his fields close to the fighting line" ' (12 October 1915). This attitude made him, Beatrice thought, an 'ideal companion' for a 'self-tortured mind', but she remained unconvinced by his reasoning. 'What I have lost,' she wrote, lamenting her lack of stamina, 'is hopefulness and enthusiasm; I no longer feel certain that the right will prevail' (10 January 1918).

After the War had ended, she looked around for the 'sag forward' that Sidney had predicted: 'Where is "the freedom broadening down from precedent to precedent," ' she asked, 'either within the British Empire or the world outside?' (25 December 1919). The War seemed to have brought an end to a long, extended era of slow but steady social progress:

Ten years ago one would have left the world feeling that human society was getting steadily more loving and more enlightened. Today it needs a robust 'Will to believe' to avoid the fear that we are sinking back into a barbarism as dark as any endured since the times deemed 'civilised'. One dreads that human life is becoming worse and not better while one is finishing one's brief spell of work. (23 October 1920)

It had become virtually impossible to hope for the achievement of a new social order, and even the vocabulary of Victorian social philosophy seemed outmoded: 'No one,' she wrote in 1921, 'now talks of Progress' (1 January 1921). Five years after the close of the War she had still not regained her faith in the future: Sidney had retained his optimism, but she was becoming 'every day *more* pessimistic'. She feared that men had ceased to be agents of construction and had been irredeemably transformed into agents of destruction: 'They are capable of destroying the existing civilisation; they are not capable of building up another social order' (11 January 1923).

She was not merely an old woman who had lost her faith and had come to despair of 'modern' life: she had witnessed the subversion of a social philosophy on which she had based all of her efforts, all of her work, even, in part, her marriage. She had dedicated her professional and personal life to the notion of evolutionary progress, to the service of humanity and to the idea that science combined with social faith would have redemptive powers. She had married with the conviction that public service must take precedence over private, 'egotistical' happiness, because public service was bound to end in the regeneration of social life. If that regeneration was never to take place, had all of her decisions been falsely taken? The Webbs had failed to woo the Liberals; they had succeeded in antagonizing other British socialists; they had undercut their own ability to influence political life; and now the War suggested to Beatrice that perhaps they had been wrong about many other things as well. Her solution to this global and personal crisis, to the World War and to her own breakdown, was to look for salvation in memory and in the affirmation of *private* progress: her solution was to write an autobiography.

MY APPRENTICESHIP: A 'BOOK OF MY LIFE'

Although *My Apprenticeship* was not published until 1926, it was conceived and begun directly after Beatrice Webb's initial six-month War crisis had ended in the winter of 1916–17. In December, she recorded in her diary that she had recovered somewhat from her 'neurasthenia' and was able to work again (2 December 1916). One month later, she reported that she had bought a small typewriter of her own, and was beginning to copy out and edit her diary 'so as to make a Book of my Life' (3 January 1916).[17] She believed herself to be at 'one of the watersheds of life', and her past had suddenly become of vital interest to her. She wanted not only to discover what she thought and dreamed and accomplished; she wanted to see *'what it all amounts to'* (22 December 1918). What was the shape of her life, what the purpose? Her curiosity was excited by the idea of 'piecing it together into a connected whole' (25 February 1920). The progress she found lacking in the evolution of society might be present in her personal history. If society had not been moving towards wholeness, perhaps she had been doing so in her own life. Her faith might be redeemed by a discovery of private meaning. The history of humankind did not now seem to her a 'connected whole', as Herbert Spencer had taught her and as she and Sidney had so fervently believed, but the writing of autobiography might prove that design and purpose could be detected at least in the *individual* life.

The writing of *My Apprenticeship* was, then, Beatrice Webb's response to the public and personal crisis of the First World War; but it was also an expression of many of the impulses and interests that had been stifled in her – with her own compliance – in the years preceding the War. The pleasure she took in the project of her autobiography was unequalled by anything else she had undertaken; for much of the time during the nine years between the beginning and the publication of the book, writing *My Apprenticeship* was all she really cared to do. 'This coming year,' she wrote in the last month of 1918, 'I shall devote myself entirely to three tasks: getting our own publications forward, helping with the advisory committees of the Labour Party, and in holiday intervals, typing out the back volumes of my diary. This latter occupation, I can hardly call it work, pleases me most' (22 December 1918). She found the job of typing and composing to be amusing and endlessly absorbing: 'I have started on a task which I delight in.' Her diary entries during these years contain repeated outbursts of enthusiasm for 'the new favorite which is absorbing most of my thoughts' (24 December 1921).

When she wrote *My Apprenticeship*, she broke out of the intellectual constraints under which she had been working for so long. 'I have done so much drudgery,' she wrote on New Year's Eve, 1922, 'that I think I have a right to let myself go in a work of art!' This was her own book, written in her own voice and her own style; this was her creation, her 'work of art', her novel. It was, at least in part, the novel she had planned to write in 1895 about a 'fully fledged woman engaged in a great career . . . pictured just as we should now picture a man'. She was the heroine of the novel, a triumphant Maggie Tulliver, and she pictured herself in an intellectual and spiritual autobiography as men like John Stuart Mill had done throughout the nineteenth century. For Beatrice

Webb, this autobiography represented an expression of those parts of herself which she considered to be bound up with the artistic, the creative, the religious, the non-rational and even the sexual: she called it 'this child of my old age' (9 June 1925).

In writing *My Apprenticeship*, based upon the diaries she had kept for some forty-five years, she was making the private public, exposing her 'other self' and asserting its importance to the world. She worried about how much private detail to include, about 'what degree of self-revelation is permissible and desirable' (9 February 1923). At times she felt as though she were engaged in 'displaying' herself 'like an actress or an opera singer', and the fear of vanity and egotism that had troubled her in adolescence asserted itself now and again (29 October 1925). But despite this nervousness and self-consciousness, she felt overwhelming satisfaction at her ability to express openly certain aspects of the other side, the underside, the 'disguised' part of her personality. Childhood breakdowns, conflicts of young womanhood, crises of identity and, above all, a search for vocation and faith, are the stuff of *My Apprenticeship*; they are not at all those kinds of human experience that the English public associated with the Mrs Sidney Webb of *Industrial Democracy* and *The History of Trade Unionism*, with Poor Law reform and Fabian technocracy.

The autobiography celebrates the years of apprenticeship and the experience of the 1880s (five out of the seven chapters focus on that decade). These years were eclipsed in the public mind – and, one should add, in the mind of the historian – by later Fabian politics, massive tomes of research and the 'firm of Webb', but they were years in which Beatrice Webb, then Potter, first enjoyed freedom to work, independence of thought and existence, expression of talent and ambition. During that decade she escaped the stultifying pressures of Victorian upper bourgeois life, and experienced the exhilaration of personal freedom. For a very few years she was neither daughter nor wife, and suffered neither the social constraints imposed by family and class nor the intellectual constraints that were the results of marriage. In *My Apprenticeship*, one has glimpses of her in transcendent moments: in Bacup, sharing cigarettes and conversation with textile workers; at Katherine Buildings, taking notes on the lives of tenants and living in a congenial community of women; in Victoria Park with Kerrigan, the Stepney School Board Visitor, listening to soap box orators; with Charles Booth in Leicestershire, planning the great work on poverty; at the London docks, watching 'casuals' fight to be taken on for work; in East End sweatshops learning to be a trouser-hand; and at Co-operative Society meetings arguing with members about the role of trade unions. Her earliest efforts at investigation, many of them made possible only through the use of disguise, had the quality of adventure, of experiment and bravado, of great personal engagement. Webb largely gave up this kind of social investigation when she turned to the historical and statistical research that she carried out with Sidney. *My Apprenticeship* is, among other things, an attempt to recover the inspiration and the satisfactions of the 'East End' years of her life.

My Apprenticeship was the first major work that Beatrice had undertaken on her own since her marriage to Sidney. (Although she served on the Royal Poor Law Commission alone, she and Sidney wrote the Minority Report together.) Sidney tolerated her involvement with the project, but showed little enthusiasm for it; he was, himself, not the 'autobiographical' sort. 'Sidney is an extrovert,' she wrote in the final years of her life, 'and has no such inclination [to write an autobiography]: "I have no insides" he asserts' (15 July 1937).[18] He was not altogether convinced of the value of his wife's revelation of *her* 'insides', and she was aware of his ambivalence:

> I don't think Sidney quite likes it: he does his best to approve, still more to help me; but there is something about it that he – not exactly resents – but which is unsympathetic. In his heart he fears I am over-valuing it, especially the extracts from the diaries – the whole thing is far too subjective and all that part that deals with 'my creed' as distinguished from 'my craft' seems to him the sentimental scribblings of a woman, only interesting just because they are feminine.   (19 March 1925)

Sidney was correct, in ways that he could not have understood, when he drew connections between his wife's 'creed', her diary and her womanly 'scribblings', when he saw something essentially 'feminine' in her autobiography; he was very far wrong, however, in undervaluing these aspects of his wife's experience.

Her husband's lack of sympathy with her autobiographical efforts inhibited her very little, in part because during the period of her greatest involvement with the book, Sidney was occupied with active political life, first as an MP from Seaham in 1922 and then as a Cabinet Minister in the first Labour government in 1924. It has generally been assumed that when Sidney was in Parliament, Beatrice had a good deal of time on her hands and so took to producing a memoir, but quite the opposite is true. She had been planning the book from 1917, and Sidney's political preoccupations and necessary absences from home gave her the opportunity to carry out her plans. 'I can get back to my little book,' she wrote after her husband's election in 1922. 'Sidney's absorption in his new life will leave me free to become absorbed in this curiously personal task' (23 November 1922). 'Fortunately,' she returned to the subject two months later, 'Sidney's life will leave me a good deal alone' (9 February 1923). They began to lead new, separate lives, he in Parliament and she, as she put it, 'in literature' (5 December 1925).

Beatrice was not merely absorbed in her own work; she was very little interested in Sidney's work and in its implications for her own career. She had enjoyed her limited involvement with the miners of Seaham, Sidney's constituents: she began a circulating library for them, wrote a newsletter for the miners' families and recalled with fondness her days in another Northern town, Bacup. But she disliked the 'daily life of a Cabinet Minister's wife' and resented the new responsibilities she was expected to take on (2 May 1924). She longed for the time when her role as political hostess would become 'sufficiently fixed' and routine enough to enable her to retire permanently to Passfield Corner and get on with her book as a full-time project (11 February 1924). 'Clothes, curtseys, parties, dances and dramatic circles, all the details of cultivating social intercourse within the Labour Party' interested her not at all. After years as a professional student, she shunned the job of professional wife.

Her lack of enthusiasm for Sidney's career in politics went deeper, however, than her resentment of 'wifely' duties; she was simply not interested in the Labour government. She might well have been expected to regard this government as a partial realization of the Webbs' goals, as the justification for all of their long years of work, as the beginning of the fulfilment of their dreams of a Socialist state. Margaret Cole, in an introduction to the second volume of her edition of Beatrice Webb's diaries, remarks that Beatrice soured on the second Labour government of 1929, and lost interest in its activities because of Sidney's failures as Minister for the Colonies.[19] It would be far more

accurate to say that she had never shown much interest in ever
the first Labour government. 'It is my *duty*,' she wrote in 1924, 'to
be interested in the Labour Party and the Labour Government
and I honestly try to show the symptoms of being interested. But I
am not really interested except in so far as Sidney's activities and
happiness are concerned' (10 July 1924). It is perplexing and
profoundly revealing that while the first Labour government in
Britain's history was being established, Beatrice Webb was
longing to be left alone to devote herself to her autobiography.

THE MEANING AND PARADOX OF *MY APPRENTICESHIP*

The process of writing *My Apprenticeship* helped Webb to overcome
the depression and paralysis of her War crisis, and satisfied her
need to create something of her own. Friends applauded the book,
and reviewers were unexpectedly enthusiastic. She had 'displayed' her life to the public, and they had received it well. The
text she produced redeemed and celebrated the notion of
progress, at least in the individual life. Without violating the
documentation of her past that she had in the form of her diary,
she managed to create out of her personal history the story of a
quest that reached a felicitous end. Synthesis and solution had
been achieved: she had found love and work, Creed and Craft,
faith and vocation. Even the debate of the 'two Egos' seemed to
have been resolved in the discovery of a 'rational' faith and in the
happy combination of service and science.

On the most profound level of experience and belief, however,
the writing of this personal work reinforced Webb's sense of
having failed to solve the problems of self and the world. The
autobiographical text concludes in absolute affirmation and
ringing optimism; the act of writing it ended in ultimate confusion
and uncertainty:

> The work on the book has . . . upset my state of mind. I have
> learnt a good deal from it – I have ruminated over my
> experience of life and the reflections have sometimes been
> pessimistic. Somewhere in my diary – 1890? – I wrote '*I have
> staked all on the essential goodness of human nature*' – I thought of

putting the entry into the book – I did not do so because it was too near the truth! Looking back I realise how permanent are the evil impulses and instincts in man – how little you can count on changing some of these – for instance the greed of wealth and power – *by any change in machinery*.   (5 December 1925)

The Great War, she admitted in her diary, had proved the 'new science, which seemed to the pioneers of 1870 to be able to solve all problems', to be absolutely 'bankrupt in directive force' (28 September 1921). The 'old religious faith' had disappeared and the 'new science' could offer no moral guidance. 'Like so many other poor souls,' Webb wrote in the year *My Apprenticeship* appeared, 'I have the consciousness of being a *spiritual outcast*' (14 April 1926).[20]

She compared herself in her diary to Mrs Moore, the old woman in Forster's *Passage to India* whose ' "twilight of the double vision" ' and sense of ' "spiritual muddledom" ' Webb believed she shared. Like Mrs Moore, she had lost her bearings and could no longer 'estimate the relative value' of all the 'thoughts and feelings streaming out of the past and into the future' (10 July 1924). This loss of balance, she went on to lament, seemed to have made all the questions to which she had devoted her life's work seem 'stale and unprofitable': 'trade unionism, local government, co-operation, political organisation, no longer interest me – I dislike reading about them, thinking about them, talking about them or writing about them'. In this state, she resembled no one so much as John Stuart Mill who, at the onset of mental crisis, realized that the fulfilment of all his professed goals for society could bring him no happiness. At this realization, Mill records in his *Autobiography*, 'the whole foundation on which my life was constructed fell down'.[21]

Webb's privately expressed doubt and continuing moral uncertainty in the years surrounding the publication of *My Apprenticeship* underscore its paradoxical and what one might call its fictional aspects. What she wrote in the autobiography and what she wrote in the diary as she composed *My Apprenticeship* were not always completely congruent. As she indicated in the diary passage quoted above, she hesitated to include certain diary entries in *My Apprenticeship* because they painfully reminded her that the optimism of her youth had not been validated by the experience of middle-age. Her youthful belief in man's goodness of nature and, therefore, in the inevitability of progress had, in truth, given way to pessimism, but it was impossible for her to represent this process of growing despair and disillusionment in her autobiography. She made the certainty of felicitous change the theme of *My Apprenticeship*, and felt the nearly insurmountable difficulty of any such change as she wrote it.

'Machinery' and the 'new science' had proven impotent means of transforming society, but what, if not 'machinery', had the Fabianism she celebrated in her autobiography become? It had begun in the 1880s as a faith, a utopian vision of social regeneration, but it had indeed ended as a philosophy of machinery, as the kind of Gradgrindism that she had criticized in *My Apprenticeship* as a feature of the *laissez-faire* Individualism she had rejected. It had been the failures of Fabianism to satisfy fully her own needs and the needs of humanity that had, in part, prompted the writing of *My Apprenticeship*. The autobiography is, on its surface, an unwavering endorsement of scientific socialism and an unequivocal celebration of the discovery of partnership, but the fact of its having been written and the continuing private doubt of its author are, paradoxically, an implicit challenge to the syntheses and resolutions it contains and affirms.

Conclusion: On the Soviet Union

Although the experience of the War seemed to have dealt Spencerian notions of progress a death blow, Beatrice Webb's indomitable will to believe did not permit her to relinquish the search for social redemption. She held onto the hope that yet to come was a salvation that would provide 'the authoritative ethics associated with faith in a spirit of love at work in the universe', as Fabian Socialism could not do. In the year that *My Apprenticeship* appeared, Webb wrote in her diary that although she had failed to solve 'the problem of life', she was possessed of 'a growing faith that it *will* be solved by a combination of truth-seeking and personal holiness – of the scientific mind with the religious life' (14 April 1926). She now imagined a leader who might unite the 'intellect of an Aristotle, a Goethe or an Einstein with the moral genius of a Buddha, a Christ or a St Francis' (14 April 1926). The peculiar search for faith, that recurrent theme in her mental life, continued to obsess and confound her. 'I am perpetually brooding,' she confessed in the diary, 'on my inability to make clear even to myself, let alone to others, why I believe in religious mysticism – why I hanker after a Church.'

Despite the affirmation of Fabianism that *My Apprenticeship* contained, Webb's hankering after 'religious mysticism' and search for a 'Purpose' to direct the hand of 'Progress' went unfulfilled by Socialist politics, Fabian programmes and what she regarded as the 'rot' of British civilization. In 1926, she had vague imaginings of a new faith, a new leader, a new Church: by 1932 she had begun the love affair with Soviet Communism that dominated most of the final decade of her life. Webb's professional and psychic involvement with Soviet Russia must be understood in the context of her post-war disillusionment, her search for 'Purpose', her long-standing and profound need for a 'Creed'. An examination of her feelings about Russia helps to unravel further

239

many of the central themes and preoccupations of Webb's life. The debates and conflicts that set the tone of her private writings – her diary and her autobiography – were recapitulated in her complex and apparently contradictory attitude toward Communism.

A NEW CIVILIZATION

Despite an initial antagonism to the Russian Revolution and a dismissal of Soviet Communism throughout the 1920s, the Webbs ultimately came to believe that a number of the fundamental aspects of their own blueprint for a socialist society had been carried out in the Soviet Union. Beatrice wrote in her diary in January 1932, a number of months before they journeyed to Russia, that the Soviet constitution bore out their own *Constitution for the Socialist Commonwealth* and corresponded to their own 'tripod' of 'political democracy, vocational organisation, and the consumers' co-operative movement' (4 January 1932). This last feature of Soviet society was, of course, of great importance to Beatrice, as her long-standing support of co-operation had often been ignored by other British socialists. The 'deliberate planning of the production of commodities and services', as the Webbs wrote in their *Soviet Communism: a New Civilisation?*, was made indispensable in Russia by the abolition of profit-making and the transfer of the means of production to collective ownership.[1]

The Webbs believed that their sphere of influence had shifted, and they transferred their hopes for social progress accordingly. Russia represented to them the possibility of a 'new civilisation', a new arena for the felicitous evolution of humanity. If the First World War had cancelled out the possibility of a gradual and inevitable progress towards social regeneration in Britain, and if the Labour governments had failed to redeem British society, then perhaps one had to look elsewhere for an object worthy of one's aspirations for mankind. The idea of Progress could be transplanted to the Soviet Union and thereby reaffirmed. For an aged Spencerian clinging to belief in the inherent perfectibility of humanity, a transfer of allegiance was a surprising but not wholly illogical solution to the 'disappearance' of optimism in Western Europe. When *Living Philosophies*, a collection of personal essays by various authors, appeared in 1939, Beatrice remarked in her diary on 'the uniform pessimism of the essays, *except those of communists*'. 'When one is on the point of leaving life', she added, 'it is happy to leave on a hopeful note about the future of the human race' (16 August 1939).

The future of the human race in Britain seemed to her to be particularly grim. The 'barbarism' of the War seemed to have taken root in her own country in the form of decadence and 'soullessness', which she thought she recognized over and over again in the literature of the period. She acknowledged, for example, the talent and originality of Virginia Woolf, but she questioned the value of Woolf's emphasis on the internal life of her characters, most of whom Webb found to be completely without interest:

> Like other work of the new School of Novelists – I do not find her work interesting outside of its craftsmanship which is excellent but 'precieuse'. Her men and women do not interest me – they don't seem worth describing in such detail – the mental climate in which they live seems strangely lacking in light, heat, visibility and variety – it is a dark mist of insignificant and monotonous thought and feelings – *no predominant aims, no powerful reactions from their mental environment* – . . . To the aged Victorian this soullessness is depressing – doubtless our insistence on a Purpose, whether for the individual or the Universe, appears to them a delusion and a pernicious delusion. (5 February 1927)

Webb's comments on Woolf do not betray a lack of sensitivity to literature or even an inability to understand what someone like Woolf was attempting to achieve in fiction, but rather an unwillingness to accept a modern art which seemed to ignore the important social and moral questions that had informed the literature of her childhood and young-womanhood.

Far guiltier, however, of this evasion of the pressing issues of collective life was, Webb believed, D. H. Lawrence, whose interest in the 'sub-human' she often lamented in her diary entries during the late 1920s and early 1930s. She judged Lawrence to be, like Huxley, Norman Douglas, David Garnett and Compton MacKenzie, a clever but 'morbid' novelist (26 October 1928). Lawrence concerned himself, she thought, with the 'animal' part of human nature, and seemed to repudiate the 'heritage of man as distinguished from that of the lower species' (30 October 1932). The 'cult of sex' and ' "phallic consciousness" ' were blasphemous to her because they ignored what she considered to be the truly 'human' qualities of existence – the aspirations, the search for 'Purpose', the striving for a harmonious communal life.

She believed that Western democracies were being destroyed and degraded by the constant din of 'sex, sensational crime, silly gossip, idle pleasure, the worship of money and the love of luxury' (4 January 1932). Young people were faced with an utter absence of 'beauty, personal dignity, sense of service, public interest or intellectual strivings'. The Great War had disgusted and depressed everyone with its 'manifestation of . . . the Will to Murder', and everyone, particularly the young, found it difficult to believe in deity *or* humanity. ' "Your generation," ' Webb recorded the words of a Cambridge undergraduate to his mother, ' "lost faith in God; our generation has lost faith in man" ' (26 October 1928). Virginia Woolf's lack of interest in politics and her dislike for the 'environmental novel', Lawrence's revelation of the significance of the sexual in human life, and the casual acceptance of the 'sub-human in art and literature and music' were, as far as Webb was concerned, all signs of this tragic loss of faith.

By contrast, the Soviet Union fostered asceticism, personal 'purity' and a puritanical attitude towards sex, drink and even food.[2] This habit of restraint seemed to her 'the exact opposite of the D. H. Lawrence cult of sex', and, though it 'lack[ed] a sense of humor as well as a sense of beauty', it seemed 'more likely to lead to a healthy mind in a healthy body than Lawrence's morbid obsessions about the "phallic consciousness" as the be all and end all of human life' (30 October 1932). In the place of the 'cult of sex', in opposition to 'egotism' and morbid introspection, the Russians proposed selflessness, self-sacrifice and a commitment to the group over the individual. The Soviet Union was involved in creating what the Webbs called a 'Communist Conscience'. '*Socially* useful work' was made 'a universal duty', and the concept of a 'universal individual *indebtedness*' to the community was imposed.[3] A new morality, affirming the faith in humanity that Britain had apparently lost, was emerging under Soviet Communism. It was precisely this perceived moral and, indeed, spiritual power that drew Webb to Communism: Russia had supplied a 'soul', she believed, to the Webbian concept of government, a religious core which their own 'paper constitution' had lacked. 'Personally being a mystic and a moralist,' she wrote in her diary in 1932, declaring her prejudice in favour of Soviet Russia, 'I always hankered after a spiritual power; always felt instinctively that there *must* be some such a force, if salvation were to be found' (4 January 1932). In Soviet Communism, as she perceived it, she had found a political system that did not leave the question of 'Purpose' or of 'Creed' to chance.

At the very centre of Russia's ethical and 'religious' power was the Communist Party, which Webb considered to be 'the most important part of the effective constitutional structure of the USSR'.[4] These 'super citizens', the members of the Party, were selected out of the entire population 'for the exercise of a special *vocation* and the fulfillment of a particular duty based upon a definite *creed*', the creed of Marxism.[5] They constituted a virtual 'religious order', and took vows of obedience and poverty. 'It is the invention of the religious order,' she admitted, 'as the determining factor in the life of a great nation, which is the magnet that attracts me to Russia' (4 January 1932). The Russians themselves might object to her characterization of the Party as an 'order' with 'its Holy Writ, its prophets and its canonised Saints', as indeed her friend Sokolnikov, the Soviet Ambassador to Britain, had done, but she regarded this 'vocation of leadership' as the Soviet Union's greatest achievement. In his work on 'fellow-travellers', David Caute includes the Webbs among those 'heirs to the pre-Marxian Enlightenment' who were drawn to the Soviet Union as a 'rational, educated and scientific society', a place where reason, order and planning had triumphed.[6] This analysis misses the real essence of Beatrice Webb's attraction to Russia, an attraction that had far more to do with a perceived ethical and spiritual power than with a taste for technocratic efficiency.

The party could provide moral guidance, establish a sound and consistent ethic, and act as an agent of social control. The discipline within the Party and that which it could enforce throughout the community might seem extreme, but it could 'lift the peoples of Russia out of the dirt, disease, apathy, superstition, illiteracy, thieving and brutishness of pre-revolutionary days'.[7] Beatrice Webb imagined the Communist Party as an élite that combined the oligarchic power of the proposed Fabian 'junta' with the moral and spiritual influence of the Dissenting Chapels of Northern England.

The institution of this 'religious order' at the hub of Soviet society was, to Webb's mind, pure 'Comteism – the religion of Humanity'. In Russia, she declared, 'Auguste Comte comes to his own' (4 January 1932). In the aftermath of the First World War, Comte had again become important to Webb: she quoted Comte on altruism at the conclusion of *Methods of Social Study*, and she found herself returning to the notion of a 'social' religion, a 'religion of Humanity'. Now the Soviet Union seemed, perhaps unwittingly, to be the resurrection and the embodiment of Comtean ideas. She wrote in her diary that she was certain that Comte and even Herbert Spencer had had a great influence among the Russian intellectuals of the 1880s; their influence seemed apparent to her in the kind of society that the Bolsheviks had created (7 March 1932). Not only did she see the Communist Party as a secular 'church', reminiscent of the Comtean church (she waited to see if, like the followers of Comte, the Party members would develop religious ritual),[8] but she also detected the Comtean creed of altruism at the heart of Communist ideals: 'It is because I believe that the day has arrived for the changeover from egotism to altruism – as the mainspring of human life – that I am a Communist' (9 November 1932).

THE 'DARK SIDE'

Even as Webb embraced the Soviet Union as a 'new civilisation', she continued to harbour doubts about certain aspects of this Communist state. Many of these doubts were expressed only in her diary: there she fretted over and condemned the repression, cruelty, violence and terrorism – physical as well as mental – that continued to exist in the society that she hoped would outgrow its 'atavistic' characteristics. From the outset of her enthusiasm for Russia, she worried about what she called the 'disease of orthodoxy', about the sinister dimensions of the very thing that drew her to Soviet Communism in the first place. The paradox was evident to her from the beginning, and she looked forward to solving it through her inquiry into this new society: 'Of course the stop in my mind,' she wrote, 'is how can we reconcile this dominance of a religious order imposing on all citizens a new orthodoxy, with the freedom of the soul of man? How can we combine religious zeal in action with freedom of thought? That is the question which we want to solve by studying Russia' (4 January 1932). She never did resolve this issue, and she never ceased to be disturbed by it, but she continued to assume that a resolution could be found.

At times, the 'denial of free thought and free expression' seemed merely a '*blemish* in the theory and practice of Soviet Communism', and at others, this denial appeared to her to be 'inconsistent with the scientific spirit of endless enquiry into the nature of things', a spirit essential to the Webbs' view of socialism (24 August 1933; 3 April 1935). She regarded certain kinds of repression as 'characteristic of a revolutionary period', but she saw others as 'menacing to [the] future'. 'There is nothing to be said in favour of the disease of orthodoxy,' she admitted; 'human parrots are not attractive animals: there are too many of them in the USSR. The *herd*, whether of wolves or sheep, is a monstrosity in the organisation of human beings' (16 August 1939). She realized that there was 'something missing in their conception of humanity': they ignored 'delicacy and warmth of sympathetic feeling, expression of individual gifts [and] personal charm'. This resulted, she recognized, in behaviour that seemed 'crude and sometimes cruel' and in art that became 'blatant and coarse' (9 November 1932).

But the retardation of scientific investigation and the stunting of artistic endeavour were not, she knew, the most devastating consequences of the 'disease of orthodoxy'. Far worse than these oppressions of the spirit was the 'physical terrorism' that the Webbs did not observe – were not allowed to observe – when they visited Russia in 1932, but which they knew to be 'present everywhere and at all times . . . according to all the available evidence'.[9] They knew of the 'trapdoor disappearance of unwanted personalities, the harrying and backbiting, the purging out of office and power of upright but indiscreet citizens', of the 'atmosphere of suspicion and fear' that was bred within the Party and the society as a whole. 'How far will these evils cease,' she asked in her diary, 'when Soviet Russia feels secure from its internal and external enemies?'[10]

Just a few years after she posed this question, the 'dark side' of

Russia, as she called it, forced itself upon the notice of the whole world in the form of the Soviet 'Show' Trials, the mock Treason Trials, of 1936. Webb withstood this 'nasty shock . . . for the defenders of Soviet Communism in foreign parts', but not without a temporary loss of confidence in the new society she had so enthusiastically welcomed:

> To reopen a criminal indictment concerning a particular episode when the principal individuals accused have already been tried, convicted and are in confinement, is repugnant. . . . One has just to shrug one's shoulders and mutter 'After all the Soviet government has only just emerged from the middle ages', which is not quite consistent with welcoming Soviet Communism as a new *civilisation*. . . . [A]ll the leading men in the USSR have been brought up in the atmosphere of violent revolution, of underground conspiracies, and ruthless killings and they cannot get out of this pattern of behavior. . . . These Soviet leaders are heroic . . . but they all have the same mentality of ruthless revolutionaries when brought up against opponents to their policy – to their particular view of social expediency – they spy and conspire – they kill and are killed.   (28 August 1936)

Such an incident did not, indeed, appear to be an indication of the coming-of-age of a 'new civilisation', and Webb was not a believer true enough to accept a justification for these trials. She was guilty, instead, of recognizing the barbarity of the episode, of trying first to explain and then to forget it.

Three years after the staging of the Soviet Treason Trials, Russia signed a non-aggression pact with Nazi Germany and agreed to the joint invasion and occupation of Poland. Once again, Webb was in despair at the seemingly inconsistent behaviour of the Soviet Union. She had often dwelt on the differences between Communism and Nazism in her diary: Hitler's Germany was a 'creedocracy' without any creed, a society led, not by reason, but by 'mere emotion, and that of a debased character'. Fascism represented 'a return to the desire to dominate and to kill, to revenge yourself, to suppress and stamp on your enemies' (24 August 1933). Leninism, on the other hand, was essentially 'humanitarian and pacifist'; it was 'based on science', not mere emotion, and it was, unlike Nazism, free of 'racial pride and prejudice'. This last point had come to be peculiarly important to Webb. During the 1930s, she can be said to have had a revival of interest in the Jews, and this interest was due, in no small part, to the rise of Hitler and to her own sense of connection to the Jews who were persecuted and murdered in Germany. In her own mind, she opposed the anti-Semitism of Germany to what she understood to be an atmosphere of receptivity and tolerance of Jews in the Soviet Union.

When Webb visited Russia, she took special note of the Jews she met there: a family from Philadelphia who were resettling in their native Russia, her guide in Leningrad who came from a rich Polish family, her interpreter and companion in Moscow who had been born in Warsaw and had spent the years between 1905 and 1917 in Chicago as an emigrée.[11] She decried the 'new fervour of anti-Semitism' that she detected in the *anti*-Communist sentiments of British acquaintances, among them her nephew-by-marriage Malcolm Muggeridge (29 March 1933). In her diary, she marvelled at the continued power and unity of the Jews 'in spite of their dispersion', and at the 'glorious spiritual and intellectual heritage' – 'Moses, David, Elijah, Jesus, Paul, Spinoza, Marx and Einstein' – of one small group of people (1 May 1933). And it was in the Soviet Union, she believed, that Jews would find their home. She mentioned repeatedly the autonomous Jewish republic that she had heard was being planned in Russia, and she and Sidney devoted a special section of their *Soviet Communism* to the improved condition of Russian Jews under Communism.[12] With peculiar voraciousness, she read the works of Jewish writers – novels by Sholem Asch and articles by Waldo Frank – and quoted from them at length in her diary. Asch seemed to her to express her 'own metaphysical background' in *Three Cities*, a novel demonstrating 'the revolutionary strain among all sections of Russian and Polish Jews' (14 November 1933). Like Frank, she believed that Jews, in order to survive, had to follow Marx and Spinoza, to pursue material safety and security first and a 'Spinozistic sense of God' second (29 December 1933). While Germany embarked on the destruction of the Jewish people with whom she had always felt a tenuous and all-but-unacknowledged identification, Russia would receive and liberate them.

How doubly chilling, then, was the news of the Nazi–Soviet Pact. Webb felt simultaneously confused and horrified. Sidney 'remained calm' at first, but Beatrice declared it 'A day of holy horrors' (23 August 1939). She tried to recover her composure by imagining that the pact would benefit China and Hong Kong, but she could not successfully delude herself to that degree. On 23 August, when she first recorded the news of the pact, she confessed only to being 'shaken as to the integrity of the international policy of the New Civilisation'; but two days later she was 'in a state of collapse' – 'knocked almost senseless' (25 August 1939). The German–Soviet Pact was 'a greater disaster to all the Webbs have stood for' and 'a tragedy . . . so far as our faith in Soviet Communism is concerned'. During the first weeks of September, she toyed with possible rationalizations for the pact, but by 18 September, she again confronted the undeniable horror of the situation. 'Satan has won hands down', she declared, condemning the villainy of Stalin and Molotov, whose broadcast to the Russian people justifying the Red Army's march into Poland she found 'a monument of international immorality – cloaked in cynical sophistry' (18 September 1939). 'To me,' she continued, 'it seems the blackest tragedy in human history.'

Sidney counselled patience and refused to be 'downcast'. He felt sure that the episode would be forgotten and the 'new civilisation' ultimately and properly established (18 September 1939). Beatrice, then eighty-one years old, never fully recovered from this blow, but for the next four years, until her death in 1943, she continued to cling with enfeebled determination to the idea of society's rebirth under Communism. In the diaries of the very last years of her life, she is concerned with the deaths of friends, the Second World War, the importance of her diary and her fear of dying long before or long after Sidney. She writes little about Russia, the subject that had dominated her diaries throughout most of the decade of the 1930s. In April 1943, however, twenty days before her death, she felt able to record that she and Sidney had finally been 'proved . . . right about *Soviet Communism*' (10 April 1943). After the Russians had defeated Germany at Stalingrad in the winter of 1942–3, the Soviet Union seemed to her the only society that could possibly survive the War.

THE CONTRADICTIONS OF BEATRICE WEBB: SOVIET UNION AS PARADIGM

In her attachment to Soviet Communism, Beatrice Webb was clearly in contradiction with herself: she was drawn to Russia because she craved an orthodoxy, and she doubted Russia because she feared orthodoxy as a 'disease'. To understand this contradiction is to understand the central problematic of Webb's life, and to explain it one must try to unravel the peculiar quest for faith that dominated her existence and her most private literary works, her autobiography and her diaries. After a close reading of these works, it becomes clear that Webb sought two distinct, though obviously connected, principles in what she variously called 'religion', 'creed', 'orthodoxy' or 'faith': (i) *morality*, or a system of ethics, and (ii) *'mysticism'*, an individual experience of spirituality or 'communion' or prayer. The community of Bacup, for example, represented a pefect synthesis of these two elements: there she detected the existence of true inner belief, or spirituality, along with a clearly determined and soundly enforced social morality to govern individual action.

At times, Webb believed that the source for moral direction, for the determination of life's 'Purpose', would be found, not in an external power or structure, but *within* each individual. 'In any case,' she and Sidney wrote at the conclusion of *Methods of Social Study*, 'it is not to the intellectual outcome of science, but to some feeling in the *individual consciousness*, that we possess.'[13] Social re-organization would not suffice in the apprehension of 'Purpose', and an internal mechanism would have to be relied upon. The problem for Webb, as for many who looked inward for a source of ethics in a secularized age (and here we think primarily of Freud), was to determine how the mechanism was established, what it reflected, how it originated. She could never identify, however, more than a vague original source: this internal ethic was, she felt, 'associated with faith in a spirit of *love* at work in the universe' (5 December 1925). Individual 'guides to conduct' emerged out of the area of 'emotive thought', out of a striving for the 'beautiful', the 'good' or the 'holy'.[14]

At other times, however, when belief in an internal moral force eluded her, she looked to an external power to provide and, indeed, enforce a morality. The Communist Party in Russia would be just such a power. The Party members, constituting a kind of 'religious order', would serve as an example of right living, and set down rules for the lives of others. Her attraction to Comteism and to the notion of a leading élite, or a Fabian 'junta', bespoke her belief that the 'mass' of individuals had to be controlled, guided, dominated by a select, exemplary group of powerful and impeccably 'moral' people. But again, the ultimate source of this power or morality remained unclear. From where, in a 'religion of Humanity', did the élite's unfailing knowledge of right and wrong derive? In the case of Russia, was it from Marxism or Leninism (or from Marxism–Leninism)? Or was it from Stalin, or from the Party itself? When Frederic Harrison took the young Beatrice Webb to the Positivist Hall in 1889 to hear a sermon on 'living for others', she found the address to be 'a valiant effort to make a religion out of nothing; a pitiful attempt by poor humanity to turn its head round and worship its tail' (p. 145). She did not always manage to maintain this perspective on philosophies that celebrated humanity and, in the process, elevated one part of humanity to godhead.

   Intimately related to this search for moral power in an external, organized structure or body of people was Beatrice Webb's habitual confusion of morality with prohibition, abstinence and asceticism. The majority of people, herself included, had to be regulated, inhibited and censored, she believed, in order to behave in an ethical manner. In her admiration for Soviet Russia, she confused the puritanical regimen of Party members with moral force. In the same spirit, using the same logic (or lack thereof), she equated 'altruism' with self-sacrifice and self-denial, and she regarded 'egotism' or self-indulgence as the equivalent of self-expression. Marriage to Sidney Webb, for example, had the virtue, she said, of constituting a 'denial' of self rather than an 'indulgence' of self. In an egalitarian state, as she believed the Soviet Union to be, everyone had to 'serve and *suffer* for the community', as if the first action was necessarily defined by or at least accompanied by the second (9 November 1932). 'You have got to serve', she wrote in the last months of her life, alluding to the need to keep alive her faith in Communism despite painful doubts, 'however much you may suffer by day and night' (10 April 1943). It was almost as if the years of agonizing over Russia's pact with Hitler made 'service' to the Communist ideal a nobler effort. These confusions were obvious too in her perception of an opposition between D. H. Lawrence's 'cult of sex' and the

Party discipline of Russian Communists. 'I prefer,' she wrote in reference to this opposition, 'the hard hygienic view of sex, and the conscious subordination of sexuality to the task of "building up Socialism" characteristic of Soviet Russia' (30 October 1932). Webb's positing of an antithetical relationship between sexuality and Socialism was not, of course, peculiar to her, but it was wholly consistent with the dichotomies, confusions and conflations that characterized her own particular understanding of ethical life.

What was the reason for this habit of thought? Why did she wish to relegate responsibility for individual morality to an absolute authority, and why did she confuse morality with asceticism? We can answer that all of this moralism is but a reflection of what we have come to call 'Victorianism', but we can also recognize in Webb the individual dynamics of personality and circumstance that made her peculiarly susceptible to this aspect of 'Victorianism'. Her search for a prohibiting, a punishing, morality in the form of a 'religion' was linked to her own continuing mistrust and fear of the nature of her own 'individual consciousness', a distinctly unreliable (she thought) source of ethical guidance. Among the instincts and impulses that caused her to doubt herself, that she hid from others and kept in confinement, were yearnings toward art, toward fiction-writing, toward public recognition and fame, toward sexual expression and fulfilment. In her adolescence, she reprimanded herself for these yearnings and for the uncontrolled daydreaming that was their expression. She called these desires 'vain' and 'egotistical', and she condemned herself for longings deemed inappropriate to her sex. She would not allow herself to 'indulge' in the writing of fiction, and she denied herself the reality of sexual feeling that she had come to associate only with men, like Joseph Chamberlain, who wished to control and suppress. She subordinated certain of her personal aspirations to Sidney's, and embraced 'partnership' as a preventive measure against 'egotism'. Demands for gratification of self were dangerous and had, ultimately, to be checked.

Webb gave up 'subjective' social investigation for a more dispassionate, more distanced form of social and historical research. She abandoned the method of disguise, the strategy that allowed for this subjective investigation and for expression of parts of the submerged self. Disguise and her earliest work – on sweated labourers and dock-workers – also enabled Webb to identify with segments of the working class and to appreciate their importance in the politics of social change. As I have suggested, it was her interest in working-class organization that first alerted Sidney and the Fabians to the significance of trade unionism. The Webbs' *History of Trade Unionism*, first published in 1894, represented an extension of the subjects, if not the techniques, of Beatrice's work with Charles Booth and of her research on Co-operation. But the core of Fabian politics and, hence, of the politics to which Beatrice Webb ultimately dedicated herself, did not assign a place of central importance to the working class. Webb's own class biases seemed to reassert their dominance in her attraction to the power of élites, whether the Fabian oligarchy or the Russian Communist Party.

We have seen how the customarily thwarted impulses of her nature erupted after two decades of marriage and contributed to her breakdown during the First World War, and we have seen how the writing of *My Apprenticeship* answered the need for creation and self-revelation. For the most part, however, she confined self-expression to two entirely private realms: diary-writing and prayer. In the diary, which she called, according to her own logic, a 'vent for my egotism', many of the mistrusted and hidden impulses found a voice. Her habit of prayer, confounding to her contemporaries and to the modern critic alike, was a form of supremely personal experience protected from the scrutiny of others, and it was, therefore, an experience of freedom. She expressed in prayer and in her diary what were, for her, both the most dangerous and the most precious, the most profane and the most holy, parts of herself. And here we arrive at the contradictions of self that were reproduced in her contradictory attitude toward Russia. Missing from Russia were 'delicacy and warmth of sympathetic feeling [and] *free expression of individual gifts*'; utterly absent was 'a *state of mind which I associate with Prayer*' (29 November 1932). Soviet Communism, the great reviver of 'orthodoxy', made the experience of real 'Prayer' an impossibility. The two different elements of religious faith that she sought – morality and mysticism, orthodoxy and personal freedom, ethical direction and spirituality – were at odds in the Soviet Union, and they were at odds within her own life. She repeatedly invested her hopes for moral regeneration in forms of political thought and in personal relationships that were sure to disappoint and even subvert her desires for personal freedom and spiritual – or creative – experience.

Her efforts to restrain her impulses to self-expression were not, of course, wholly successful, for she wrote *My Apprenticeship*, continued to pray and kept her diary until eleven days before her death at eighty-five. She privately celebrated her 'authorship' of the diary, and recognized it as the enduring, uninterrupted part of herself that she would leave 'unfinished' for future generations to read. 'Authorship seems to be a profession from which you cannot retire,' she wrote in the year before she died; 'you long to carry on, however unfit you may be to do so. G.B.S. and H. G. Wells can not stop writing: they will die with an unfinished book on their desk. And *I* shall die with my diary, pen and ink, in a drawer by the side of my bed' (26 August 1942).

Her insistent need to keep writing was not, however, only the result of what Samuel Hynes has called 'self-expression . . . thrust out by the front door . . . [and] come in by the scullery window'.[15] 'Authorship', as Webb referred to her literary profession, also enabled her to express the problematic feelings of doubt, confusion and self-contradiction. In the realms of politics and social science, those realms inhabited by her public persona, she did not allow herself to indulge in uncertainty or equivocation. Post-war despair and disillusionment, doubts about the success of Soviet Communism, uncertainty about her marriage and her childlessness, reservations about Fabianism – these were the stuff of 'literature' and of her diary. The diary released her from rigidity and absolute self-confidence; it freed her, as the strategy of disguise had done, from the constraints of class, of gender and of her own tenuously-held prejudices.

In *My Apprenticeship*, as distinguished from the diary, conflict and contradiction were not only exposed but transcended. Webb chose an autobiographical form that gave intellectual and spiritual debate a central role, a place of prominence. The careful reader of *My Apprenticeship* must reject the 'grim, inhuman [Webb] legend . . . of infallibility . . . [and] omniscience' and put in its place a Beatrice Webb vexed by the problems of what to believe and what to be, of faith and identity. But if she chose this Victorian genre because it allowed her to expose conflict and inner debate, she also chose it for its insistence upon reconciliation and resolution. In the conclusiveness of *My Apprenticeship*, Webb did not shut out or ignore contradiction, as she did in her political and professional life: she created out of contradiction a grand synthesis, a fiction that lent shape and purpose to the chronology of her early life. The disorientation of Webb's post-war years and her final, strained effort to embrace Soviet Communism as the 'new civilisation' confirmed the fictionality of the neat resolutions of *My Apprenticeship*, of its novelistic conclusiveness and its affirmation of Fabianism. The crises, conflicts and spiritual odysseys that informed Beatrice Webb's life were unmasked and traced in her diary and transcended only in the fiction of her autobiography.

Notes

Introduction

1. Ellen Moers, *Literary Women* (Garden City, NY: Doubleday, 1976) p. 11.
2. Dorothy L. Sayers, 'Are Women Human?', in *Unpopular Opinions* (New York: Harcourt Brace, 1947) p. 136.
3. Lytton Strachey, *Eminent Victorians* (New York: Modern Library, 1918) p. 131.
4. Ibid., p. 168.
5. Michael Holroyd, *Lytton Strachey and the Bloomsbury Group: His Work, Their Influence* (London: Penguin, 1971) p. 317.
6. Anne Olivier Bell (ed.), *The Diary of Virginia Woolf* (New York & London: Harcourt Brace Jovanovich, 1977) vol. I, p. 196 (23 September 1918).
7. Gerald Gould, review of *My Apprenticeship*, *Daily Chronicle*, 26 February 1926. A collection of reviews of *My Apprenticeship* can be found among the Passfield Papers, XII.A.2.
8. *The New Machiavelli* was first published in 1911. Two other Wells novels of this period, *Ann Veronica* and *Tomo-Bungay*, also contain attacks on the Fabians.

    In *The New Machiavelli*, Wells includes a thinly disguised rendering of the events surrounding his break with the Fabians. The Fabians distrusted Wells' desire to remake them and to assert control over their Society, but they also disliked his views on marriage and 'free love', and they regarded him as a 'sexual anarchist' (see Samuel Hynes, 'The Fabians': Mrs Webb and Mr Wells', in *The Edwardian Turn of Mind* (Princeton, NJ: Princeton University Press, 1968). They got all the proof they thought they needed of his suspected libertinism when Amber Reeves, the daughter of two leading Fabians, was found to be expecting Wells' child. In his novel, Wells attacks the small-mindedness of those who ostracized him, and defends his own actions as 'human', normal and inevitable. Part of the defence that the narrator, Remington, offers for having left his wife and established a new family with his mistress and child is his 'feminism', which involves the notion that the 'special function' of the modern woman is 'conscious, deliberate motherhood and mothering'. The narrator is able, therefore, to suggest that his wife's childlessness and his mistress' fertility are justification for his change of allegiance. In the light of this peculiar brand of 'feminism' and of the events that prompted the writing of *The New Machiavelli*, Altiora Bailey's 'unwomanliness' takes on a more specific, and an ironic, meaning.
9. H. G. Wells, *The New Machiavelli* (Harmondsworth: Penguin, 1966) p. 158.
10. Ibid., p. 155.

11. Robert J. Scally, *The Origins of the Lloyd George Coalition: The Politics of Social-Imperialism, 1900–1918* (Princeton, NJ, & London: Princeton University Press, 1975) pp. 81–2. Scally's depiction of Beatrice Webb as a skilled hostess is particularly amusing in view of the austerity of the meals served by her: 'a soup, a plain fish, and mutton or boiled fowl and milk pudding, with nothing to drink but whisky and soda, and hot and cold water, and milk and lemonade' (Wells, *The New Machiavelli*, p. 161).

12. Bell, *Diary of Virginia Woolf*, vol. I, p. 26 (3 January 1915).

13. Wells, *The New Machiavelli*, p. 159.

14. Malcolm Muggeridge, *In a Valley of this Restless Mind* (London: George Routledge, 1938) p. 118.

15. See 'My Aunt Bo', the introduction to Kitty Muggeridge and Ruth Adam, *Beatrice Webb, A Life, 1858–1943* (London: Secker & Warburg, 1967). Kitty Muggeridge's mother, Rosy Potter, was never on the best of terms with her older sister Beatrice, particularly during the years after their mother's death when Rosy was in Beatrice's charge. It would be difficult for ill-feeling *not* to play a part in Muggeridge's description of her aunt, and her inevitable bias illustrates the limitations of 'definitive' biographies written by relatives.

16. Ibid., p. 13.

17. Ibid., p. 14. One wonders if Muggeridge is alluding here to her great-grandmother, Mary Seddon Potter, said by some members of the family to have been a gipsy and by others, among them Beatrice Webb, to have been a Jew. See Chapter 6 below.

18. Ibid., p. 14.

19. Shirley Robin Letwin, *The Pursuit of Certainty* (Cambridge: Cambridge University Press, 1965) pp. 348–9.

20. Ibid., p. 357.

21. Review of a reissue of *My Apprenticeship*, *Daily Herald*, 11 April 1929.

22. Review of a reissue of *My Apprenticeship*, *Newcastle Daily Journal*, 11 April 1929.

23. Review of a reissue of *My Apprenticeship*, *Methodist Recorder*, 18 April 1929.

24. R. H. Tawney, 'Beatrice Webb', in *Proceedings of the British Academy, 1943* (London: Oxford University Press, 1943) p. 307.

25. Desmond MacCarthy, 'The Webbs as I Saw Them', in Margaret Cole (ed.), *The Webbs and their Work* (London: Frederick Muller, 1949) p. 128.

26. Bertrand Russell, *Portraits from Memory and Other Essays* (New York: Simon & Schuster, 1951) p. 106.

27. Ibid., pp. 106, 107, 109.

28. Ibid., p. 105.

29. Leonard Woolf, *Sowing, 1880–1904* (New York & London: Harcourt Brace, 1960) p. 48.

30. Ibid., p. 48.

31. F. R. Leavis, introduction to *Mill on Bentham and Coleridge* (London: Chatto & Windus, 1950) p. 18.

32. Ibid., p. 18.

33. Ibid., p. 19.

34. Ibid., p. 26.

35. Hynes observes that among the great modern diarists, only Virginia Woolf is Webb's rival.

36. Samuel Hynes, 'The Art of Beatrice Webb', in *Edwardian Occasions* (New York: Oxford University Press, 1972) p. 158.
37. Ibid., p. 154.
38. Ibid.
39. Ibid., pp. 170–1.
40. At this time, only the first volume has been published. See Norman and Jeanne MacKenzie (eds), *The Diary of Beatrice Webb*, vol. I: *Glitter Around and Darkness Within, 1873–1892* (Cambridge: Harvard University Press; London: Virago Press, 1982).
41. A recent study of the Fabians' relation to the arts tries to correct the impression of the presumed aridity of Fabian aesthetics. In *Fabianism and Culture: A Study in British Socialism and the Arts* (Cambridge University Press, 1982), Ian Britain goes to very great lengths to prove that the Fabians were not the Philistines those like Wells claimed them to be. Britain may be overreacting to certain distortions in historical representations of the Fabians, but he is right to blur the rigid distinctions traditionally perceived between humanist and utilitarian strains of nineteenth-century socialism.
42. Webb's upbringing, the MacKenzies assert, engendered in her a 'profound conflict between . . . her feminine instincts and her desire to be . . . successful in a man's world; and that ambivalence led to the *first great crisis* of her life, when she conceived an obsessive passion for the Radical politician Joseph Chamberlain' (*Diary of Beatrice Webb*, p. xii). The MacKenzies' editing of the diary tends to overestimate, I think, the influence of the Chamberlain episode on Webb's decisions about her work and life, and to minimize both the continuity of her professional aspirations and the centrality of spiritual crises and preoccupations to her youth.
43. Patricia Meyer Spacks, *The Female Imagination* (New York: Avon-Discus, 1976) p. 365.
44. There have been recent efforts made to discuss *My Apprenticeship* in the context of Victorian autobiographical writing. In 'Beatrice Webb's Two Voices: *My Apprenticeship* and Victorian Autobiography' (*English Studies in Canada*, II, 1 (Spring, 1976) pp. 83–96), Ira Nadel analyses the 'historical' and the 'fictional' narrative modes in Webb's autobiography. Alan Mintz makes *My Apprenticeship* the focus of the epilogue to his suggestive study, *George Eliot and the Novel of Vocation* (Cambridge & London: Harvard University Press, 1978). Mintz asserts that Webb, a 'latter-day Dorothea', departed from the classic Victorian idea of vocation in her autobiography by making 'craft', rather than 'calling' or 'divinely inspired mission', her goal. I would argue that Mintz does not fully take into consideration the equally important theme of 'creed' in *My Apprenticeship*, and that Webb's notion of interdependent faith and work is the equivalent of a mid-Victorian concept of vocation. I would agree, however, that history had created new circumstances for the discovery and practice of vocation (particularly for women) by the 1880s and 1890s.

Chapter 1: A Tradition of Victorian Autobiography

1. Southey coined the term 'autobiography' in 1809, but, as Keith Rinehart has pointed out in his essay 'The Victorian Approach to Autobiography' (*Modern Philology*, 51 (February, 1954) pp. 177–87), the word was not firmly established until the 1860s. Rinehart's analysis of the publication dates of 171 major Victorian autobiographies suggests that the number of autobiographies published each year increased steadily throughout the century.

2. M. H. Abrams, *Natural Supernaturalism: Tradition and Revolution in Romantic Literature* (New York: Norton, 1971) pp. 95–6 (my italics). I owe a great deal to Abrams' definition of the 'crisis-autobiography' in the second chapter of his book. For another discussion of this genre, see John Nelson Morris, *Versions of the Self: Studies in English Autobiography from John Bunyan to John Stuart Mill* (New York: Basic Books, 1966).

3. See Beatrice Webb, *My Apprenticeship* (New York: Longman, 1926) p. 139, and Beatrice Webb's Diaries (Passfield Papers), March 1886, June 1878, January 1873, December 1879, March 1877 and March 1878. Many of Webb's reading notes have been left out of the typescript version of her Diaries, and must be read in the original manuscript.

4. Frank D. McConnell, *The Confessional Imagination: A Reading of Wordsworth's 'Prelude'* (Baltimore & London: Johns Hopkins University Press, 1974) pp. 2, 9.

5. See Alan Mintz's *George Eliot and the Novel of Vocation* (Cambridge & London: Harvard University Press, 1978) p. 21, on the idea of vocation as a 'principle of biographical design' for both biographers and autobiographers.

   I use the male pronoun here and elsewhere in this chapter with deliberate intention as it is my point to argue that, until *My Apprenticeship*, this particular form of autobiography was one used by male writers.

6. Jerome Buckley sees this pattern of conversion in much of Victorian literature. See Chapter 5 of *The Victorian Temper* (Cambridge: Harvard University Press, 1951).

7. Avrom Fleishman, *Figures of Autobiography: The Language of Self-Writing in Victorian and Modern England* (Berkeley & Los Angeles: University of California Press, 1983) p. 118.

8. Edmund Gosse, *Father and Son: A Study of Two Temperaments* (New York: Norton, 1963) pp. 231–2.

9. Avrom Fleishman makes great claims for the centrality of *Sartor* to the autobiographical tradition of the nineteenth century: '*Sartor* becomes the paradigmatic text for a line of autobiographical novels of crisis and conversion while the most significant autobiographies of the time (Mill's, Ruskin's, and even Newman's) are written, as it were, in its margins' (*Figures of Autobiography*, p. 135).

10. 'Mark Rutherford' (William Hale White), *Autobiography and Deliverance* (New York: Humanities Press; Leicester University Press, 1969) pp. 36–7.

11. Both Gosse and 'Rutherford' find a substitute for the Deity of their fathers in the Deity of Wordsworthian nature. Mill finds in Wordsworth's 'Immortality' ode a reflection of his own mental crisis, and seeks sustenance in the 'cultivation of the feelings' that Wordsworth's poetry inspires.

12. Thomas Carlyle, 'Goethe', in *Critical and Miscellaneous Essays*, centenary edn

(London: Chapman & Hall, 1899) vol. I, p. 210. This essay was published originally in 1828 in the *Foreign Review* (my italics).

13. Thomas Carlyle, 'Goethe's Helena', in *Critical and Miscellaneous Essays*, vol. I, p. 158.
14. Thomas Carlyle, *Sartor Resartus*, centenary edn (London: Chapman & Hall, 1897) vol. I, p. 133.
15. Abrams, *Natural Supernaturalism*, p. 134.
16. Herbert Spencer, *Autobiography* (New York: Appleton, 1904) vol. I, p. x. H. G. Wells had no such qualms about egoism when he came to write his memoirs: 'If you do not want to explore an egoism,' he warned his readers, 'you should not read autobiography.' See H. G. Wells, *Experiment in Autobiography* (New York: Macmillan, 1934) p. 347.
    John Stuart Mill, *Autobiography* (New York: Columbia University Press, 1924) p. 1.
17. Gosse, Preface to *Father and Son*.
18. Gosse, *Father and Son*, p. 9.
19. Carlyle, *Sartor*, vol. I, p. 2.
20. Gosse, *Father and Son*, p. 19.
21. Ibid., p. 11.
22. John Stuart Mill, 'Coleridge', in J. B. Schneewind (ed.), *Mill's Essays on Literature and Society* (New York: Collier, 1965) p. 293.
23. Ibid., pp. 323–4.
24. Mill, 'Bentham', in *Mill's Essays*, p. 259.
25. Mill, *Autobiography*, p. 117.
26. See Willard Wolfe, *From Radicalism to Socialism* (New Haven, Conn. & London: Yale University Press, 1975) pp. 36ff.
27. Mill, 'Coleridge', in *Mill's Essays*, pp. 340–1.
28. Mill, *Autobiography*, pp. 32–3.
29. 'Mark Rutherford', *Autobiography and Deliverance*, pp. 227–8 (my italics).

Chapter 2: 'My Apprenticeship': the Shape of a Life

1. Beatrice Webb, Diary, 6 October 1885. Hereafter, references to the Webb diaries will be indicated parenthetically in the text by a date. Diary excerpts included in *My Apprenticeship* will be noted to that text.
2. Beatrice Webb, *My Apprenticeship* (New York: Longman, Green, 1926) p. 92. All references to *My Apprenticeship* will be indicated parenthetically in the text by a page number.
3. Beatrice Potter was reading *Dombey and Son* as she tended her dying father, shortly before her marriage to Sidney Webb, and she wrote to Sidney about its effect on her: 'I cried over "Dombey and Son" yesterday evening – I got it down to look at the scene of Mrs Dombey "making the effort" – and found myself running through the whole story. Why are his books so like nightmares in spite of the realism?' (Letter to Sidney Webb, November 1891, Passfield Papers, II.3.ii.)
4. See F. R. Leavis' introduction to *Mill on Bentham and Coleridge* (London: Chatto & Windus, 1950) pp. 23–4, 28.
5. Charles Dickens, *Hard Times* (New York: Norton, 1966) pp. 120–1.

6. Throughout this text, Beatrice Webb will be referred to as 'Webb' rather than 'Potter', and as 'Beatrice' when confusion with Sidney Webb is a possibility.
7. See Georgina Meinertzhagen, *From Ploughshare to Parliament: A Short Memoir of the Potters of Tadcaster* (London: Chiswick Press, 1895).
8. The British Museum Catalogue lists the following works by Lawrence Heyworth: *The Expansion of the Suffrage*, 1861; *Fiscal Policy: Direct and Indirect Taxation Contrasted*, 1861; *Glimpses at the Origin, Mission and Destiny of Man*, 1866; *Mr Heyworth's Address to the Members of the Bacup Mechanics*, 1861; *On the Corn Laws and Other Legislative Restrictions*, 1843.
9. Sarah A. Tooley, 'The Growth of a Socialist: an Interview with Mrs Sidney Webb', in *The Young Woman*, February 1895.
10. Letter from Margaret Harkness to Beatrice Potter, winter 1875–6 (n.d.), Passfield Papers, II.1.ii.
11. In the following chapter, I shall suggest that this crisis and conversion were connected to distress at the emergence of adolescent sexuality and followed a pattern common to other nineteenth-century female autobiographers.
12. Owen Chadwick notes that both Webb and Charles Darwin had their traditional Christian beliefs shaken by the study of Eastern religion. He mentions specifically the influence of Brian Hodgson and Max Muller, both scholars of Sanskrit and Eastern religions. Hodgson, considered the founder of the scholarly study of Buddhism, was the Potters' neighbour in Gloucestershire, and discussed his research with Beatrice, encouraging her to 'question the superiority of Western over Eastern civilization'. See *My Apprenticeship*, pp. 81–4, and Owen Chadwick, *The Victorian Church* (London: Adam & Charles Black, 1970) vol. II, pp. 35–7.
13. Informal will of Beatrice Potter, inserted in MS Diary and dated 1 January 1886.
14. Letter from *Pall Mall Gazette* pasted in MS Diary, 13 February 1886.

Chapter 3: Female Traditions of Autobiography: Memoir and Fiction

1. Of particular interest in this connection are three pieces in Estelle C. Jellinek (ed.), *Women's Autobiography: Essays in Criticism* (Bloomington & London: Indiana University Press, 1980): Jellinek's own introductory essay, 'Women's Autobiography and the Male Tradition', Elizabeth Winston's 'The Autobiographer and her Readers' and Patricia Meyer Spacks' 'Selves in Hiding'. Even as women like Emma Goldman, Eleanor Roosevelt and Golda Meir tell of 'unusual accomplishment' in their memoirs, Spacks comments, 'they finally hide from self-assertion' (p. 132).
2. Nancy K. Miller, 'Women's Autobiography in France: for a Dialectics of Identification' in Sally McConnell-Ginet, Ruth Borker and Nelly Furman (eds), *Women and Language in Literature and Society* (New York: Praeger, 1980) p. 265 (my italics).
3. Cynthia S. Pomerleau, 'The Emergence of Women's Autobiography in England' in Jellinek, *Women's Autobiography*, p. 37. Spacks makes a similar observation: 'Women, for obvious social reasons, have traditionally had

more difficulty than men about making public claims of their own importance. They have excelled in the writing of diaries and journals, which require no such claims, more than in the production of total works offering a coherent interpretation of their experience' ('Selves in Hiding', p. 112).

4. Northrop Frye, *Anatomy of Criticism: Four Essays* (Princeton, NJ: Princeton University Press, 1957) p. 307.

5. *Memoirs of Lady Fanshawe, wife of Sir Richard Fanshawe, Bart., Written by Herself* (London: Henry Colburn & Richard Bentley, 1830) p. 46 (written 1676; first published 1829). For a discussion of women's autobiographies in the seventeenth century, see Chapter x of Paul Delany, *British Autobiography in the Seventeenth Century* (London: Routledge & Kegan Paul, 1969). Four of the six women's memoirs that Delany discusses are biographies of husbands: those by the Duchess of Newcastle, Lady Fanshawe, Lady Ann Halket and Mary, Countess of Warwick. The two others were written by Quaker women, Lucy Hutchinson and Mary Penington.

6. *Memoirs of Mrs Laetitia Pilkington, wife to the Rev. Mr Matthew Pilkington, Written by Herself* (London: R. Griffith, 1748) pp. 1, 302.

7. *A True Relation of the Birth, Breeding and Life of Margaret Cavendish, Duchess of Newcastle, Written by Herself* (Kent: Johnson & Warwick, 1814) pp. 28–31 (written 1656).

8. Delany, *British Autobiography*, p. 158.

9. Harriet Beecher Stowe, introduction to Charlotte Tonna's *Personal Recollections*, in *The Works of Charlotte Elizabeth* (New York: M. W. Dodd, 1849).

10. The best source for a full list of British women's autobiographies is William Matthews, *British Autobiographies* (Berkeley & Los Angeles: University of California Press, 1955).

11. Quoted in Elizabeth Gaskell, *The Life of Charlotte Brontë* (London & New York: Everyman, 1908) p. 102.

12. An English translation of St Theresa's *Life*, published in 1851, revived interest in her among the Victorians. See Ellen Moers, *Literary Women* (Garden City, NY: Doubleday, 1976) pp. 123–4, for a discussion of Theresa's importance to Victorian women, especially George Eliot, and to certain twentieth-century women writers like Gertrude Stein.

13. Harriet Martineau, *Autobiography* (London: Smith, Elder, 1877) vol. I, p. 45; George Sand, *Histoire de ma vie* (Paris: Calmann-Levy, 1925) vol. III, p. 195; Kitty Muggeridge and Ruth Adam, *Beatrice Webb, A Life* (London: Secker & Warburg, 1967) p. 250.

14. *The Life of St Theresa of Jesus*, trans. David Lewis (London: Thomas Baker, 1932) pp. 8–9.

15. Tonna, *Personal Recollections*, p. 3.

16. Edmund Gosse, *Father and Son* (New York: Norton, 1963) pp. 25–6.

17. Martineau, *Autobiography*, vol. II, p. 150.

18. Sigmund Freud, *A General Introduction to Psycho-Analysis*, trans. Joan Riviere (New York: Liveright, 1935) p. 88.

19. Ibid., p. 88.

20. Florence Nightingale, 'Cassandra', reprinted in Ray Strachey, *Struggle* (New York: Duffield, 1930). Cecil Woodham-Smith, Nightingale's biographer, describes 'Cassandra' as a short autobiographical fiction (*Florence Nightingale, 1820–1910* (New York, London, Toronto: McGraw-Hill, 1951) p. 63).

The title of this fragment seems to refer to the subject of dreaming and to the prophetic aspect of Nightingale's own insights into the position of women. Jane Addams wrote her graduating essay at the Rockford Seminary on Cassandra's 'tragic fate always to be in the right, and always to be disbelieved and rejected'. See Jane Addams, *Twenty Years at Hull House* (New York: Signet, 1960) p. 57.

21. Elaine Showalter, 'Florence Nightingale's Feminist Complaint: Women, Religion and *Suggestions for Thought*', *Signs*, vol. 6 (Spring 1981) pp. 395–413.

22. Nightingale, 'Cassandra', p. 397.

23. Herbert Spencer, *Autobiography* (New York: Appleton, 1904) vol. I, p. 86.

24. H. G. Wells, *Experiment in Autobiography* (New York: Macmillan, 1934) p. 74.

25. Bertrand Russell, *Portraits from Memory and Other Essays* (New York: Simon & Schuster, 1951) p. 19.

26. Nightingale, 'Cassandra', p. 397.

27. Ibid., p. 413.

28. W. H. Channing *et al.* (eds), *Memoirs of Margaret Fuller Ossoli* (Boston: Phillips, Sampson, 1852) vol. I, p. 99.

29. Martineau, *Autobiography*, vol. I, pp. 42–3.

30. Annie Besant, *An Autobiography* (Philadelphia: Henry Altemus, 1897) p. 32.

31. Ibid., p. 52.

32. Sand, *Histoire de ma vie*, vol. III, p. 195. Part of this book was translated into English by Maria MacKaye and published as *The Convent Life of George Sand* in Boston in 1893.

33. Sand, *Histoire de ma vie*, vol. III, p. 229.

34. Channing, *Memoirs*, II, 101. Showalter suggests that Florence Nightingale too was attracted to the idea of convent life because she saw it as the 'only real opportunity for the training and hard work she craved' ('Florence Nightingale's Feminist Complaint', p. 405).

35. Nightingale, 'Cassandra', p. 404.

36. The value of these activities was not merely ornamental but practical and pecuniary as well. Such occupation constituted training for a good and advantageous match.

37. Woodham-Smith, *Florence Nightingale*, p. 43.

38. Nightingale, 'Cassandra', p. 406.

39. Martineau, *Autobiography*, vol. I, p. 101.

40. Ibid., vol. I, p. 145.

41. Addams, *Twenty Years at Hull House*, pp. 61–4, 72. Beatrice Webb met Jane Addams when she visited Hull House on her American trip in 1898. She recorded in her 'American Diary' that she was much impressed with Addams and found her 'an interesting combination of the organizer, the enthusiast and the subtle observer of human characteristics'. 'It is she,' Webb continued, 'who has created whatever spirit of reform exists in Chicago.' See David A. Shannon (ed.), *Beatrice Webb's American Diary* (Madison: University of Wisconsin Press, 1963) p. 108.

42. Besant, *An Autobiography*, p. 98.

43. Martineau, *Autobiography*, vol. I, p. 133.

44. Nightingale, 'Cassandra', p. 407.

45. Channing, *Memoirs*, vol. I, p. 229.

46. Ibid., vol. I, p. 11.

47. Beatrice Webb, contemplating what her relations must think of her as she carried out her social investigations and circulated among London socialists before her marriage, speculated that her friends and family probably shook their heads resignedly and thought, ' "We know no more of Beatrice than we should were she a man" ' (27 December 1891).

48. Woodham-Smith, *Florence Nightingale*, p. 280. Showalter suggests that when Nightingale took to her bed, she was turning her mother's and sister's weapons against them ('Florence Nightingale's Feminist Complaint', p. 401).

49. In an article called 'They Stayed in Bed' (*Listener*, 16 February 1956, pp. 245–6), Cecil Woodham-Smith discusses the illnesses of Nightingale, Martineau, Elizabeth Barrett Browning and Charles Darwin as strategies for creating a 'climate in which they could work'. Invalidism was their only means to the peace and solitude necessary for concentrated study.

50. Martineau, *Autobiography*, vol. II, pp. 146–51 (my italics).

51. One woman who suffered almost a complete dissociation of personality while sitting at the bedside of her dying father was Bertha Pappenheim, Freud's 'Anna O.'. In their account of her case of hysteria, Freud and Josef Breuer take note of the tedium of Pappenheim's life, her stifled intelligence and her chronic habit of daydreaming. Pappenheim was born into a middle-class Jewish family in Vienna in 1859, the year after the birth of Beatrice Webb; she became a prominent social worker, philanthropist and feminist. See Sigmund Freud and Josef Breuer, *Studies on Hysteria (1893–1895)*, in *The Standard Edition of the Complete Psychological Works of Sigmund Freud*, trans. James Strachey (London: Hogarth Press, 1953) vol. II, p. 22.

52. Addams, *Fifty Years at Hull House*, p. 75.

53. Ibid., p. 60.

54. Sand, *Histoire de ma vie*, vol. III, p. 269. Sand was raised by two parents, her mother and her grandmother, her father having died when she was four, and it was her grandmother who encouraged her in her studies and in the value of rational pursuits: '*Toute pleine de Jean-Jacques et de Voltaire, elle eût démoli sans pitiés tout l'édifice enchanté de ma imagination.*' Sand's mother, on the other hand, represented to her daughter poetry, music, joy, religious faith and imagination: '*Elle est née en musique et dans le rose: elle aura du bonheur.*' Sand therefore associated the split between reason and imagination, not with a difference between father and mother, but with a difference between grandmother and mother (Ibid., vol. II, p. 273).

55. Virginia Woolf, *A Room of One's Own* (New York & Burlingame: Harcourt, Brace & World, 1929) p. 83.

56. Charlotte Brontë, *Jane Eyre* (Oxford: Shakespeare Head Press, 1931) vol. II, ch. XXIV, p. 45.

57. Ibid., vol. II, ch. XXXV, p. 240.

58. George Eliot, *The Mill on the Floss*, in *The Complete Works of George Eliot* (Edinburgh & London: William Blackwood, 1878–80) vol. II, bk 4, ch. III, p. 35. In *Memoirs of a Dutiful Daughter*, Simone de Beauvoir records her girlhood fantasy of being 'a nun, confined in a cell, confounding my jailer by singing hymns and psalms'. She interprets the fantasy in this way: 'I conveyed the passivity to which my sex had condemned me into active

defiance' (*Memoirs of a Dutiful Daughter*, trans. James Kirkup (Penguin, 1963) p. 134).

59. Eliot, ii, bk 7, ch. v, p. 400. Recent feminist criticism of *The Mill on the Floss* has stressed the logic, appropriateness and even the liberating nature of Maggie's death. See especially Mary Jacobus, 'The Question of Language: Man of Maxims and *The Mill on the Floss*', *Critical Inquiry*, vol. 8 (winter 1981), and Gillian Beer, 'Beyond Determinism: George Eliot and Virginia Woolf', in Mary Jacobus (ed.), *Women Writing and Writing About Women* (London: Croom Helm, 1979).

60. Charlotte Brontë, *Villette* (Oxford: Shakespeare Head Press, 1931) vol. i, ch. vii, pp. 92–3.

Chapter 4: 'My Apprenticeship': Autobiographical Resolution

1. When Richard Potter died in January of 1892 (his daughter Beatrice was then thirty-four), *The Times* obituary described his nine daughters in the following way: 'Mr Potter leaves nine daughters, eight of whom are married, the remaining one being Miss Beatrice Potter, the well-known writer on the co-operative and other movements'. (*The Times*, 4 January 1892, p. 10.)

2. From a number of accounts, it is clear that Laurencina Heyworth Potter was, in Herbert Spencer's words, 'somewhat of a notability' and an exceptionally impressive woman. As a girl, she was active in Anti-Corn Law agitation and acted as secretary of a committee to get signatures from women for a petition to send to Parliament.

   After her marriage, Mrs Potter was less active politically, but took up an extensive study of languages. Hippolyte Taine, in his *Notes sur l'Angleterre*, remarks on the superior intellectual seriousness of the English woman, and describes the following incident by way of an example: 'M——, being invited to the country, discovered that the mistress of the house knew much more Greek than himself, apologised, and retired from the field; then, out of pleasantry, she wrote down his English sentence in Greek. Not that this female Hellenist is a woman of the world, and even stylish. Moreover, she has nine daughters, two governesses, servants in proportion, a large, well-appointed house, frequent and numerous visitors. . . . These gatherings of faculties might make us reflect.' (Hippolyte Taine, *Notes on England*, trans. W. F. Rae (New York: Henry Holt, 1885) p. 93.) Webb tells us in her autobiography (p. 15) that 'M——' was Michel Chevalier, whose work her mother translated. The woman in question is, of course, Laurencina Potter.

   One of Mrs Potter's accomplishments was the authorship of a novel, *Laura Gay*, published anonymously in 1856, which tells the fictionalized story of Richard and Laurencina Potter's courtship. Laura Gay, the heroine, is said to be 'killing herself with study' and to be disillusioned by the idea that men would take offence at an intellectual woman: 'Laura, having lived all her life in the most unreserved intimacy with a man of superior mind [her father], whose chief solace and delight it had been to cultivate her intellectual faculties, had no conception that the nobler sex were capable of jealousy on this subject.' See *Laura Gay, A Novel* (London: Hurst & Blackett, 1856) pp. 131–2, 253.

3. Margaret Mead, a pioneering social scientist of a later generation, wrote of her mother in *her* autobiography: 'In my life I realized every one of her unrealized ambitions.' See Margaret Mead, *Blackberry Winter: My Earliest Years* (New York: Pocket Books, 1975) p. 28.

4. Richard Potter invited Daniel Meinertzhagen, a young banker, to Standish as a possible match for one of his daughters. When Georgina showed some interest, Potter 'coerced the family firm into increasing Daniel's share of the proceeds of their merchant banking business'. (Kitty Muggeridge and Ruth Adam, *Beatrice Webb, A Life* (London: Secker & Warburg, 1967) p. 45.)

5. Webb refers to a 'secularist friend' who once cross-examined her as to what exactly she meant by 'prayer'. This friend was Leonard Woolf, whose humorous account of his conversations with Beatrice about religion and prayer, during which her violent arguing once caused her skirt to fall to her feet, appears in his memoirs. Leonard Woolf, *Sowing: An Autobiography of the Years 1880 to 1904* (New York & London: Harcourt Brace, 1960) pp. 46–7, 49–50.

6. Shirley Letwin, having read Webb's diaries (which are, to my mind, inconclusive on the question of a Chamberlain proposal), declares with some authority that the idea of such a proposal is pure myth. Letwin's animus against Webb leads her to imply that such a myth originated out of Webb's own chagrin at Chamberlain's failure to propose. See Shirley Letwin, *The Pursuit of Certainty* (Cambridge University Press, 1965) p. 358.

   Kitty Muggeridge records in her biography of her aunt that according to 'family legend', Chamberlain did indeed propose and Beatrice did in fact turn him down: 'On one occasion . . . Chamberlain was seen hurrying away from York House, pale-faced and distraught, while Beatrice was discovered weeping indoors. "I've just refused him," she sobbed.' See Muggeridge and Adam, *Beatrice Webb, A Life* (London: Secker & Warburg, 1967) p. 93.

   Norman and Jeanne MacKenzie give a brief but accurate account of the relationship with Chamberlain in Chapter 8 of *The Fabians* (New York: Simon & Schuster, 1977). See, too, Jeanne MacKenzie's *A Victorian Courtship: The Story of Beatrice Potter and Sidney Webb* (Oxford University Press, 1979) and Part II of the MacKenzies' edition of the Webb diaries (vol. I).

7. As this diary entry suggests, Webb lost her desire to work or to study in the wake of her relationship with Chamberlain. 'It is true my personal ambition is dead,' she wrote later that same year, 'and I feel now that the time and strength devoted to its fulfilment was wasted. . . . But though I was deceived by my conceit, my motive was pure – sprang from a desire to do honest work and to live sincerely according to my nature' (6 November 1884). When, in their introduction to *The Diary of Beatrice Webb*, the MacKenzies suggest that Webb took refuge 'in the anodyne of work' after the Chamberlain affair, they overlook this temporary reaction against her own ambition, and they underestimate the importance of work to Webb before Chamberlain appeared on the scene (see *The Diary of Beatrice Webb*, vol. I, p. xii).

8. Informal will of Beatrice Potter, dated 1 January 1886, inserted in Diary (Passfield Papers).

9. Letter to Vanessa Bell, June 1911, quoted in Quentin Bell, *Virginia Woolf, A Biography* (New York: Harcourt Brace Jovanovich, 1972) vol. I, p. 176.

When one considers Webb from the point of view of her sexual identity, one is struck by the similarities between Webb and Virginia Woolf, rather than by the differences that reading Woolf's letters and diaries suggests. Much attention has been paid to the harshly critical comments about Webb in Woolf's writing (see, for example, letters numbered 770, 771, 812, 984, 1121 in *The Letters of Virginia Woolf*, vol. II, ed. Nigel Nicolson and Joanne Trautmann (New York & London: Harcourt Brace Jovanovich, 1976)); and there is no question that Webb found Woolf an alien creature in return. Still, it is worth quoting Webb's diary entry on hearing of Woolf's suicide: it reveals something about Webb's awareness of Woolf's feelings about her and a certain humility about their differences: '7 April 1941   In the morning news: "Mrs Virginia Woolf": "missing from her home since Friday 28": "assumed drowned in the River Ouse". During the day and for some days afterwards, ghosts from the past haunt me – that talented tall woman with her classic features – her father Leslie Stephen . . . with whom I used to discuss in the '80s, English History in the house of Alice Green. . . .

'Virginia was a beautiful woman and a writer of great charm and finesse – in her *uniqueness* the most outstanding of our women novelists. . . . [W]e never became sympathetic friends. I think we liked them better than they liked us. In a way which I never understood I offended Virginia. I had none of her sensitiveness, her understanding of the inner life of the subjective man.'

The one thing the two women seemed to have agreed upon, in fact, was the moral justification of suicide. 'We enjoyed our Sunday with you and Mr Webb so much,' Woolf wrote to Mrs Webb in the spring of 1931, 'I wanted to tell you, but was too shy, how much I was pleased by your views upon the possible justification of suicide. Having made the attempt myself [in 1913], from the best of motives I thought – not to be a burden on my husband – the conventional accusation of cowardice and sin has always rather rankled. So I was glad of what you said.' (*The Letters of Virginia Woolf*, vol. IV, p. 305.)

10. In Chapter 5, I shall discuss in some detail these 'strong women' Webb came to know in the East End.

11. Letter from Beatrice Potter to Sidney Webb, January 1892 (Passfield Papers, II.3.ii).

12. Letter from Beatrice Potter to Sidney Webb, 2 May 1890 (Passfield Papers, II.3.ii).

13. Numerous English and American women writers in the eighteenth and nineteenth centuries married non-Anglo-Saxon men, thereby facilitating their own unconventional existences, as marrying a man of a lower class did for Webb. Ellen Moers alludes to this phenomenon in *Literary Women*, and mentions as examples the marriages of Hester Thrale Piozzi, Fanny Burney D'Arblay, Margaret Fuller Ossoli, Bessie Parkes Belloc and Virginia Stephen Woolf. It might be said that Leonard Woolf's Jewishness acted to loosen the bonds of conventional marriage as Sidney Webb's lower middle-class origins did.

14. Letter from Ella Pycroft to Beatrice Potter, 10 January 1892 (Passfield Papers, II.1.ii). When Beatrice and Sidney were finally married, Kate Potter Courtney made the following entry in her diary: 'Our Beatrice is

married to Sidney Webb in the St Pancras Vestry Hall – a prosaic almost sordid ceremony – our civil marriages are not conducted with much dignity and seem rather to suggest a certain shadiness in the contracting partners.' (Diary of Kate Courtney, Courtney Papers, British Library of Political and Economic Science.)

15. Letter from Mary Playne to Beatrice Potter, January 1892 (Passfield Papers, II.1.ii).

16. Letter from Charles Booth to Beatrice Potter, 15 October 1890 (Passfield Papers, II.1.ii).

17. Although Webb did not foresee that Herbert Spencer would dismiss her as his literary executor after her marriage to Sidney, she did realize that aligning herself with a Fabian was a kind of treason against Spencer's teachings. While staying in Spencer's London flat in his absence, during a period when her engagement to Sidney was still a secret, she recorded with some glee the irony of working in the flat with Sidney while Spencer's spirit looked on: 'Poor Herbert Spencer: if he had seen us evening after evening working away together, undermining the Individualism of the British race, with intervals of human nature [Webb's euphemism for lovemaking]. His bust and portrait look down on us beneficently with philosophical resignation to the inevitable' (19 August 1891).

18. Letter from Arabella Fisher to Beatrice Potter, no date, but likely summer 1890 (Passfield Papers, II.1.ii).

19. Letter from Arabella Fisher to Beatrice Potter, 10 October 1890 (Passfield Papers, II.1.ii).

20. Letter from Beatrice Potter to Sidney Webb, 6 October 1890 (Passfield Papers, II.3.ii). See also the new edition of Webb letters, Norman MacKenzie (ed.), *The Letters of Sidney and Beatrice Webb* (Cambridge University Press, London School of Economics and Political Science, 1978) vol. I.

21. Letter from Beatrice Potter to Sidney Webb, 6 October 1890 (Passfield Papers, II.3.ii). It is interesting to compare the courtship letters of Beatrice Potter and Sidney Webb with those of Virginia Stephen and Leonard Woolf. The men in both cases were persistent supplicators, the women hesitant, frank about their lack of sexual desire and conscious that if they could but love these suitors they would be wise to do so. 'Again, I want everything,' Virginia wrote to Leonard, 'love, children, adventure, intimacy, work. . . . So I go from being half in love with you . . . to the extreme of wildness and aloofness. I sometimes think that if I married you, I could have everything – and then – is it the sexual side of it that comes between us? As I told you the other day, I feel no physical attraction in you. There are moments – when you kissed me the other day was one – when I feel no more than a rock. And yet your caring for me as you do almost overwhelms me.' (Quoted in Bell, *Virginia Woolf*, vol. I, p. 185.)

22. Letter from Beatrice Potter to Sidney Webb, May 1890 (Passfield Papers, II.3.ii).

23. The second volume of Webb's autobiography, which covers the years 1892 to 1911, is entitled *Our Partnership*. It lacks the thematic coherence of *My Apprenticeship*, and is essentially a memoir, rather than an autobiography.

Chapter 5: Women's Work

1. For a recent account of Webb's ambivalent feminism, see Barbara Caine, 'Beatrice Webb and the "Woman Question" ', *History Workshop Journal*, 14 (Autumn 1982) pp. 23–43.

2. Hippolyte Taine, *Notes on England*, trans. W. F. Rae (New York: Henry Holt, 1885) p. 91.

3. See Geoffrey Best, *Mid-Victorian Britain, 1851–1875* (New York: Schocken, 1972) p. 101, and Ray Strachey, *Struggle* (New York: Duffield, 1930) p. 187.

4. G. M. Young, *Victorian England: Portrait of an Age* (London: Oxford University Press, 1960) pp. 90–1.

5. Frances Power Cobbe, 'Social Science Congresses, and Women's Part in Them', *Macmillan's Magazine* (December 1861) pp. 88–9.

6. Annie Besant, 'Political Status of Women', in John Saville (ed.), *A Selection of the Social and Political Pamphlets of Annie Besant* (New York: Augustus M. Kelley, 1970) p. 6.

7. Strachey, *Struggle*, p. 208.

8. Ibid., p. 304.

9. Viola Klein, 'The Emancipation of Women: its Motives and Achievements', in *Ideas and Beliefs of the Victorians* (New York: Dutton, 1966) p. 265.

10. Gareth Stedman Jones, *Outcast London* (Oxford: Oxford University Press, 1971) pp. 269–70.

11. E. J. Hobsbawm, 'The Fabians Reconsidered', in *Labouring Men: Studies in the History of Labour* (Garden City, NY: Doubleday, Anchor, 1967) pp. 295–321. Between 1851 and 1881, the number of people in professions and related services increased by a third, between 1881 and 1911 by two thirds (ibid., p. 316).

12. Ibid., p. 303. In 1890, forty-nine out of a total membership of 188 were female; in 1906, 253 out of 1060 were female. The decrease in percentage of females from 1890 to 1906 might suggest a tendency for active women to join suffrage movements in the first decade of the twentieth century, rather than socialist movements.

13. For the influence of the young Beatrice Webb on Shaw's heroines, see Kitty Muggeridge and Ruth Adam, *Beatrice Webb, A Life* (London: Secker & Warburg, 1967) p. 142.

14. Biographical information on Octavia Hill was taken from C. E. Maurice (ed.), *Life of Octavia Hill* (London: Macmillan, 1913) and E. Moberly Bell, *Octavia Hill* (London: Constable, 1942).

15. Octavia Hill, 'Four Years' Management of a London Court', *Macmillan's Magazine*, July 1869, reprinted in *Homes of the London Poor* (London: Macmillan, 1883) pp. 29–30.

16. Jones, *Outcast London*, p. 256.

17. Hill, 'Four Years' Management of a London Court', p. 55.

18. Ibid., pp. 26–7. For a fuller description of Hill's scheme for the management of working-class dwellings, see Jones, *Outcast London*, pp. 193–6, and for a more general discussion of housing schemes, p. 179ff.

19. Hill, 'Four Years' Management of a London Court', p. 37.

20. Octavia Hill, 'The Work of Volunteers in the Organization of Charity',

Macmillan's Magazine, October 1872, reprinted in *Homes of the London Poor*, p. 66.

21. Bell, *Octavia Hill*, p. 257.

22. Letter from Octavia Hill to Mr S. Cockerell, 22 November 1890, as quoted in Maurice, *The Life of Octavia Hill*, p. 515. Hill disliked the use of the word 'slums' and preferred the euphemism 'courts' to 'slum dwellings' and 'tenements'.

23. Ella Pycroft eventually turned to teaching and became an educational advisor to the Technical Education Board of the London County Council in 1893. Maurice Paul, like Webb, later worked with Charles Booth on his study of the London poor and, much later, became active in the International Socialist Movement.

24. Highest rent, for two large rooms on the ground floor: 6s. 6d. Lowest rent, for one small room on the fourth floor: 1s. 1d. (*Katherine Buildings, A Record of the Inhabitants*, Collected Miscellany no. 43, British Library of Political and Economic Science).

25. Quoted in Webb, *My Apprenticeship*, pp. 253–4.

26. Report, January 1886, from Ella Pycroft to Edward Bond, director of the East End Dwelling Company (*Katherine Buildings, A Record of the Inhabitants*).

27. John Law (Margaret Harkness), *A City Girl, A Realistic Story* (London: Vizitelly, 1887) pp. 10–11.

28. Ibid., p. 11.

29. In another novel, *George Eastmont* (London: Burns & Oates, 1905), Harkness refers to the female medical students, journalists and artists among whom she lived in London as 'she-boys'.

30. A number of the early suffragists campaigned first for votes for unmarried women. See, for example, M. O. W. Oliphant, 'The Grievances of Women', *Fraser's Magazine*, n.s. XXI (May 1880) pp. 678–710. Mrs Oliphant argues that if householding and rate-paying are the conditions for suffrage, then a married woman 'votes in her husband', but a single woman householder is completely unrepresented.

31. Best, *Mid-Victorian Britain*, p. 101.

32. Josephine E. Butler (ed.), *Woman's Work and Woman's Culture* (London: Macmillan, 1869).

33. Ibid., Introduction, p. xxxv.

34. Frances Cobbe, 'Social Science Congresses', p. 89.

35. Ibid., p. 90.

36. George Gissing, *The Odd Women* (New York: Norton, 1971) p. 37.

37. Letters from Ella Pycroft to Beatrice Potter (Passfield Papers, II.l.ii).

38. Edward Bond, one of the original directors of the East End Dwelling Company, was also one of the leaders of the COS and served for a few years on the London County Council.

39. See Rose Squire, *Thirty Years in the Public Service: an Industrial Retrospect* (London: Nisbet, 1927), and Mary Augusta Ward, *A Writer's Recollections* (New York & London: Harper, 1918).

40. Squire, *Thirty Years in the Public Service*, p. 116.

41. Much of the information on Harkness is gleaned from her letters to Beatrice Potter in the Passfield Papers, Section II.1.ii. See also John Goode,

'Margaret Harkness and the Socialist Novel', in Gustav Klaus (ed.), *The Socialist Novel in Britain* (New York: St Martin's Press, 1982) pp. 45–67.

42. Letter from Ella Pycroft to Beatrice Potter, 4 May 1890 (Passfield Papers). Peter Keating has noted that Harkness was remarkable among Victorian novelists for her conscious effort to write about the poor from a working-class point of view. See Keating, *The Working Classes in Victorian Fiction* (New York: Barnes & Noble, 1971) pp. 242, 245.

43. Quoted in Vineta Colby, *The Singular Anomaly* (New York: New York University Press, 1970) p. 74.

44. See Yvonne Kapp, *Eleanor Marx* (New York: Pantheon, 1976) vol. II, p. 258.

45. Eleanor Marx, like Amy Levy, was a suicide.

46. For Eleanor Marx in the East End, see ibid., vol. II, pp. 261–4; for Marx and the Jews see ibid., vol. II, pp. 510ff.

47. Letter from Beatrice Potter to Richard Potter, August 1885 (Passfield Papers).

48. Letter from Ella Pycroft to Edward Bond, 6 January 1886 in *Katherine Buildings, A Record of the Inhabitants*.

49. Letter from Beatrice Potter to Richard Potter, August 1885 (Passfield Papers).

50. Ibid.

51. This essay on 'social diagnosis' was never published but appears as Appendix 'A' of *My Apprenticeship*. A reading notebook of Webb's from 1886 contains notes on the history of the Corn Laws, the Factory Bill of 1851, the work of Lords Grey and Salisbury, unemployment in 1870, the Trades Union Bill, the use of statistics, Education Bills, the School Enquiry Commission, the history of Ireland and its penal laws, Toynbee and Fawcett on Political Economy, the Agricultural Employment Bill, Ricardo's theory of rents, Foreign Trade in 1871, Adam Smith, Jevons and Marshall on economics (Passfield Papers).

52. Ellen Moers has written suggestively on the peculiar affinity nineteenth-century women writers felt for the subjects of money-making and jobs, and she attributes it, in part, to their fascination with those realities of life that were denied them. (Moers, *Literary Women*, p. 83, and see all of Chapter 4, 'Money, The Job and Little Women: Female Realism'.)

53. For Charlotte Elizabeth Tonna, see Wanda Fraiken Neff, *Victorian Working Women* (New York: Columbia University Press, 1929) pp. 16–17, 114; and Ivanka Kovačević and S. Barbara Kanner, 'Blue Book Into Novel: The Forgotten Industrial Fiction of Charlotte Elizabeth Tonna', *Nineteenth Century Fiction*, 25 (1970) pp. 152–74.

54. For Harriet Martineau, see her *Autobiography*, 3 vols (London: Smith, Elder, 1877), and R. K. Webb, *Harriet Martineau, A Radical Victorian* (New York: Columbia University Press, 1960). R. K. Webb actually draws certain parallels between Martineau and Beatrice Webb: they both had the upper-middle-class custom of 'setting people straight', he remarks, and they both wished to exercise this habit on a national scale (p. 48). Dickens described Martineau as ' "grimly bent upon the enlightenment of mankind" ' (ibid., p. 231), and she in turn criticized Dickens's 'vigorous erroneousness' on matters political, legal and economic (Martineau, *Autobiography*, vol. II, p. 378).

55. Virginia Woolf, *A Room of One's Own* (New York & Burlingame: Harcourt, Brace & World, 1929) p. 70.

In *The Feminization of American Culture*, Ann Douglas entitles a chapter on Margaret Fuller's choice of vocation 'Margaret Fuller and the Disavowal of Fiction'. In this chapter, Douglas attempts to explain why, in a 'period when ambitious American women were increasingly seeking careers in literature', Fuller rejected fiction in favour of history. Fuller's predilection for the historical and the real, engendered by the education she received from her father, caused her to find the 'burgeoning ladies' culture' of sentimental literature both unsympathetic and constraining. 'The difficulty for Margaret Fuller from the start,' Douglas asserts, 'was in reconciling her historical consciousness with her feminine identity. . . . "I love best to be a woman," she lamented in her early thirties, "but womanhood is at present too straightly-bound to give me scope." '

As I have been suggesting here and in Part II, and as Virginia Woolf's comment implies, women's attitudes toward fiction and the question of their sexual identities were very much connected, especially for women like Fuller, Martineau and Webb, who had talents and interests which were considered to be 'masculine'.

See Ann Douglas, *The Feminization of American Culture* (New York: Avon, 1978) pp. 313–49.

56. Beatrice Potter, 'A Lady's View of the Unemployed at the East', *Pall Mall Gazette*, 18 February 1886.

57. Stedman Jones observes that in the 1880s the attention of people concerned with chronic poverty shifted from the evil influences of indiscriminate charity, drink, early marriages and lack of thrift to the insidious influences of the city itself: 'the savage and brutalized condition of the casual poor was the result of long exposure to the degenerating conditions of city life'. A common preoccupation was the fear that the influx of people from the country would increase the numbers of working people exposed to the city's influences and would thus enlarge a degenerate stratum of the poor with 'feeble and tainted constitutions'. See Jones, *Outcast London*, pp. 286–7.

58. Potter, 'A Lady's View'.

59. Ibid. See Jones, *Outcast London*, pp. 152–9, on the 'crisis of the inner industrial perimeter'.

60. *Katherine Buildings, A Record of the Inhabitants*.

61. *Katherine Buildings, A Record of the Inhabitants*, list of occupations of men in Katherine Buildings, January 1886.

62. *Katherine Buildings, A Record of the Inhabitants*, list of occupations of women in Katherine Buildings, January 1886.

63. All descriptions of tenants to be found in *Katherine Buildings, A Record of the Inhabitants*.

64. Brian Harrison, *Separate Spheres: the Opposition to Women's Suffrage in Britain* (New York: Holmes and Meier, 1978) p. 22. Harrison also has an interesting analysis of the role of party politics in the mounting of the Appeal (see pp. 115–16).

65. Woodham-Smith, *Florence Nightingale*, pp. 310–12.

66. Martineau, *Autobiography*, vol. I, pp. 400–1.

67. *The Times*, July 1910, as quoted in Bell, *Octavia Hill*, p. 271.

68. Ward, *A Winter's Recollections*, p. 204.
69. Such women believed, as Brian Harrison remarks, that ' "citizenship" for women lay not through possessing a vote, but through promoting the good of the community' (Harrison, *Separate Spheres*, p. 59).
70. Ibid., p. 112.
71. One among many of the ironies of Webb's position as a non-feminist yet 'emancipated' woman was her estrangement even from those women of an older generation who had shared her own attitude toward suffrage. In a diary entry of 13 January 1891, Webb pondered with some humility her sense that Octavia Hill and Florence Nightingale distrusted her and her methods of work.
72. Webb wrote a series of articles on women's rights for the *New Statesman*, 1913–14, and yet recorded – with some amazement at herself – that she had never mentioned the enfranchisement of women in her diary in 1918 (Diary, 16 June 1918). She dissented from suffragist doctrine on factory legislation in *Women and the Factory Acts* (1896) and *The Case for the Factory Acts* (1901), and wrote a pamphlet defending equal pay for men and women, *The Wages of Men and Women: Should they be Equal?*, in 1919.
73. In their history of the suffrage movement, *One Hand Tied Behind Us* (London: Virago, 1978), Jill Liddington and Jill Norris have accomplished the important task of distinguishing between different strands of suffragism. They maintain that the history of women's suffrage has too often been told with emphasis on the largely middle-class militant *suffragettes*. Even the Northern, working-class radical suffragists of whom Liddington and Norris write in their book, however, opposed factory legislation or any other legislation 'that put any restrictions upon women's right to work' (p. 240).

Chapter 6: Social Investigation

1. Webb's essay on dock labour first appeared in *Nineteenth Century*, vol. XXII (October 1887) pp. 483–99, as 'The Dock Life of East London', and her piece on the tailoring trade appeared in the same journal (vol. XXIV (August 1888) pp. 161–83) as 'East London Labour'.
2. See Chapter 5 above, and Jones, *Outcast London*, pp. 258ff. Edward Denison, Oxford graduate and son of the Bishop of Salisbury, went to live in Stepney, where he taught Bible classes, built and endowed a school and lectured to workmen. He 'reported' his experiences back to members of his own class in the form of letters. See Sir Baldwyn Leighton, Bart. (ed.), *Letters and Other Writings of the Late Edward Denison* (London: Richard Bentley, 1872).
3. Webb shared Booth's enthusiasm for certain aspects of Positivism. It was the Positivist Frederic Harrison who first alerted Webb to the value of trade unionism when she was a very young woman (see Webb, *My Apprenticeship*, p. 140). Booth, too, developed an early sympathy for the organization of labour because of the influence of his cousins, followers of the English Positivist Richard Congreve. For a discussion of the connections between English Positivists and trade unions, see Royden Harrison, *Before the Socialists: Studies in Labour and Politics, 1861–1881* (London: Routledge & Kegan Paul, 1965), especially ch. VI, 'The Positivists: a Study of Labour's Intellectuals'.

4. See Eileen Yeo, 'Mayhew as Social Investigator', in E. P. Thompson and Eileen Yeo (eds), *The Unknown Mayhew* (Penguin, 1973) p. 100.

5. Sarah A. Tooley, 'The Growth of a Socialist. An Interview with Mrs Sidney Webb', *The Young Woman*, February 1895.

6. In *The Country and the City*, Raymond Williams compares Booth's 'deliberate impersonality' to Henry Mayhew's more 'personal' style of social investigation: Mayhew's method, he writes, 'belonged to an earlier world, before the scale of the problem and the sustained consideration of systematic remedies had altered social vision'. Booth's method, he continues, 'is deficient in many respects . . . but it has two . . . strengths. It is a mode which belongs with the substitution of social services for random charity: the services themselves . . . are a response of a new kind to the problems of the city. Moreover, the statistical mode itself, which to Dickens and other early Victorian humanists had seemed destructive and hateful, was a necessary response to a civilisation of this scale and complexity.' Raymond Williams, *The Country and the City* (London: Chatto & Windus, 1973) p. 222.

7. Charles Booth (ed.), *East London*, vol. I of *Labour and Life of the People* (London: Williams and Northgate, 1889), p. 158.

8. A fully adequate account of Booth's life and work does not as yet exist, but the most comprehensive study of his inquiry is to be found in T. S. Simey and M. B. Simey, *Charles Booth, Social Scientist* (Oxford University Press, 1960). Mary Booth's biography of her husband, *Charles Booth, A Memoir* (London: Macmillan, 1918) is also useful; and Noel Annan's 'The Intellectual Aristocracy', in J. H. Plumb (ed.), *Studies in Social History* (London: Longman, 1955) pp. 241–87 gives an interesting account of the connections among the families – Booths, Potters, Macaulays, Trevelyans, Arnolds and Huxleys – of the Victorian intelligentsia.

9. Quoted in Simey and Simey, *Charles Booth*, pp. 40–1.

10. See ibid., pp. 51–3.

11. Letter from Mary Booth to Beatrice Potter, 1889, as quoted in ibid., pp. 103–4.

12. Booth, *East London*, p. 158.

13. Ibid., p. 160.

14. Both Webb and Booth had problems with digestion, always ate sparingly and took up vegetarianism (see Simey and Simey, *Charles Booth*, p. 61). Webb alternated, at times, between fasting and vegetarianism.

15. Stephen Yeo has written suggestively on the intensity of late-Victorian middle-class revolt in his analysis of the religious element in socialist 'conversions' at the end of the century ('A New Life: the Religion of Socialism in Britain, 1883–1896', *History Workshop Journal* (Autumn 1977) pp. 5–57). In this context, he quotes the following passage from the memoirs of the SDF leader, W. H. Nevinson: 'To myself, though I naturally belonged to the comfortable classes, the attraction of repulsion was very strong, and during those years (1885–1897) my shamed sympathy with working people became an irresistible torment, so that I could hardly endure to live in the ordinary comfort of my surroundings.' (Quoted in ibid., p. 10.)

16. The typescript version of Webb's diary has her reading 'Makin' in August 1887. Obviously, Webb's handwriting confused her secretary here, as in various other places.

17. Eileen Yeo maintains that Mayhew's work was methodical, thoroughgoing and conclusive about the connection between certain kinds of exploitation and unemployment (Thompson and Yeo, *The Unknown Mayhew*, p. 81). She quotes H. J. Dyos, however, who finds Mayhew's work a 'form of higher journalism, not of social analysis' (p. 72). In her instructive and illuminating monograph on Mayhew, Anne Humphreys reviews recent scholarly assessments of him, and concludes that Mayhew's best work combined social analysis with artistic representation: 'The artistic qualities of selection, order, and direction,' she writes, 'not only gave Mayhew's work force and effectiveness, but they also rendered it more precise, more accurate – more scientific.' See Anne Humphreys, *Travels Into the Poor Man's Country: the Work of Henry Mayhew* (Athens: University of Georgia Press, 1977) pp. 198–200.

18. Beatrice Potter, 'The Docks', in Booth, *East London*, p. 184.

19. See Beatrice Potter, 'The Dock Life of East London', *Nineteenth Century*, vol. XXII (October 1887) p. 458.

20. Potter, 'The Docks', p. 189.

21. Ibid., pp. 189–90.

22. Harriet Martineau, 'The Magic Troughs at Birmingham', *Household Words*, 25 October 1851, p. 115.

23. George Orwell, *The Road to Wigan Pier* (London: Victor Gollancz, 1937) p. 33.

24. Potter, 'The Docks', p. 190.

25. Henry Mayhew, 'The Dock-Labourers', in John Rosenberg (ed.), *London Labour and the London Poor*, reprint of the 1861 edition (New York: Dover, 1968) p. 309.

26. Potter, 'The Docks', p. 199.

27. Ibid., p. 204.

28. Ibid., p. 205.

29. Ibid.

30. Ibid., p. 206.

31. Ibid.

32. Ibid., p. 207.

33. Ibid., p. 208.

34. In this chapter, I shall discuss those aspects of Webb's Bacup visit which are connected to her use of disguise. In the following chapter, I shall return to the Bacup visit in the context of Webb's political 'conversion'.

35. When Webb went to Bacup in 1886, she told her Aked cousins that she was Beatrice Potter, their rich relation. They reacted, according to her account, happily: 'I feared they would be offended,' she wrote, 'on the contrary, they were delighted, and glad that I had not told them before they had got to know me.' (Diary, 31 October 1886.)

36. Letter from Beatrice Potter to Richard Potter, October 1886 (Passfield Papers).

37. Beatrice Potter to Richard Potter, October 1886 (Passfield Papers), and Webb, *My Apprenticeship*, pp. 162–3.

38. Beatrice Potter to Richard Potter, 9 November 1883 (Passfield Papers).

39. Ibid.

40. Orwell, *The Road to Wigan Pier*, p. 163. The notion, which both Webb and Orwell acted upon in their lives, of leaving off some aspect of a real identity in order to overcome the barriers and constraints of class appeared often as a motif in certain kinds of literature in the last decades of the nineteenth century and first decades of the twentieth. The political and social consciousness of these decades, the 'rediscovery' of poverty and the attempt to narrow the destructive distance between classes lie behind the appearance of this latter-day 'pastoral'. Dickens' *Our Mutual Friend* stands as an early example of the literary exploration of class disguise; and Walter Besant's *All Sorts and Conditions of Men*, Shaw's *The Millionairess*, *Major Barbara* and *Mrs Warren's Profession*, and Orwell's own *Road to Wigan Pier*, *Down and Out in Paris and London* and *A Clergyman's Daughter* all deal in some way with the theme of tainted inheritance.

41. See Webb, *My Apprenticeship*, p. 316 for a summary of conventional notions about 'sweating'.

42. *Mechanical Magazine*, vol. xxxix (1843) p. 443 (*OED*).

43. Charles Kingsley, *Alton Locke, Tailor and Poet* (London: Cassell, 1967) pp. 100, 101, 200.

44. See Lloyd P. Gartner, *The Jewish Immigrant in England, 1870–1914* (London: George Allen & Unwin, 1960) pp. 81–93, on the immigrant tailoring trade. Jews had been involved in the second-hand clothing and rag trade since the eighteenth century, and in the late 1850s and 1860s, when the Singer sewing machine was introduced, Jewish tailors did create a kind of middle-ground between skilled tailors and slop-workers.

45. See, for example, Arnold White, 'The Invasion of Pauper Foreigners', *Nineteenth Century*, vol. xxxiii (1888) pp. 414–22.

46. Beatrice Webb may not have wanted to call attention to her interest in Jews because of the common misconception that Sidney Webb was Jewish. Beatrice herself thought him 'Jewish-looking' when she first described him in her diary (13 February 1890), and the Webbs' hagiographer, Mary Hamilton, took great pains to deny what 'many people, both when he was young and throughout his career, have assumed', that Sidney Webb was a Jew. Mary Agnes Hamilton, *Sidney and Beatrice Webb* (Boston and New York: Houghton Mifflin, 1933) p. 16.

47. The Potter family did not like to speak of Mary Seddon as a Jew, and when Georgina Meinertzhagen wrote her story of the Potters, she described Mary Seddon as 'gipsy-like'. See Georgina Meinertzhagen, *From Ploughshare to Parliament* (London: Chiswick Press, 1895) p. 55.

48. Others remarked on Beatrice Webb's Jewish appearance. Her sister Kate Courtney described all of her sisters in her diary on the occasion of Richard Potter's funeral: Beatrice, she wrote, was 'handsome, . . . Jewish looking with a very intellectual face'. (Diary of Kate Courtney, 3 January 1892, Courtney Collection, vol. 26.) Mary Hamilton suggests that Beatrice got her 'vivid darkness of colouring' and her 'finely aquiline nose' from her Jewish grandmother (Hamilton, *Sidney and Beatrice Webb*, p. 41).

49. Beatrice Potter, 'Pages from a Work-girl's Diary', *Nineteenth Century*, vol. xxv (September 1888) p. 313.

50. 'Wholesale Clothing Trade' (1887) ms. notebook (Passfield Papers VII.1.8).

51. Tooley, 'The Growth of a Socialist'.

52. Letter from Beatrice Potter to Mary Playne, 30 April 1888 (Passfield Papers II.1.i).

53. Beatrice Webb's anti-Semitism has been the subject of debate in recent letters-to-the-editor of *Encounter* magazine. The series of letters began in March 1976 with a long statement on Socialist anti-Semitism written by Max Geltman in response to a previously published article on Marx. Mr Geltman, whose aim is to discredit Socialism by revealing the anti-Semitic leanings of leading European socialists, said that Webb 'found much virtue in the Soviet constitution under Stalin, and nothing but a lust for greedy profit among the poorest of the poor among the Jews of Whitechapel'. Margaret Cole replied to defend her colleague and friend (May 1976) in a way that ignored the kernel of truth in Geltman's exaggerated accusations. More balanced views then came in from Robert Wistrich (August 1976) and George Feaver (September 1976); they both were accurate about Webb's racialist thinking, and they put that kind of thinking in some perspective. What neither tried to account for and analyse was the 'other side' of her racialism – her peculiar sense of identification with the Jews. The debate did not end there: Margaret Cole wrote again, as did Geltman (November 1976), and a final round of Wistrich and Feaver, joined by Shirley Letwin, finished off the ten-month long controversy (January 1977). Letwin's final word displays her customary animosity towards Webb: Webb did not merely dislike Jews, Letwin maintains, she hated 'all concrete human beings', and, what's more, this antipathy is shared by all those who adhere to 'socialism, . . . Communism, Nazism, and all varieties of Manicheism'.

54. Beatrice Potter, 'The Jewish Community', in Booth, *East London*, p. 589.

55. 'Of the interesting study of the Jewish East End Community,' a reviewer in the *Jewish Chronicle* wrote, 'it would be impossible to speak too highly. Written with considerable literary power and enlivened by touches of humour and observation, it is by far the ablest account of our poor brethren in the East End that has yet been given to the world.' ('Jewish East London', *Jewish Chronicle*, 26 April 1889). A reviewer in the *Jewish World* commented that Webb's article on 'sweating' 'results practically in a vindication of our local and immigrant brethren from all the serious charges brought against them by Protectionist alarmists and sensational demagogues'. 'It is gratifying', the reviewer continued, 'to find such competent observers agreeing in almost every main point with the main contentions we have been striving for during the past two or three years. It seems to be granted that the body of Jewish immigrants are not by any means the mass of human refuse which it has pleased sensational writers . . . to style them' (26 April 1889). For reviews of *East London*, see the Booth Collection, A58, British Library of Political and Economic Science.

56. Potter, 'Pages from a Work-girl's Diary', p. 303.

57. Ibid., pp. 308–9.

58. Ibid., p. 304.

59. Ibid., p. 307.

60. Ibid., p. 310.

61. Ibid.

62. Ibid.

63. Ibid., p. 311.
64. Ibid., p. 313.
65. See Beatrice Potter, 'How Best to Do Away with the Sweating System', a paper read at the 24th Annual Conference of Co-operative Societies, Rochdale, June 1892, and Webb, *My Apprenticeship*, pp. 319–20.
66. From the Fifth Report of the Select Committee of the House of Lords on the Sweating System, 1888–9: Conclusions and Recommendations, pp. xlii, xliii, as quoted in Webb, *My Apprenticeship*, p. 318.
67. Beatrice Potter, 'The Tailoring Trade', in Booth, *East London*, p. 228.
68. Ibid., p. 215.
69. Ibid., pp. 226–7.
70. Ibid., p. 228.
71. Ibid., p. 230.
72. Kingsley, *Alton Locke*, p. 101.
73. Potter, 'The Tailoring Trade', p. 238.
74. Beatrice Potter, 'East London Labour', *Nineteenth Century*, vol. XXIV (August 1888) p. 181.
75. Ibid., p. 182.
76. Ibid., p. 183.
77. Quoted in Simey and Simey, *Charles Booth*, p. 116.
78. Booth calculated that employment (lack of work or low pay) was the reason for poverty in 55 per cent of all 'very poor' families and in 68 per cent of 'poor' families (*East London*, p. 146).
79. Ibid., p. 160. Peter Keating asserts that Booth's 'greatest single achievement was that once and for all he destroyed the view that the working classes were "debased" ' (Keating, *The Working Classes*, p. 119).
80. Booth, *East London*, p. 166.
81. Ibid., p. 167.
82. See Harold Pfautz (ed.), *Charles Booth on the City* (Chicago & London: University of Chicago Press, 1967) p. 71, and Albert Fried and Richard M. Ellman (eds), *Charles Booth's London* (New York: Pantheon Books, 1968) p. xxv.
83. J. W. Burrow notes that Beatrice Webb was one of the very few English social scientists who were conscious of the need for both 'social amelioration' and 'ethical and political theory'. It was having one foot in the Spencerian camp and one in the Boothian camp, Burrow asserts, that afforded her this perspective, almost unique among British social thinkers. See J. W. Burrow, *Evolution and Society: a Study in Victorian Social Theory* (Cambridge University Press, 1970) pp. 91–3.

Chapter 7: Fabian Socialism

1. Royden Harrison, *Before the Socialists: Studies in Labour and Politics, 1861–1881* (London: Routledge and Kegan Paul, 1965) p. 254.
2. Willard Wolfe, *From Radicalism to Socialism: Men and Ideas in the Formation of Fabian Socialist Doctrines, 1881–1889* (New Haven & London: Yale University Press, 1975) p. 13.
3. Others have analysed Comte's appeal in similar ways. See, for example,

W. M. Simon, *European Positivism in the Nineteenth Century* (Ithaca: Cornell University Press, 1963).

4. Gertrud Lenzer (ed.), *Auguste Comte and Positivism: the Essential Writings* (New York and London: Harper and Row, 1975) p. xxxiii.

5. Ibid., p. xxxii.

6. J. W. Burrow, *Evolution and Society*.

7. Ibid., p. 111.

8. Herbert Spencer, *Social Statics, the conditions essential to human happiness specified and the first of them developed* (New York: Robert Schalkenbach Foundation, 1954 (1851)) p. 4.

9. Ibid., p. 9.

10. Webb, *My Apprenticeship*, p. 38.

11. Spencer, *Social Statics*, p. 20.

12. Ibid., pp. 58–60.

13. Ibid., p. 14.

14. Ibid., pp. 241, 248.

15. Ibid., p. 268.

16. Herbert Spencer, *Autobiography* (New York: Appleton, 1904) vol. I, p. 487.

17. Spencer, *Social Statics*, p. 396.

18. See Chapter 6.

19. Beatrice Potter, *The Co-operative Movement in Great Britain* (London: Swan Sonnenschein, 1899 (1891)) p. 221.

20. Ibid., p. 221.

21. Ibid., p. 206.

22. The following Fabians wrote works on Robert Owen: Frank Podmore, Elizabeth Lucy Hutchins, C. E. M. Joad, G. D. H. Cole and Margaret Cole. Two of the works, by Hutchins and Joad, were published as Fabian Tracts, in 1912 and 1917.

23. Potter, *The Co-operative Movement*, p. 16.

24. Ibid., pp. 18–19.

25. Ibid., p. 19.

26. Ibid., p. 18.

27. Ibid., p. 15.

28. See ibid., Chapter III, 'The Store', especially pp. 63–7, for Webb's explanation of the 'dividend on purchase' system.

29. Potter, *The Co-operative Movement*, p. 77.

30. Ibid., p. 209.

31. Ibid., pp. 203–4.

32. Beatrice Potter, 'The Relationship between Co-operation and Trade Unionism', paper read at Tynemouth, 15 August 1892 (Manchester: Co-operative Union, 1892) p. 13.

33. Potter, *The Co-operative Movement*, p. 227.

34. Ibid., p. 228.

35. Ibid., p. 238.

36. Ibid.

37. Potter, 'The Relationship between Co-operation and Trade Unionism', p. 9.

38. J. M. Winter, *Socialism and the Challenge of War: Ideas and Politics in Britain 1912–1918* (London & Boston: Routledge & Kegan Paul, 1974) p. 34.

39. I have found useful the following works on Fabianism: Edward Pease, *The*

History of the Fabian Society (1918); Margaret Cole, *The Story of Fabian Socialism* (1961); A. M. McBriar, *Fabian Socialism and English Politics, 1884–1918* (1966); E. J. Hobsbawm, 'The Fabians Reconsidered', in *Labouring Men* (1967); Willard Wolfe, *From Radicalism to Socialism* (1975); and Norman and Jeanne MacKenzie, *The Fabians* (1977).

40. See especially Wolfe, *From Radicalism to Socialism* and Norman and Jeanne MacKenzie, *The Fabians*.

41. See Wolfe, *From Radicalism to Socialism*, pp. 156–7, and also Stephen Yeo's 'A New Life: the Religion of Socialism' for an examination of the strong religious content of much British socialism in the last two decades of the nineteenth century.

42. See N. & J. MacKenzie, *The Fabians*, Part One, for descriptions of these groups and the connections among them.

43. Wolfe, *From Radicalism to Socialism*, p. 151.

44. Ibid., p. 168.

45. N. & J. MacKenzie, *The Fabians*, p. 18. See also Ian Britain's *Fabianism and Culture* (Cambridge University Press, 1982) on the Fabians' 'literary and artistic' origins.

46. George Bernard Shaw, *Sixteen Self Sketches* (London: Constable, 1949) pp. 56–9.

47. Wolfe, *From Radicalism to Socialism*, pp. 233, 241.

48. Shaw, *Sixteen Self Sketches*, pp. 58, 66.

49. Edward R. Pease, *The History of the Fabian Society* (New York: Barnes & Noble, 1963 (1918)) p. 44.

50. See N. & J. MacKenzie, *The Fabians*, p. 64. The Fabians who belonged to the Karl Marx Club were Shaw, Edward Pease, Sydney Olivier, Graham Wallas and Sidney Webb.

51. Shaw, *Sixteen Self Sketches*, p. 67.

52. N. & J. MacKenzie, *The Fabians*, p. 84.

53. Pease, *The History of the Fabian Society*, p. 81.

54. Ibid., p. 82.

55. Webb clipped and saved an article from the *Pall Mall Gazette* some time in 1892 in which W. T. Stead compared her husband to her ex-suitor in the following manner: 'Since Mr Chamberlain arose in Birmingham there has been no man so like him as Mr Sidney Webb, who aspires to be Mr Chamberlain of London – only more so. For to all the energy and perseverance and municipal spirit of Mr Chamberlain, Mr Sidney Webb adds a great literary gift and a philosophic conception of social progress to which Mr Chamberlain can lay no claim.' (Passfield Papers, XIIIA.1.iii.)

56. A. M. McBriar, *Fabian Socialism and British Politics, 1884–1918* (Cambridge: Cambridge University Press, 1966) p. 26.

57. Pease, *The History of the Fabian Society*, p. 88.

58. McBriar, *Fabian Socialism and British Politics*, p. 348 and Pease, *The History of the Fabian Society*, p. 89.

59. Ibid., pp. 90–91.

60. E. J. Hobsbawm, 'The Fabians Reconsidered', in *Labouring Men: Studies in the History of Labour* (Garden City: Doubleday, 1967) p. 311.

61. See McBriar, *Fabian Socialism and British Politics*, pp. 31ff. for a discussion of Fabian economics and the 'theory of value' debate.

62. Shaw, *Sixteen Self Sketches*, p. 81.
63. McBriar, *Fabian Socialism and British Politics*, p. 35.
64. Similarly, when Sidney reviewed Booth's *East London* earlier that year in the *Star*, he observed that ' "the only contributor with any literary talent is Miss Beatrice Potter" '.
65. Wolfe, *From Radicalism to Socialism*, p. 184.
66. Sidney Webb, Lecture on George Eliot (Passfield Papers, Section VI, Item 6).
67. Ibid.
68. Sidney Webb, 'Historic Basis of Socialism', in G. Bernard Shaw (ed.), *Fabian Essays and Socialism* (London: Fabian Society and George Allen and Unwin, 1931 (1889)) p. 29.
69. Ibid., p. 29.
70. Ibid., p. 32.
71. Ibid., pp. 42–3.
72. Ibid., p. 43.
73. Ibid., p. 56.
74. N. & J. MacKenzie, *The Fabians*, p. 151.

Chapter 8: The Writing of 'My Apprenticeship'

1. Letter from Beatrice Potter to Sidney Webb, January 1892 (Passfield Papers, II.3.ii).
2. Samuel Hynes, 'The Art of Beatrice Webb', in *Edwardian Occasions* (New York: Oxford University Press, 1972) p. 161.
3. See Chapter 4.
4. 'Today, and ever since I first began to read William James's works, I find him the truest of all metaphysicians.' When Webb met William James during her American trip in 1898, she was 'prejudiced against him as the brother of Henry James', whom she had known in London and 'heartily disliked'. The dislike was apparently 'reciprocated'.
5. William James, *The Will to Believe, and other essays in popular philosophy* (New York: Dover Publications, 1956) p. 22.
6. Webb inserted a clipping about Mrs Chamberlain in vol. xiii of her diary, and wrote beneath it: 'Every Romance has a conclusion. This is the end to the romance of four vols. of my life.'
7. Almost all of Webb's manuscript diaries were typed out, at first by herself and then by her secretary, with a view to autobiographical publication. This particular passage was left in manuscript and inserted in the typescript volume.
8. Samuel Hynes maintains that marriage to Sidney Webb ended Beatrice's longings to write a novel once and for all: 'The "vulgar wish" [to write fiction] came in September 1889. In October, she was sent a copy of the recently published *Fabian Essays*, and read it through. In January 1890 she met Sidney Webb, and on February 1 she wrote in her diary: "At last I am a socialist!" From this time on there are no more yearnings toward literary work. . . . Fabianism and Sidney Webb had entered her life and driven out the novel.' (Hynes, 'The Art of Beatrice Webb', p. 157). Hynes' rather neat

account is not accurate for, as her diary indicates, she did contemplate writing a novel after her marriage, and the writing of *My Apprenticeship* surely expresses 'yearnings toward literary work'.

9. See Beatrice Webb, *Our Partnership* (London, New York, Toronto: Longman, Green, 1948) p. 423.

10. She had been similarly affected, though for a briefer period, by the Dreyfus Affair in the summer of 1899. 'I took a feverish interest in the Dreyfus trial,' she wrote in October, 'Sidney grew impatient and would not read [about] it, but to me it had a horrible fascination – became a morbid background to my conscious activities.' (Diary, 10 October 1899.)

11. Diary, 13 September 1916, and note appended to 24 July 1916 entry, dated June 1919. This note explains the progress of Webb's self-diagnosis.

12. 'Neurasthenia and Shell Shock', *Lancet*, 8 March 1916, pp. 627–8.

13. See Charles Rosenberg's introduction to the 1972 Arno Press reprint of George M. Beard, *American Nervousness* (New York: Putnam, 1881).

14. See Leonard Woolf, *Beginning Again* (New York: Harcourt Brace Jovanovich, 1963) pp. 75–6.

   Virginia Woolf's second major breakdown, during 1914–15, seems to have had little to do with 'war neurosis' and probably had much to do with her recent marriage (she began to have symptoms on her honeymoon). See ibid., p. 148. By contrast to Beatrice Webb, Woolf's relationship to the events of the war was one of extreme detachment. The following passage from a letter to Margaret Llewelyn Davies, written after her recovery, expresses that detachment rather well: 'I become steadily more feminist, owing to the Times, which I read at breakfast and wonder how this preposterous masculine fiction [the war] keeps going on a day longer – without some vigorous young woman pulling us together and marching through it – Do you see any sense in it? I feel as if I were reading about some curious tribe in Central Africa.' See Nigel Nicolson and Joanne Trautmann (eds), *The Letters of Virginia Woolf* (New York & London: Harcourt Brace Jovanovich, 1976) vol. II, p. 76.

15. Leonard Woolf, 'Political Thought and the Webbs', in Margaret Cole (ed.), *The Webbs and their Work* (London: Frederick Muller, 1949) p. 261.

16. As Paul Fussell has phrased it, the Great War proved 'a hideous embarrassment to the prevailing Meliorist myth which had dominated the public consciousness for a century. It reversed the Idea of Progress.' (*The Great War and Modern Memory* (London, Oxford & New York: Oxford University Press, 1975) p. 8.)

17. In the memoir of his early life, Robert Graves writes that when he returned home from the Front in 1916, he began to write the first chapters of an autobiographical novel, which he then scrapped. He later used these chapters as the basis for the memoir he published in 1929, *Goodbye to All That*. Robert Graves, *Goodbye to All That* (Penguin, 1960), p. 191.

18. 'Let me say at once,' Sidney wrote in a 1928 'reminiscence' in the *St Martin's Review*, 'that I have no intention of writing an autobiography; I am, I believe, "not that sort".' Indeed I have very little knowledge of what has happened to me internally.' (*St Martin's Review*, October 1928, p. 478.)

19. Margaret Cole (ed.), *Beatrice Webb's Diaries, 1924–1932* (London, New York & Toronto: Longman, Green, 1956) p. xiii.

20. 'Philosophy was out of touch with life,' Robert Graves wrote of a post-war world, '[and] science could provide the means of satisfying people's desires, but it assumed no responsibility for distinguishing between good and bad desires. People were hostile to established religion, and yet in need of faith.' See Robert Graves and Alan Hodge, *The Long Weekend* (London: Faber & Faber, n.d.) p. 203.
21. John Stuart Mill, *Autobiography* (New York: Columbia University Press, 1924) p. 94.

Conclusion: On the Soviet Union

1. Sidney and Beatrice Webb, *Soviet Communism: a New Civilisation?* (New York: Scribners, 1936) vol. II, p. 1123.
2. To a woman who tended to vegetarianism and bouts of fasting, the Soviets' Spartan eating habits, whether real or imagined, were of great importance.
3. Ibid., vol. II, pp. 1125, 1136.
4. Ibid., vol. I, p. 339.
5. Ibid. (my italics).
6. David Caute, *The Fellow-Travellers* (New York: Macmillan, 1973) p. 251. Caute's portrait of the Webbs makes them into prime candidates for his theory of fellow-travelling as a 'postscript to the Enlightenment': 'They were energetic, ambitious, worthy, intelligent, unimaginative and impatient with the vagaries of human emotion. . . . The arts didn't interest them. Only facts, statistics and blueprints interested them' (ibid., p. 81).
7. Mrs Sidney Webb, 'What I Have Learnt About Russia', BBC Broadcast, 22 September 1932; published in the *Listener*, 28 September 1932 (Passfield Papers, Section VI, item 86).
8. Diary, 14 May 1932.
9. Appendix to vol. 46 of Diaries (1932).
10. Ibid.
11. Soviet Diary, 1932 (Passfield Papers, VII.1.58).
12. For mention of the proposed Jewish republic, see Soviet Diary and Diary, 1 May 1933. See also S. & B. Webb, *Soviet Communism*, vol. 1, pp. 149–53.
13. Sidney and Beatrice Webb, *Methods of Social Study* (London: Cambridge University Press & London School of Economics and Political Science, 1975; originally published 1932) p. 258 (my italics).
14. Ibid., pp. 256–7.
15. Samuel Hynes, 'The Art of Beatrice Webb', in *Edwardian Occasions* (New York: Oxford University Press, 1972) p. 154.

Bibliography

The following bibliography of works by and about Beatrice Webb includes only a small number of the sources consulted in the writing of this book. Bibliographical information for any works not listed below can be found in the notes.

UNPUBLISHED MATERIAL

Diary of Kate (Potter) Courtney, Courtney Papers, British Library of Political and Economic Science.

Katherine Buildings, a Record of the Inhabitants, Collected Miscellany 43, British Library of Political and Economic Science.

Letters to Beatrice Potter from friends (Arabella Fisher, Margaret Harkness, Ella Pycroft), Passfield Papers, Section II.1.ii, British Library of Political and Economic Science.

Reviews of *East London*, Section A58, Booth Collection, British Library of Political and Economic Science.

Reviews of *My Apprenticeship*, Passfield Papers, Section XII.A.2, Group xiv, British Library of Political and Economic Science.

Webb, Beatrice, Diary, Passfield Papers, British Library of Political and Economic Science.

Webb, Beatrice, Letters, Passfield Papers, Section II, British Library of Political and Economic Science.

Webb, Beatrice, Soviet Diary, 1932, Passfield Papers, Section VII.1.58, British Library of Political and Economic Science.

Webb, Beatrice, 'What I Have Learnt About Russia', BBC Broadcast, 22 September 1932, Passfield Papers, Section VI.86, British Library of Political and Economic Science.

*Webb, Beatrice, 'Wholesale Clothing Trade', MS notebook, 1887, Passfield Papers, Section VII.1.8, British Library of Political and Economic Science.

Webb, Sidney, Lecture on George Eliot, Passfield Papers, Section VI.6, British Library of Political and Economic Science.

* Designates works written or published under the name Beatrice Potter.

PUBLISHED WORKS BY BEATRICE WEBB

Beatrice Webb's American Diary, ed. David. A. Shannon (Madison: University of Wisconsin Press, 1963).

Beatrice Webb's Diaries, 1912–1924, ed. Margaret Cole (London & New York: Longman, Green, 1952).

Beatrice Webb's Diaries, 1924–1932, ed. Margaret Cole (London & New York: Longman, Green, 1956).

The Diary of Beatrice Webb, vol. I: *1873–1892: Glitter Around and Darkness Within*, ed. Norman and Jeanne MacKenzie (Cambridge, Mass.: Harvard University Press, 1982).

The Letters of Sidney and Beatrice Webb, ed. Norman MacKenzie, 3 vols (London & Cambridge: Cambridge University Press & The London School of Economics and Political Science, 1978).

Webb, Beatrice, 'The Awakening of Women', *New Statesman*, Special Supplement (1 November 1913) pp. iii–v.

Webb, Beatrice (ed.), *The Case for the Factory Acts*, with Preface by Mrs Humphry Ward (London: Grant Richards, 1901).

*Webb, Beatrice, *The Co-operative Movement in Great Britain* (London: Swan Sonnenschein, 1899; first published 1891).

*Webb, Beatrice, 'The Dock Life of East London', *Nineteenth Century*, vol. XXII (October 1887) pp. 483–99.

*Webb, Beatrice, 'The Docks', in *East London*, ed. Charles Booth (London: Williams & Northgate, 1889) part II, ch. ii.

*Webb, Beatrice, 'East London Labour', *Nineteenth Century*, vol. XXIV (August 1888) pp. 161–83.

*Webb, Beatrice, 'How Best to Do Away with the Sweating System', a paper read at the 24th Annual Conference of the Co-operative Societies (Rochdale, June 1892).

*Webb, Beatrice, 'The Jewish Community', in *East London*, ed. Charles Booth (London: Williams & Northgate, 1889) part III, ch. iii.

*Webb, Beatrice, 'A Lady's View of the Unemployed at the East', *Pall Mall Gazette*, 18 February 1886.

*Webb, Beatrice, 'The Lords and the Sweating System', *Nineteenth Century*, vol. XXVII (June 1890) pp. 885–905.

Webb, Beatrice, *My Apprenticeship* (New York: Longman, Green, 1926).

Webb, Beatrice, *Our Partnership* (London & New York: Longman, Green, 1948).

*Webb, Beatrice, 'Pages from a Work-Girl's Diary', *Nineteenth Century*, vol. XXV (September 1888) pp. 301–14.

Webb, Beatrice, 'Personal Rights and the Woman's Movement', *New Statesman*, Series (February–August 1914).

*Webb, Beatrice, 'The Relationship between Co-operation and Trade Unionism', paper read at Tynemouth, 15 August 1892 (Manchester: Co-operative Union, 1892).

*Webb, Beatrice, 'The Tailoring Trade', in *East London*, ed. Charles Booth (London: Williams & Northgate, 1889) part II, ch. iii.

Webb, Beatrice, *The Wages of Men and Women: Should they be Equal?* (London: The Fabian Society & George Allen, 1919).

Webb, Beatrice, *Women and the Factory Acts* (London: Fabian Society, 1896).

Webb, Sidney and Beatrice Webb, *Methods of Social Study*, introduction by T. H. Marshall (London: Cambridge University Press & London School of Economics and Political Science, 1975; reprint of 1932 edition).

Webb, Sidney and Beatrice Webb, *Soviet Communism: A New Civilisation?*, 2 vols (New York: Scribners, 1936).

WORKS ABOUT BEATRICE WEBB, THE WEBBS AND FABIANISM

Adam, Ruth, and Kitty Muggeridge, *Beatrice Webb, A Life* (London: Secker & Warburg, 1967).

Caine, Barbara, 'Beatrice Webb and the "Woman Question" ', *History Workshop Journal*, 14 (Autumn 1982) pp. 23–43.

Cole, Margaret, *Beatrice Webb* (New York: Harcourt, Brace, 1946).

Cole, Margaret, *The Story of Fabian Socialism* (Stanford: Stanford University Press, 1961).

Cole, Margaret (ed.), *The Webbs and Their Work* (London: Frederick Muller, 1949).

Gould, Gerald, Review of *My Apprenticeship*, *Daily Chronicle*, 26 February 1926.

Hamilton, Mary Agnes, *Sidney and Beatrice Webb* (Boston & New York: Houghton Mifflin, 1933).

Hobsbawm, E. J., 'The Fabians Reconsidered', in *Labouring Men: Studies in the History of Labour* (Garden City, NY: Doubleday, 1967).

Hynes, Samuel, 'The Art of Beatrice Webb', in *Edwardian Occasions* (New York: Oxford University Press, 1972) pp. 153–73.

Leavis, F. R., introduction to *Mill on Bentham and Coleridge* (London: Chatto & Windus, 1950).

Letwin, Shirley Robin, *The Pursuit of Certainty* (Cambridge: Cambridge University Press, 1965).

McBriar, A. M., *Fabian Socialism and English Politics, 1884–1918* (Cambridge: Cambridge University Press, 1966).

MacKenzie, Norman and Jeanne MacKenzie, *The Fabians* (New York: Simon & Schuster, 1977).

Meinertzhagen, Georgina, *From Ploughshares to Parliament: A Short Memoir of the Potters of Tadcaster* (London: Chiswick Press, 1895).

Mintz, Alan, *George Eliot and the Novel of Vocation* (Cambridge, Mass. & London: Harvard University Press, 1978).

Nadel, Ira Bruce, 'Beatrice Webb's Two Voices: *My Apprenticeship* and Victorian Autobiography', *English Studies in Canada*, vol. II, no. 1 (1976) pp. 83–96.

Pease, Edward, *The History of the Fabian Society* (New York: Barnes & Noble, 1963; first published 1918).

Russell, Bertrand, *Portraits from Memory and Other Essays* (New York: Simon & Schuster, 1951).

Shaw, George Bernard (ed.), *Fabian Essays in Socialism* (London: Fabian Society & George Allen, 1931 (1889)).

Spacks, Patricia Meyer, *The Female Imagination* (New York: Avon-Discus, 1976).

Tawney, R. H., 'Beatrice Webb', in *Proceedings of the British Academy, 1943* (London: Oxford University Press, 1943) pp. 285–311.

Wolfe, Willard, *From Radicalism to Socialism: Men and Ideas in the Formation of Fabian Socialist Doctrines, 1881–1889* (New Haven & London: Yale University Press, 1975).

Woolf, Leonard, *Sowing: An Autobiography of the Years 1880 to 1904* (New York & London: Harcourt Brace, 1960).

Index

287